Six of Monty's Men

This one is for you, Amy, and I do hope you like it.

Six of Monty's Men

ADRIAN STEWART

Pen & Sword
MILITARY

First published in Great Britain in 2011 by
Pen & Sword Military
an imprint of
Pen & Sword Books Ltd
47 Church Street
Barnsley
South Yorkshire
S70 2AS

Copyright © Adrian Stewart, 2011

ISBN 978 1 84884 371 4

The right of Adrian Stewart to be identified as the author of this work has been asserted by him in accordance with the Copyright, Designs and Patents Act 1988

A CIP catalogue record for this book is available from the British Library

All rights reserved. No part of this book may be reproduced or transmitted in any form or by any means, electronic or mechanical including photocopying, recording or by any information storage and retrieval system, without permission from the Publisher in writing.

Typeset in Ehrhardt by Chic Media Ltd

Printed and bound in England
by CPI

Pen & Sword Books Ltd incorporates the imprints of
Pen & Sword Aviation, Pen & Sword Maritime,
Pen & Sword Military, Pen & Sword Family History,
Wharncliffe Local History, Wharncliffe True Crime,
Wharncliffe Transport, Pen & Sword Discovery, Pen & Sword Select,
Pen & Sword Military Classics, Leo Cooper, Remember When,
The Praetorian Press, Seaforth Publishing and Frontline Publishing

For a complete list of Pen & Sword titles please contact
PEN & SWORD BOOKS LIMITED
47 Church Street, Barnsley, South Yorkshire, S70 2AS, England
E-mail: enquiries@pen-and-sword.co.uk
Website: www.pen-and-sword.co.uk

Contents

Maps vi

Chapter 1   Master and Pupils 1

Chapter 2   'That Little Tiger' 15

Chapter 3   The Guardsman 45

Chapter 4   'Berthier' 76

Chapter 5   'Enthusiasm, Enthusiasm' 107

Chapter 6   Plans and Operations 140

Chapter 7   The Armoured Commander 171

Chapter 8   Latter Days 201

Retropect 210

Acknowledgements & Bibliography 213

Index 218

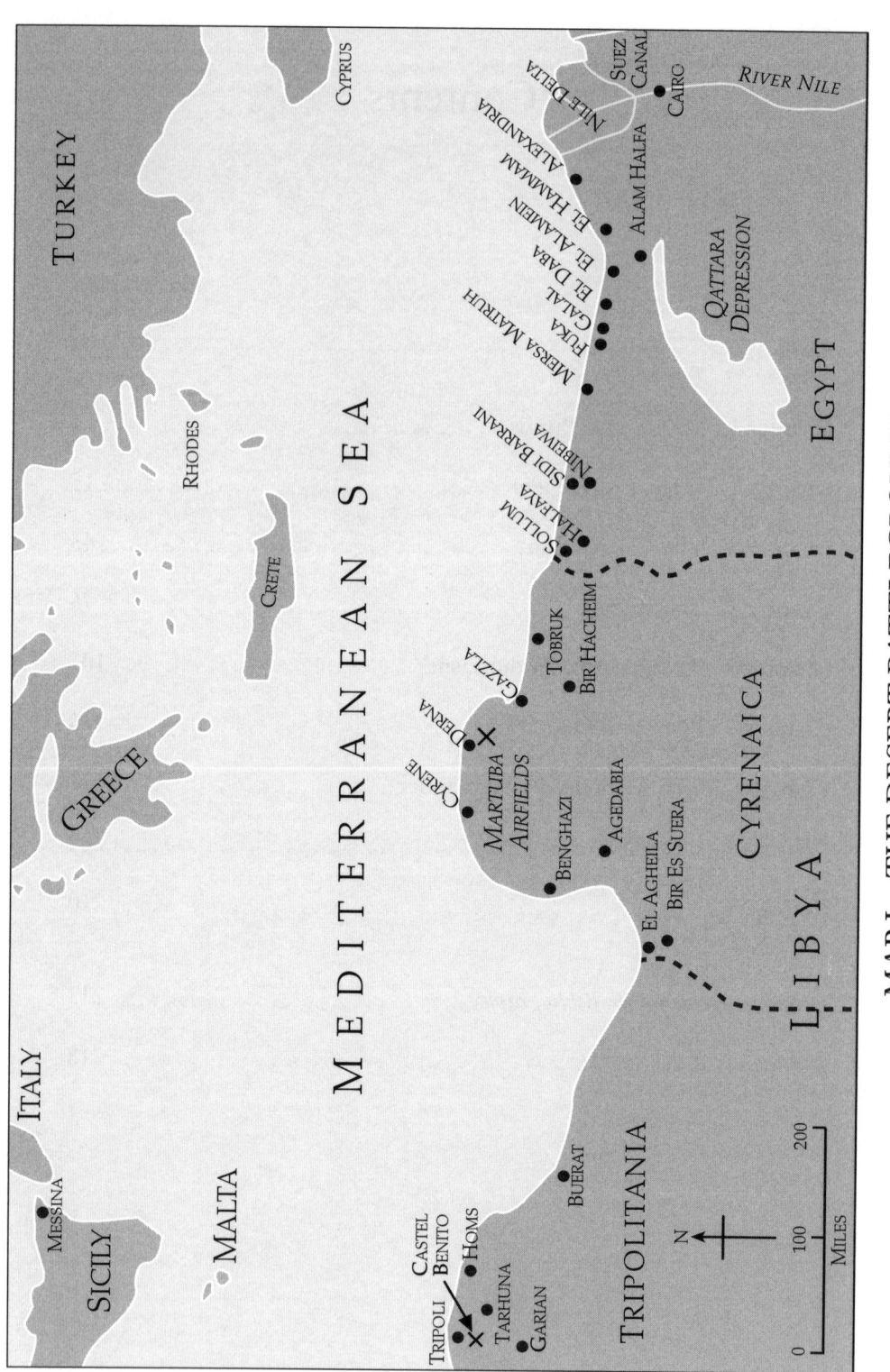

MAP I – THE DESERT BATTLEGROUND

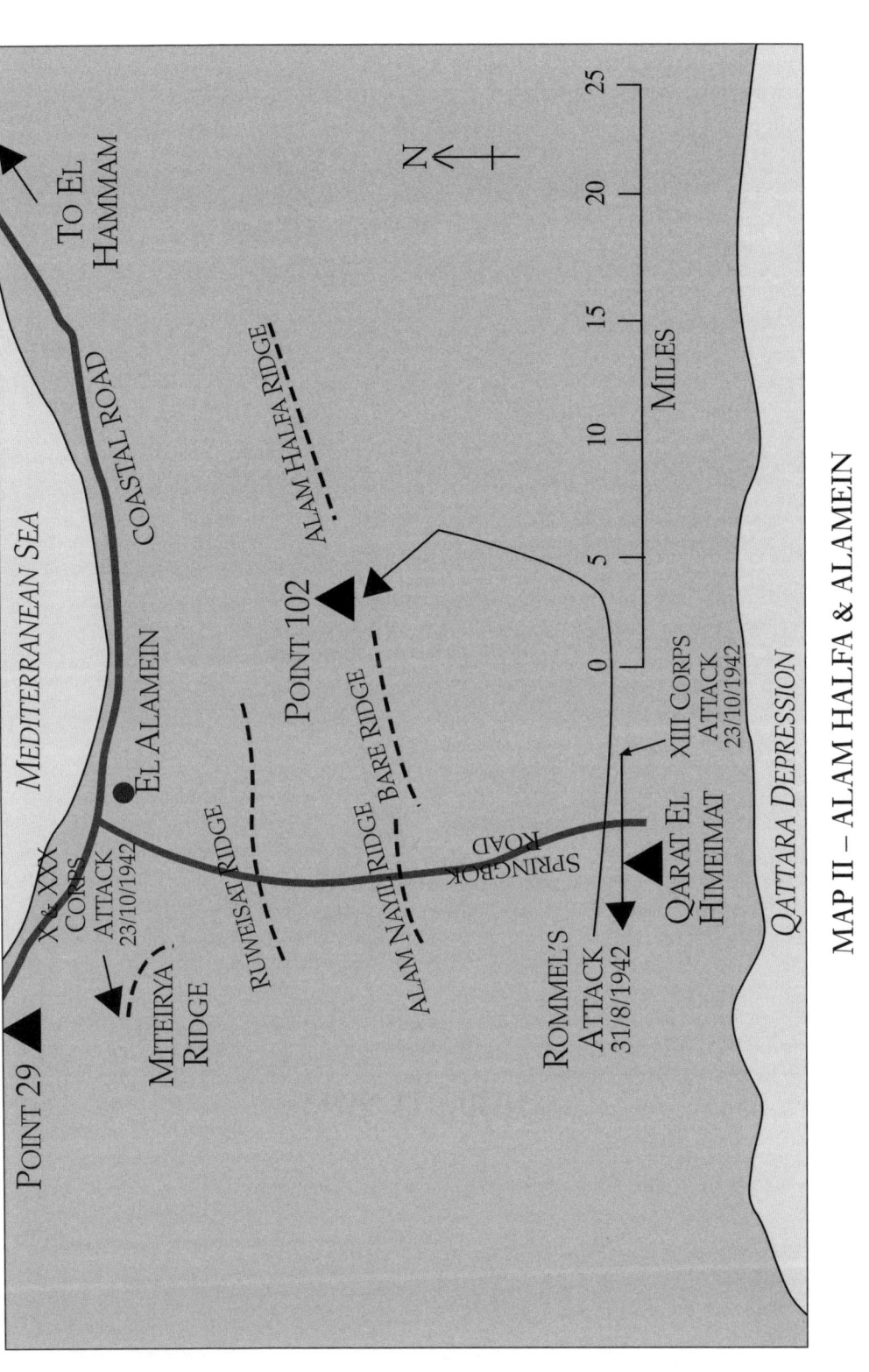

MAP II – ALAM HALFA & ALAMEIN

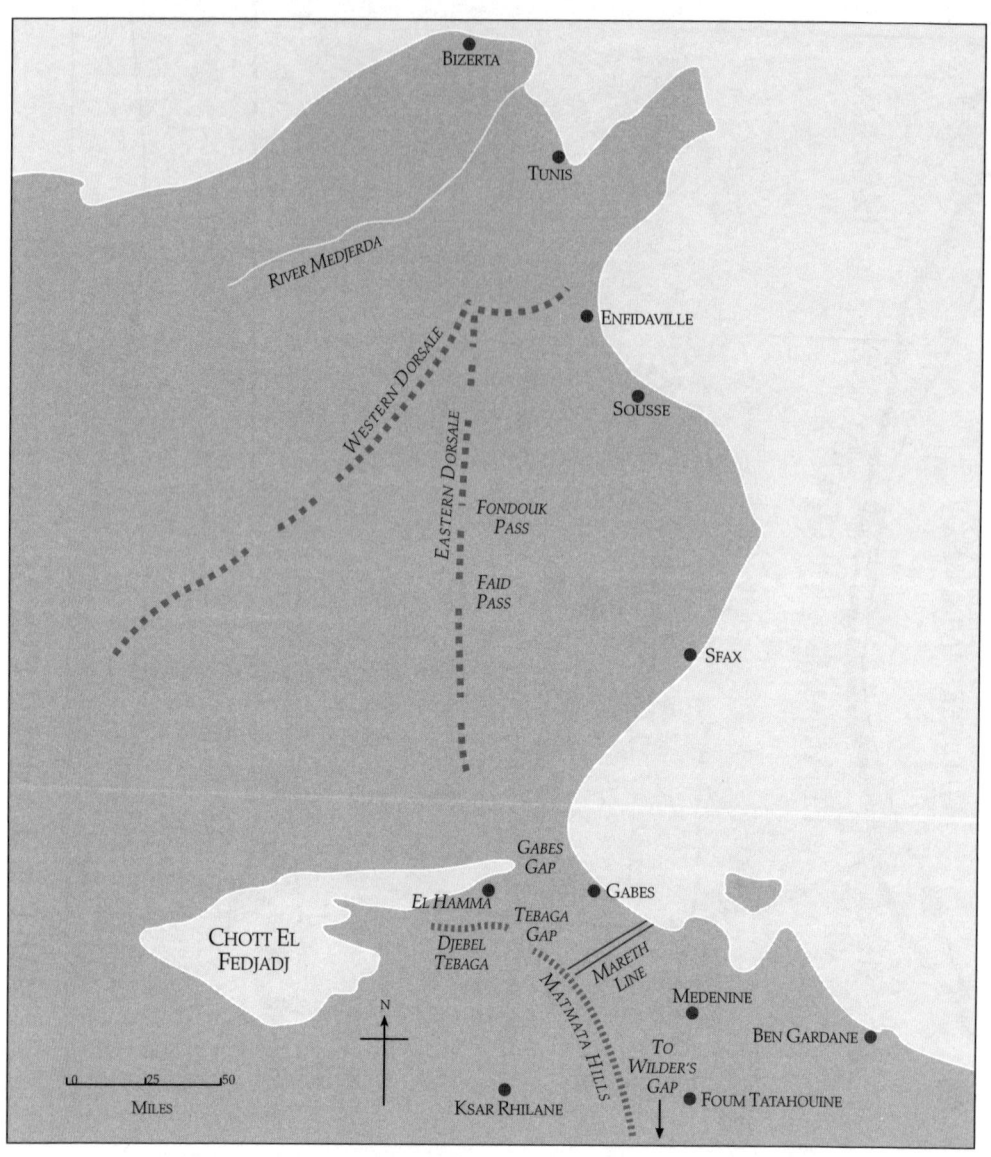

MAP III – TUNISIA

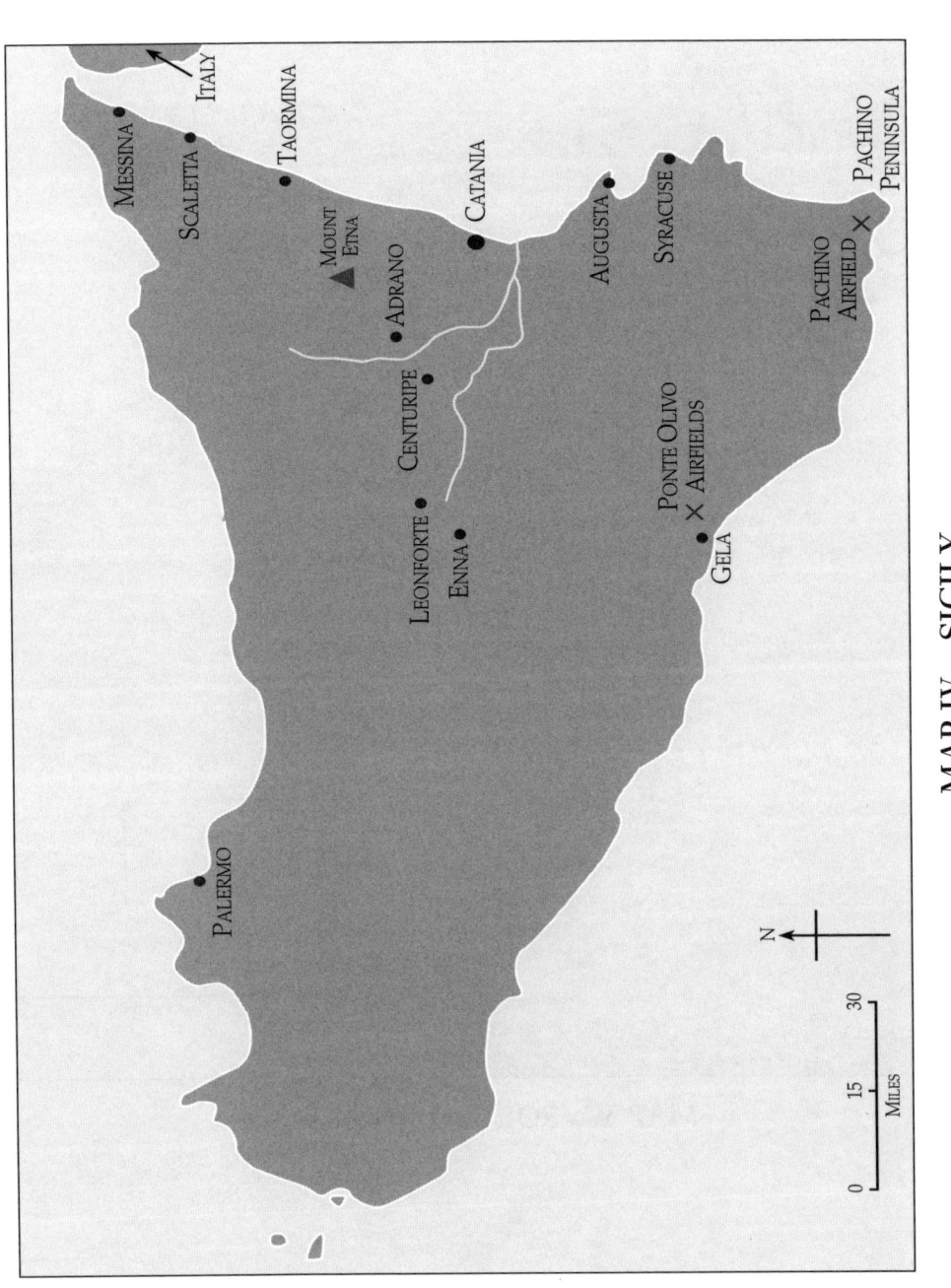

MAP IV – SICILY

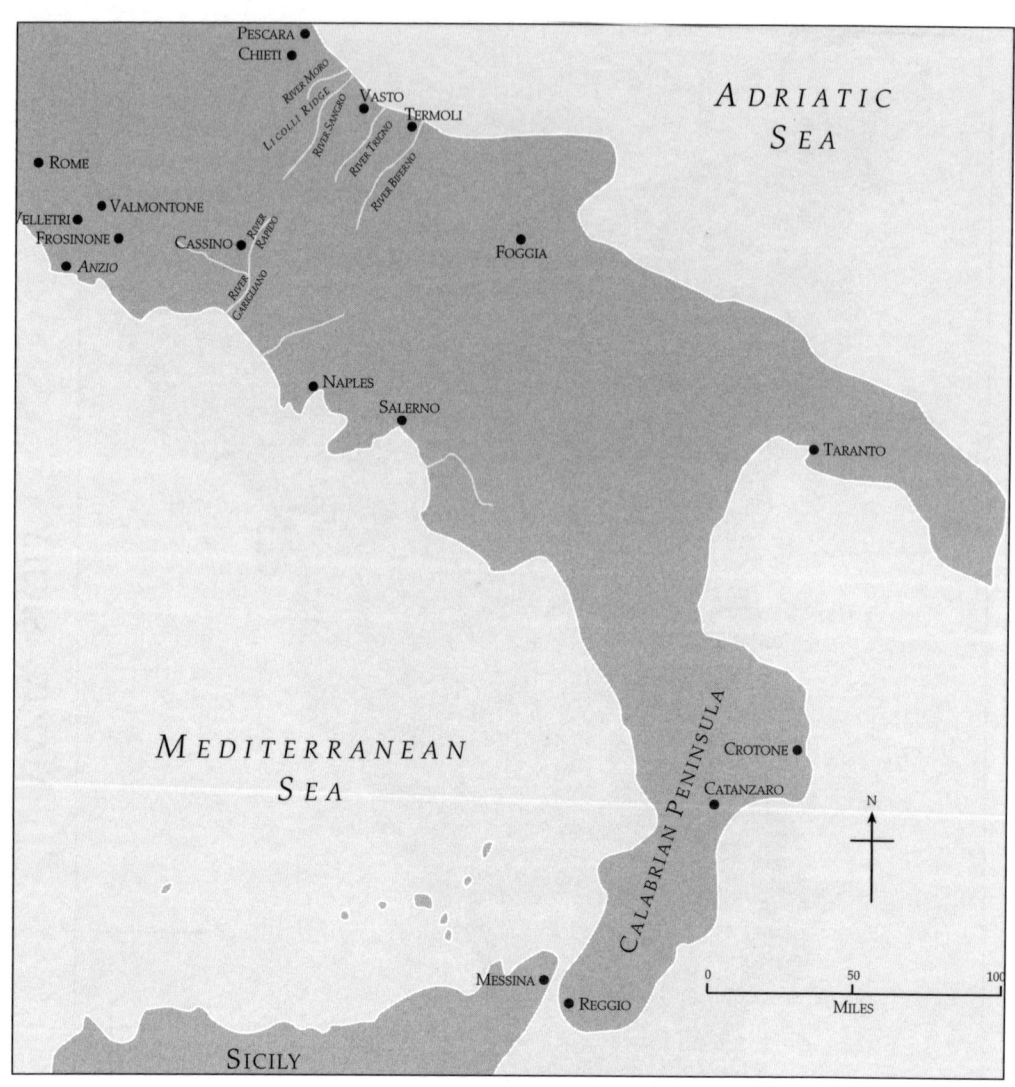

MAP V – SOUTHERN ITALY

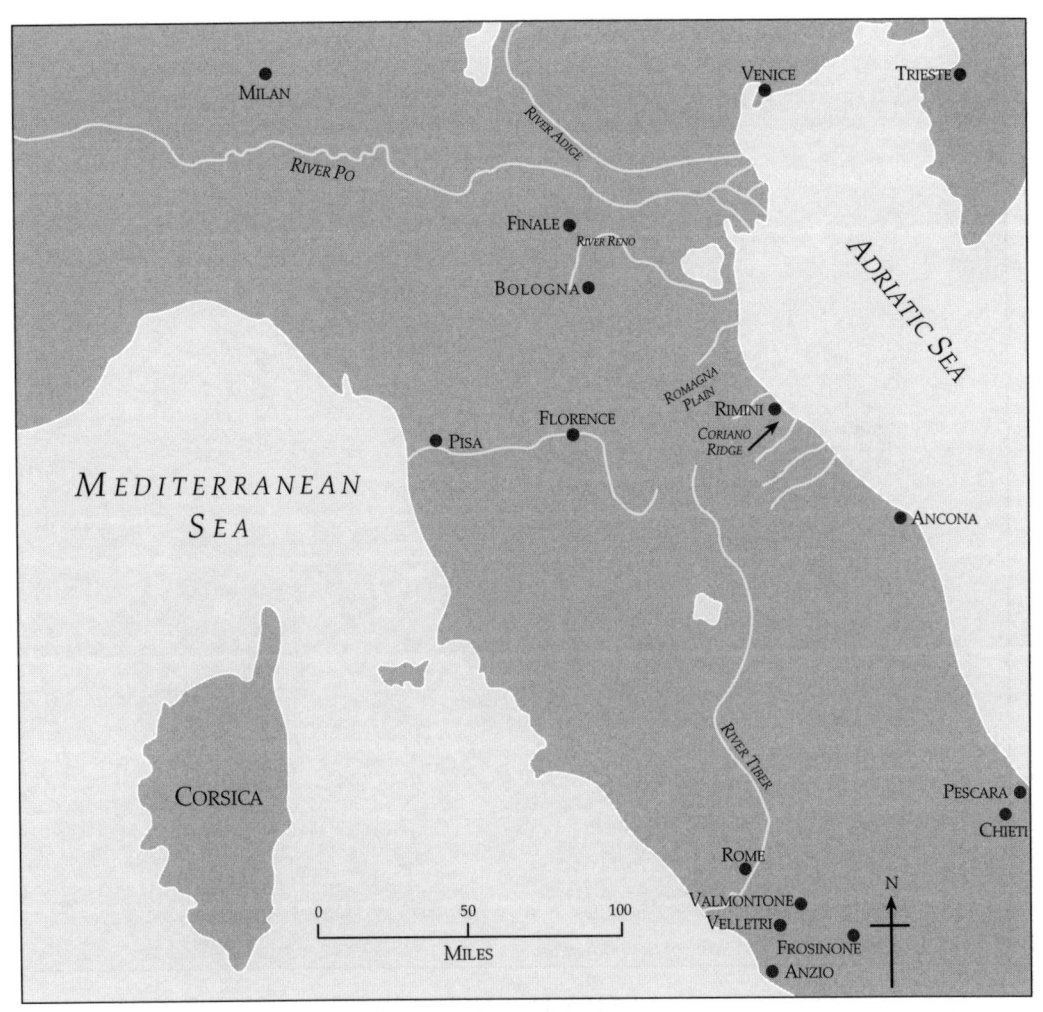

MAP VI – NORTHERN ITALY

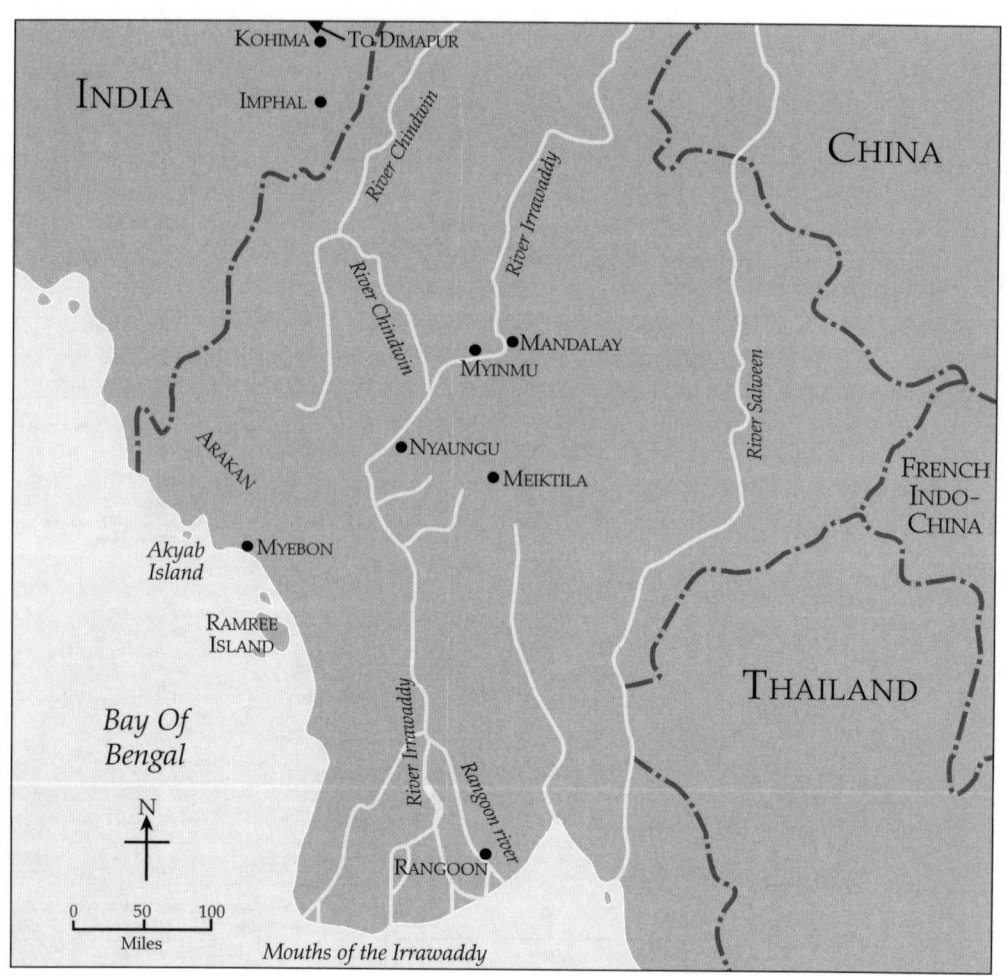

MAP VII – BURMA

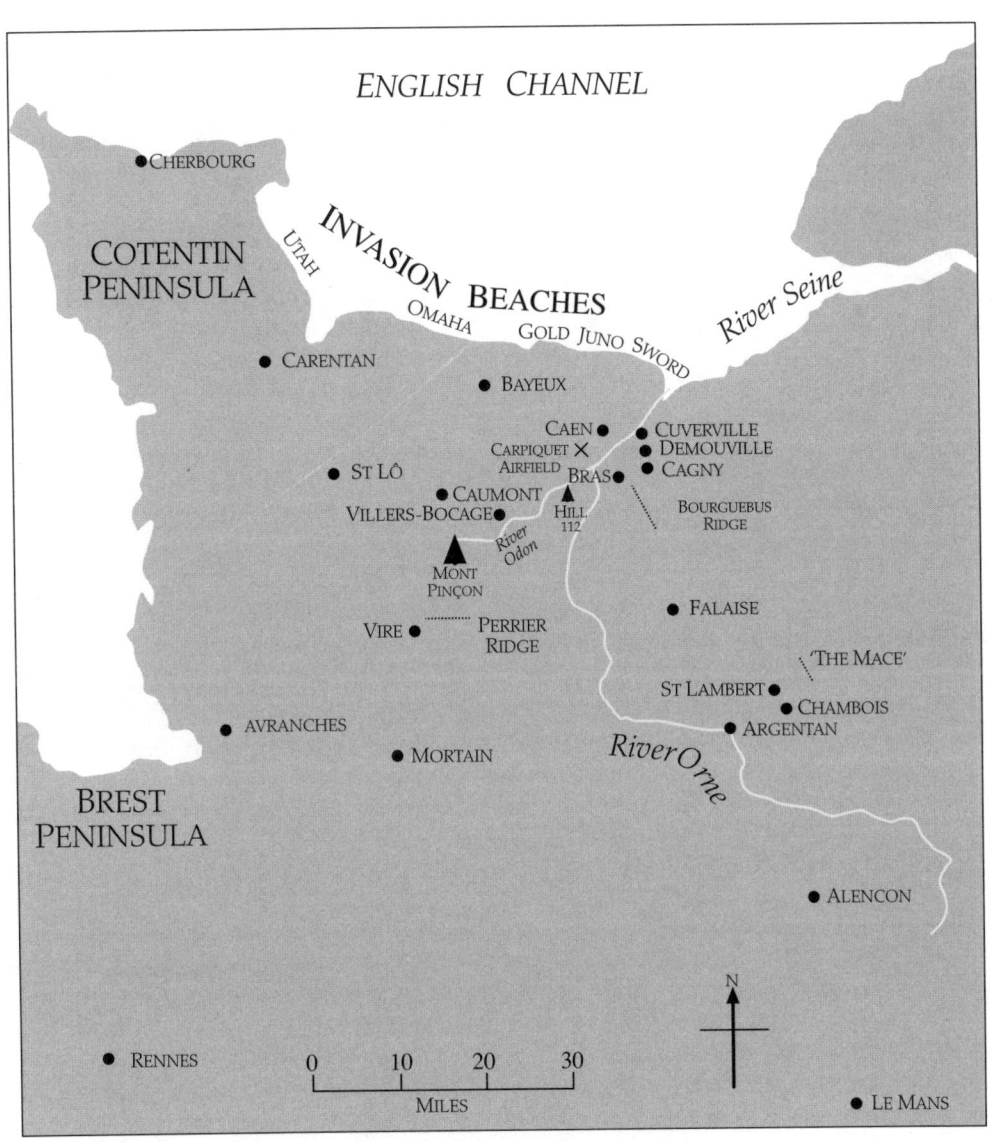

MAP VIII – NORMANDY

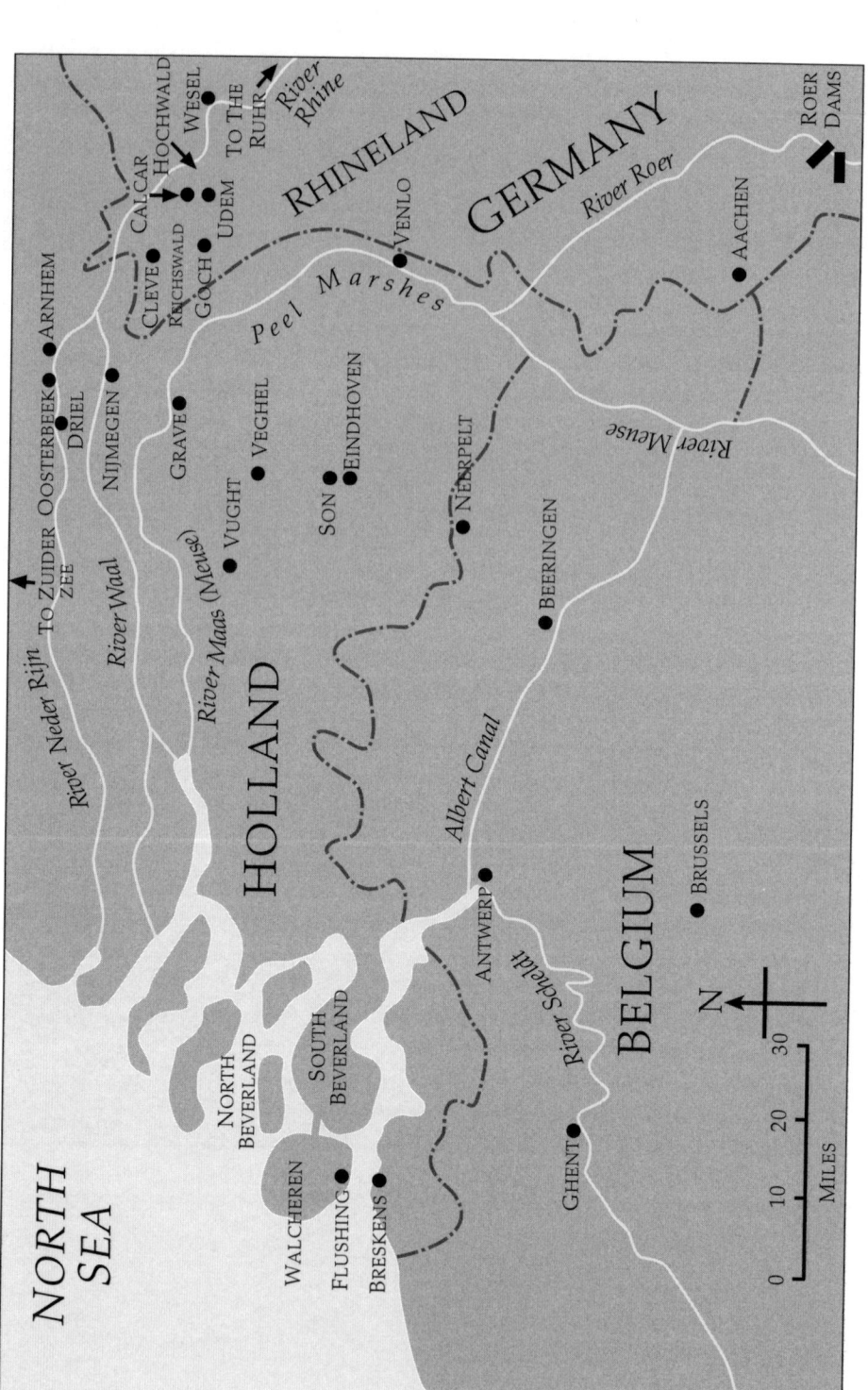

MAP IX – THE ADVANCE TO THE RHINE

Chapter 1

Master and Pupils

In August 1942, an encyclopaedia called *The New Book of Knowledge* produced an extra volume entitled *War Supplement*. Among its 1,270 articles was one that dealt briefly with an officer who had shown immense skill and resolution during the harrowing retreat to Dunkirk and subsequently won deserved praise for his thorough and realistic training methods, yet was still virtually unknown outside his own profession. It read as follows:

> Montgomery, Lt-Gen Bernard Law CB, DSO, (b 1887). He was appointed GOC-in-C, South Eastern Command in November 1941, in succession to Lt-Gen Paget. From 1938 to 1940, when he became specially employed, he was a Divisional Commander.

There would be a different story when *Supplement 2* of the encyclopaedia came out in 1947. Its frontispiece would be a painting of Montgomery, he would be mentioned in many of its 1,900 articles and appear on the photographs accompanying them, and the article dealing specifically with him would run to a full two-column page, followed by half a page of illustrations bearing the general caption: 'From Alamein to Germany He Led the Empire's Men'.

It was an appropriate reminder not only of Montgomery's immense achievements but of the debt that he owed to the soldiers who had followed him and fought his battles. This, to his credit, he was always quick to acknowledge, declaring of his Eighth Army: 'My only fear was that I myself might fail these magnificent men'; and of his Twenty-First Army Group: 'Few commanders can have had such loyal service.'

Montgomery discharged his debt by the care he lavished on those under his command. On taking over Eighth Army, he cancelled orders preventing nursing sisters being brought up to the forward areas, explaining, with typical bluntness, that the wounded 'then knew they would be properly nursed. No male nursing orderly can nurse like a woman, though many think they can.' He arranged for dentist's chairs to be landed over the Normandy beaches, so that the men's teeth could be checked regularly. Throughout the campaigns in North-West Europe, he demanded that every soldier must have at least one hot meal a day, and strongly, if no doubt tactlessly, urged his American allies to follow his example. He took all possible precautions that might reduce casualties, and ignored any political or military superior who wanted him to act before his preparations were complete; his attitude would lead to his being accused of over-caution, but not by those whose lives it would save.

Nor was Montgomery's concern inspired solely by a prudent reflection that his troops would fight better if they were well looked after, as is the impression given by some other successful commanders. Alan Moorehead, the Australian War Correspondent, states in his book *Eclipse* that Montgomery 'treated his army as a kind of family. He delighted in being with the soldiers and he drove among them for hours every day.' Montgomery himself in his *Memoirs* calls the British soldier 'my friend and comrade in arms' and would build up a partnership with his men, based on mutual respect and trust.

Yet it is often forgotten that there was a third member of this partnership: a group of exceptionally able officers, both on the staff and in the field, who formed the link between the general and his soldiers. They were deservedly liked and admired by their juniors and the men in the ranks for the example they provided, for the efficiency with which they carried out their duties, and for the loyal support that they gave to the common cause. Their merits were equally recognized by Montgomery, who gave them his confidence and did his best to further their careers. For their part, his chosen officers regarded themselves as not only his subordinates but also his pupils and were committed to following and passing on to others the precepts he had taught. They would continue to do so even when serving well away from his immediate control; they thereby extended still further the enormous contribution that Montgomery would make towards the winning of the Second World War.

As representatives of the officers and men who followed and were inspired by Montgomery, it is proposed to examine the careers of six of these chosen subordinates. They differed widely in character, background, the branches of the Army from which they came and the tasks that they performed during Montgomery's campaigns and elsewhere. Yet all of them played crucial roles during those latter months of 1942 when the tide turned; the moment that Prime Minister Winston Churchill would call 'The Hinge of Fate', and after which, as General Sir David Fraser would declare in *And We Shall Shock Them; The British Army in the Second World War*, the previously unknown general 'dominated the collective consciousness' of that Army; the moment when 'Montgomery, Lt-Gen Bernard Law' became 'Monty'.

Of those six officers, the one who would reach the greatest heights in his profession was John Harding, who would ultimately become Field Marshal the Baron Harding of Petherton – South Petherton being the small country town in Somerset where he was born on 10 February 1896. The first interesting, if perhaps unimportant fact to relate about him is that his real name was not John. He was christened Allan Francis but when, in September 1919, he joined the 12th Battalion of the Machine-Gun Corps, he was told by the adjutant that for some unexplained reason, perhaps because the name was shared by a number of other officers, he could not possibly continue to be known as Allan: 'We'll call you John.' Thereafter Harding was so universally known by his adopted name that none of his later acquaintances had any idea that it was not his true one. This caused some complications when Harding was knighted in the field by King George VI in July 1944 and he subsequently changed his name to John by Deed Poll.

A small man, often playfully teased about his lack of inches, but good-looking and invariably good-tempered, Harding was educated at Ilminster Grammar School but he left this at the age of 15 and went to live with relatives in London, where he filled minor positions in the Post Office Savings Bank. By May 1914, however, he had become interested in military matters and that month he joined the Territorials as a Second Lieutenant in the 1st Battalion of the 11th London Regiment; later applying successfully for a commission in the Regular Army.

During the First World War, Harding saw action against Germany's ally, Turkey. In 1915, he commanded his battalion's machine-gun platoon in the Gallipoli campaign and was wounded by shrapnel in his left leg. 1/11th Londons formed part of 162nd Brigade and by 1917, the machine-gun platoons of every battalion had been concentrated in a brigade machine-gun company. That March, Harding, now a captain, commanded this in the First Battle of Gaza and was again wounded by shrapnel, this time in his right leg.

Promoted to acting major, Harding then joined the staff of 54th Division, with responsibility for co-ordinating the support provided by all the division's machine-gun units; his services earning him a Military Cross. Later he performed a similar task for the whole of XXI Corps, helping to plan the final British offensive in the Middle East that would lead to the capture of Damascus and Beirut. Before this commenced on 19 September 1918, however, Harding left Corps Headquarters to take an active part in the fighting as an officer in 54th Machine-Gun Battalion. By July 1919, at the age of 22, he was himself in command of this battalion as an acting lieutenant colonel, but, like so many officers at that time, he now reverted to his substantive rank and it was as a captain that he joined the Machine-Gun Corps' 12th Battalion in September and, as previously mentioned, received a new name. He would not make lieutenant colonel again until July 1939, when he took over 1st Battalion, Somerset Light Infantry, which at the start of the Second World War was stationed on the North-West Frontier of India.

In the meantime, in April 1927 Harding had married and in January 1928, he had first become a pupil of Montgomery – literally, for he now attended the Staff College, Camberley, where Montgomery was an instructor. Harding found him 'a brilliant teacher of tactics'. He would pose problems and form the students into 'syndicates' to answer them, and Harding always retained 'vivid recollections' of one such occasion when he was his syndicate's spokesman. He was soon interrupted by the comment: 'That's interesting – continue.' Harding recognized 'the first warning shot' but he gallantly did continue, to hear: 'Now, that's very interesting.' 'Then,' says Harding, 'I knew I was in trouble, but he let me finish and then said: "Well Harding, your syndicate's solution is very interesting but in my view it could have only one result – a scene of intense military confusion."'

It was just this sort of comment that in later years would make enemies for Montgomery, but what impressed Harding was that Montgomery 'didn't leave it at that'. Instead, 'in clear and simple terms' Montgomery explained why the solution offered was likely to have the result stated and then provided an alternative answer that everyone had to admit was a sound one. For his part, Montgomery recognized

Harding's 'intelligence, hard work and energy' and would remember him for the future.

A year before Harding had entered Camberley, a very different officer had become a student there. Oliver William Hargreaves Leese, who would become Sir Oliver Leese when he succeeded to his father's baronetcy in January 1937 and Lieutenant General Sir Oliver Leese in the course of time, was born in Westminster on 27 October 1894. He was educated at Eton, where he joined the Officers Training Corps, and he was with this, as a cadet officer, at a camp run by the Brigade of Guards, when the First World War began in August 1914. He promptly applied for and received a commission in the Coldstream Guards – 'one of the happiest decisions of my life' he later decided – and by mid-October was in France, serving as a Second Lieutenant in the Coldstreams' 3rd Battalion.

In contrast to Harding, Leese was a very tall and powerfully built man with a bushy moustache. The account of him so far may have suggested that he was 'very British'; if so, it will surprise some to learn that he had a dark complexion and jet black hair, which he had inherited from his grandmother, a Portuguese lady.

Regarding Leese's character there are conflicting judgements. Air Chief Marshal Sir Harry Broadhurst who, as Commander of the Western Desert Air Force, knew Leese well in North Africa and Sicily, has left an unedifying picture of him swearing at and generally bullying his staff. There is also an anecdote describing how a senior officer complained to Montgomery about Leese's language ('I don't care what he calls you as long as he wins his battles,' retorted the Eighth Army Commander). On the other hand, there are innumerable accounts of Leese's good humour and good nature. Brigadier C.E. Lucas Phillips in his *Alamein* describes Leese as 'having an easy and friendly manner' and being able to 'laugh, and joke with anyone'. Even more to the point, his staff do not seem to have felt that Leese's behaviour was intolerable. Many of them who joined him when he first came to Eighth Army, including his senior staff officer, Brigadier George Walsh, remained with him until the end of the war and became his close friends. When at the beginning of October 1944, Leese left his command in Italy for the Far East, he was touched to learn that all his staff wanted to come with him.

The explanation would appear to be that Leese did have a temper that occasionally 'exploded' but which was quickly over and was not taken too seriously by those who knew him. And there was certainly one short period when the strains of Leese's responsibilities had an adverse effect. Montgomery, arranging leave for such a 'very valuable officer', informed General Sir Alan Brooke, Chief of the Imperial General Staff, that Leese had begun 'to get irritable with his staff and difficult with them after Sicily was over. . . You would not think it, but he is of a nervous disposition and temperament – and there have been times when his staff found him very difficult.' Perhaps Broadhurst's opinion was unduly influenced by having witnessed Leese's untypical attitude at this particular time.

No one appears to have complained of Leese's attitude during his service in the First World War and no one could possibly have complained of his conduct. Like Harding, he did not come through the fighting unscathed; indeed, he had only been in France a few days when he was wounded by shrapnel, one piece of which had to be removed from his spine and left him with a slight, but permanent stoop. Undaunted by this experience or by multiple, though minor wounds in the face in July 1915, Lieutenant Leese would be found leading a platoon of the Coldstreams' 2nd Battalion during the dreadful Battle of the Somme and winning a DSO 'for conspicuous gallantry in action' on 15 September 1916. The citation rather unemotionally records that:

> He led the assault against a strongly held part of the enemy's line, which was stopping the whole attack. He personally accounted for many of the enemy and enabled the attack to proceed. He was wounded during the fight.

The wound was caused by a pistol bullet in Leese's stomach, fired by a German officer at point-blank range. This passed clean through a silver whisky flask that had been given to Leese by his mother in the previous year as a 21st birthday present. Her gift probably saved her son's life, but his injury was still serious enough to prevent any further service abroad prior to the close of hostilities.

The next phase of Leese's life presented a number of parallels to that of Harding. He also married – in 1933; he also was taught by Montgomery at the Staff College. Leese got to know Montgomery well at this time, was enthusiastic about his abilities as an instructor and liked him 'immensely'. Judging from future events, his feelings were reciprocated. Leese would take the opportunity of passing on some of

Montgomery's ideas when, in September 1938, he became a full colonel and took up the post of Chief Instructor at Quetta, India, which he was still holding when the greatest of all wars commenced a year later.

Montgomery had himself been Chief Instructor at Quetta from 1934 to 1937 and it was in the first of those years that he 'pulled strings' to ensure that a young captain, not highly valued elsewhere, was nominated for another Staff College. He assured his protégé that he 'ought to do very well' and when the future Major General Sir Francis Wilfred de Guingand entered Camberley in 1935, he found that Montgomery had written to many of the instructors to commend him (de Guingand) to them.

This was perhaps as well. Though born in London on 28 February 1900, to an English mother, and educated at Ampleforth College, York and the Royal Military College, Sandhurst, de Guingand's unusual surname gave notice that he was as far removed as is possible from the typical British officer. Pronounced 'dee ging-gang' by his school-fellows, it was really more like 'de gang-gone', and it served as a reminder that his grandfather had been a Frenchman who had sought safety in England in 1848, following the overthrow of the last French king, Louis Philippe.

The refugee's son, who had been born in England, changed his nationality on becoming 21, and Francis Wilfred could only speak French badly, with a shocking accent. In appearance, however, he was very French with his pale face, dark hair, dark eyes and small dark moustache. At Sandhurst, his looks and his name combined to ensure that, like Harding, he would always be known by a name other than the one with which he had been christened – in his case 'Freddie' after a cartoon character of the day, 'Freddie the Frog'.

Too young to see service in the First World War, de Guingand was commissioned in 1919 and joined the 2nd Battalion, West Yorkshire Regiment on the North-West Frontier of India, where he was desperately bored. He was therefore not sorry when he was soon sent home, though the reason for this, a serious bout of fever, at first considered life-threatening, was scarcely the one that he would have chosen. On recovering, he went with his battalion to Southern Ireland, where he first met 'a most efficient and experienced staff officer' of the 17th Infantry Brigade, to which 2nd West Yorkshires and six other battalions belonged – but Major Montgomery hardly noticed him at this time.

Their next contact was longer and more fruitful. In late 1922, de Guingand was posted to the Regimental Depot at York. The Headquarters of 49th (West Riding) Division of the Territorial Army was also stationed there and Montgomery had been appointed to its staff. This time he 'quickly spotted' de Guingand as 'a very intelligent young officer' and enlisted his help in training the Territorials. For his part, de Guingand considered Montgomery, who was thirteen years older, to be 'extremely outspoken and provocative' but with a 'happy knack of making us young officers think about our profession and become interested in the military art'. They struck up a close friendship and spent many off-duty hours together playing bridge or golf, at both of which de Guingand found that Montgomery was very capable.

It was not surprising that Montgomery liked de Guingand; it is difficult to find anyone who did not. It is much to his credit, however, that he should have perceived de Guingand's potential, for that young man's life, in Montgomery's own words, 'revolved round wine, women and gambling – in all of which he excelled'. Montgomery, on the contrary, according to de Guingand, was 'looked upon as rather a novelty, in that he unblushingly proclaimed that soldiering was his one and only love. I'm afraid at that time such an attitude was somewhat rare, or at least unfashionable.' Perhaps it was because they were so different that they got on so well.

Montgomery's belief in de Guingand's abilities was confirmed in 1933. In that year, both were stationed in Egypt, Captain de Guingand being the Adjutant of his battalion and Lieutenant Colonel Montgomery commanding the 1st Battalion of the Royal Warwickshire Regiment. Both formed part of the Canal Brigade, whose commander, Brigadier 'Tim' Pile, conducted a series of intensive training exercises in the desert, in which he gave each of his battalion commanders in turn an opportunity to control the brigade and different junior officers a chance of acting as Brigade Major.

On one such occasion, Montgomery was entrusted with the brigade with de Guingand as his Brigade Major. Their task was to destroy an 'enemy' force attempting to raid their camps. Having arranged the defences of these, Montgomery formed a mobile striking group and, when the 'enemy' had not been located during daylight hours, he impulsively proposed to deliver a night attack without exact knowledge of his opponents' whereabouts. De Guingand, who had persuaded the RAF to co-operate by laying on an aerial reconnaissance, convinced him, after some argument, that it would be wiser to wait for definite news. When this was at last forthcoming, Montgomery delivered his attack with the help of flares dropped from the air, and was credited with a complete victory. He accepted that much of the credit for this was due to the good information and good advice of his Brigade Major, and next year he would take the necessary steps to get de Guingand into Camberley.

At Camberley, de Guingand was regarded as brilliant but unusual, a combination that, in June 1939, earned him the approval of another colourful, controversial character. He was selected by Mr Leslie Hore-Belisha, the Secretary of State for War, as his Military Assistant, apparently because de Guingand, then a lieutenant colonel, was 'less like a regular officer' than any Hore-Belisha had ever met. In November of that year, with Britain now at war with Germany, both men visited the British Expeditionary Force (BEF) in France, where Hore-Belisha decided that the 3rd Division gave him the best 'feel' as far as efficiency was concerned. Since it was commanded by Major General Montgomery, de Guingand had expected nothing less.

If de Guingand had got to know Montgomery very well before the war, and Leese and Harding at least reasonably well, the same could not be said for any of the other three officers with whose careers we are concerned – a fact which demonstrates that it was not necessary to be one of Montgomery's long-time favourites in order to win his approval and support. When Lieutenant Colonel Brian Gwynne Horrocks arrived in Louvain, Belgium on 13 May 1940, to take command of 2nd Middlesex, a machine-gun battalion coming directly under the control of the HQ of Montgomery's 3rd Division, he had met his general only once before and that only in passing, and regarded him with some disquiet. As he would later remark:

> He (Montgomery) was probably the most discussed general in the British Army before the war, and – except with those who had served under him – not a popular figure. Regular armies in all countries tend to produce a standard type of officer, but Monty, somehow or other, didn't fit into the British pattern. His methods of training and command were unorthodox, always a deadly crime in military circles. He was known to be ruthlessly efficient,

but somewhat of a showman. I had been told sympathetically that I wouldn't last long under his command, and, to be honest, I would rather have served under any other divisional commander.

Horrocks was born on 7 September 1895, of an English father and Northern Irish mother, at Ranniket, a hill station in India at which his father, an officer in the Royal Army Medical Corps, was serving at the time. 'There was never any question of my entering a profession other than the army,' according to Horrocks, and after his father had been posted home in 1909, he was educated at Uppingham, 'where I gravitated automatically into the army class', and subsequently, Sandhurst.

In later years, Horrocks, with his fine, almost aesthetic features and silver hair, was thought by many to have the appearance of a bishop – but certainly not the character of one. Curiously enough, he was not greatly liked by some of his subordinates – though all held him in great respect – possibly because, as Field Marshal Lord Carver rather unkindly puts it in *El Alamein*, he 'could turn on suave charm or biting anger with equal facility'.

Still at Sandhurst when the First World War began, Horrocks was commissioned immediately and led a platoon of the 1st Middlesex during the retreat from Mons. A few weeks later, on 21 October, at the start of the First Battle of Ypres, he was badly wounded in the stomach, as Leese was to be later, and taken prisoner. Despite repeated attempts to escape, he spent the next four years in seemingly endless captivity.

During these, Horrocks got to know and like a number of Russian officer-prisoners and since they had taught him their language and he was desperately eager for action, he was no sooner released at the war's end than he volunteered to help train the Russian White armies for their struggle with the Bolsheviks. Arriving in Vladivostok in April 1919, he quickly discovered that the White officers, in sharp contrast to the ones he had met previously, were of an 'abysmally low' standard and deliberately unhelpful. He was not surprised when their forces were routed and he, along with other British officers and NCOs, was once again captured. Kept under house arrest, they were fortunate to be spared the nearest prisoner of war camp where the White Russians were dying at the rate of 200 a day, but Horrocks was almost killed by an attack of typhus, and on recovering, he and his fellow British captives were transported to Moscow. Here 'the prison fare was slow starvation' and 'from time to time someone would depart from the camp "without baggage"', never to be seen again. The nightmare ended in October 1920, when the British contingent, freed under an exchange agreement, crossed the frontier into Finland.

In 1928, Horrocks married; in 1931, he entered Camberley; and surprisingly for one always thought of as a battlefield commander, he held a whole succession of staff appointments, culminating in his becoming an instructor at Camberley himself in 1938. He was Chief Instructor by 1940 but was already in the process of handing over to his replacement when on 10 May, the German invasion of the Low Countries led to his departure for the Continent a fortnight earlier than planned.

Less than two hours after his arrival in Louvain, Horrocks was visited by Montgomery. He makes no mention of the impression that he made on his general but his virtues – confidence, energy, an ability to simplify and explain problems and an overwhelming enthusiasm – were exactly those best calculated to earn Montgomery's approval. Horrocks would fight the great majority of his battles under Montgomery's command and all of them under Montgomery's inspiration, and at the end of the war he had become a lieutenant general and had won a knighthood.

Like Horrocks, Charles Leslie Richardson was born – on 11 August 1908 – of English and Northern Irish parents, but in his case it was his mother who was English, 'for which' he would later remark, 'I have always been grateful: a little of the Irish temperament goes a long way.' Like Horrocks, he had an Army background for his father was a lieutenant colonel in the Royal Regiment of Artillery. And like Horrocks, there was never any question that Richardson would not be a soldier, though his father did not wish him to follow in his own footsteps, preferring that he join the Royal Corps of Engineers. When asked why, he replied: 'If you ever get tired of the Army, or more likely the Army gets tired of you, as a sapper you can always turn your hand to something else.'

Young Charles – it seems he was always called by the formal version of his name – never did get tired of the Army, and he would ultimately progress even further than Horrocks, earning not only a knighthood but the rank of full general. He would become a great friend and admirer of de Guingand but, though both were extremely versatile and capable of assessing all kinds of situations quickly and accurately, Richardson for all his 'Irish temperament', was a quieter, steadier character, who felt that de Guingand's more frenzied lifestyle, particularly his 'powerful gambling urge', 'did not match my idea of happiness'. Amusingly, Richardson was able to 'score' over 'the Compte de Guingand' in at least one respect: having lived in the French-speaking part of Switzerland for two years as a boy, he was bilingual.

Richardson's intellectual qualifications were also higher than those of many of his contemporaries. He was educated at Wellington, to which he went on a scholarship, and the Royal Military Academy, Woolwich, from which he passed out first, being awarded the King's Medal as the cadet best qualified in military subjects. He was commissioned in the Royal Corps of Engineers in 1928 and was then sent on a two-year course to Clare College, Cambridge, where his tuition fees were paid by the War Office and where he achieved a First-Class Honours Degree in Mechanical Sciences.

In 1931, Richardson volunteered for service in India, the Army of which was strong in men and equipment – in marked contrast to the situation in Britain. Apart from one brief spell of leave, he did not return home until 1938, by which time he had reached the rank of captain, had learned Urdu, and had carried out the many varied duties of a sapper officer. He continued to do so on the outbreak of war, when he crossed over to France with a Territorial Engineer unit entrusted with the task of building a row of concrete pillboxes that would extend the Maginot Line defences along the Franco-Belgian frontier. By May 1940, over 400 had been completed together with supporting trenches and anti-tank ditches, but by that time it had in any case been decided that if the Germans invaded the Low Countries, as everyone was certain they would, the BEF and northern French armies would leave these defences and wheel into Belgium to meet them.

In January 1940, Richardson was sent on a short 'War Course' at Camberley, where he would later 'remember particularly the verve and instructional skill of a Lieutenant Colonel Horrocks'. The course ended at the beginning of May and Richardson returned to France; here he met Montgomery for the first time but both men had forgotten the encounter by August 1942. Richardson was then a lieutenant colonel himself and the Eighth Army staff officer responsible for plans. On learning that Montgomery had been chosen to lead that Army, he asked the Brigadier General Staff what his new chief was like; 'Freddie' de Guingand 'cautiously painted a picture of a commander who was very sharp, supremely confident and most decisive'.

On the evening of 13 August, Montgomery addressed the assembled Eighth Army staff; Richardson later described him as 'a slight figure with a pale face and formal uniform, which was seldom worn in the Desert'. Richardson's first thought was: 'Doesn't look the part.' But that was before Montgomery started speaking.

Over the next few days, Montgomery would visit every unit in the front line and, incidentally, would have acquired the Eighth Army's informality of dress. It was now that he first encountered Brigadier (later Major General) George Philip Bradley Roberts. 'Pip' Roberts, born on 5 November 1906, educated at Marlborough and Sandhurst, was, like Harding, a small, neat, athletic man. Unlike Harding but like Horrocks and Richardson, he came from a military background, being the son of a colonel in the Indian Army. He was commissioned in the Royal Tank Corps in January 1926 and two years later went to Egypt, where he joined the 3rd Armoured Car Company.

Though rather retiring, Roberts was calm, clear-sighted and totally unperturbed by a crisis, to which he was always able to react with speed and efficiency. He was thus ideally suited for a career with the fast-moving armour. Prior to the Second World War, when not actually serving with an armoured unit, he would be found at the Royal Tank Corps Depot at Bovington, first as a student, later as an instructor. As a result, he would become, in the words of Horrocks, 'probably the most experienced British armoured commander and certainly one of the best'.

It was also a great advantage to Roberts, and to his superiors such as Horrocks, that most of his career outside the Depot was spent in Egypt, where he gained a considerable knowledge of its Western Desert. Unlike de Guingand and Richardson, both of whom were bachelors at the start of the war, Roberts had married in 1936 and, partly for financial reasons, had decided that it would be best if he sought service abroad thereafter. His original wish was to go to India, but fate decreed that he should return to the Middle East, where he became a captain in the 6th Battalion of the Royal Tank Regiment, with which he was serving on 3 September 1939. Shortly afterwards, he was promoted to major and, as Deputy Assistant Quartermaster General, he joined the staff of the Middle East's 'Mobile Division' which, on 7 February 1940, would become the 7th Armoured Division with its famous badge of the jerboa, the desert rat.

Further promotions followed at regular intervals, and Roberts was in command of 22nd Armoured Brigade when, early on 16 August 1942, he made ready to meet the recently-appointed Eighth Army Commander – and the recently-appointed XIII Corps Commander, Lieutenant General Horrocks – on the Alam Halfa Ridge. Roberts naturally arrived in good time and was soon joined by Horrocks, his chief staff officer, Brigadier George 'Bobby' Erskine, de Guingand and, says Roberts, 'several other characters including a little man with knobbly knees, an Australian hat and no badges of rank, whom I took to be a newly-arrived war correspondent'.

Since he had never met Montgomery and had no idea what he looked like, Roberts approached de Guingand and was just about to ask him when the Army Commander would make his appearance, 'when the gentleman in the Australian hat said to me "Do you know who I am?"' 'Yes, sir!' replied Roberts promptly, having quickly concluded that the Army Commander had appeared already.

Chapter 2

'That Little Tiger'

When Montgomery first arrived in Egypt, well before he met Roberts, some time before he gave the talk that so impressed Richardson, he had spoken to Major General 'John' Harding, Deputy Chief of the General Staff at GHQ, Cairo. General Sir Harold Alexander, who had been chosen as the new Commander-in-Chief, Middle East, was also present, and both he and Montgomery were fortunate to be briefed by an officer who had had such a wide and varied experience of the confused and bitter struggle that had previously swung backwards and forwards across the Western Desert.

It had begun at midnight on 10 June 1940, when the Italian dictator, Benito Mussolini, had declared war on a Britain he believed was already doomed. Harding was then still in India, but in October he arrived at Suez in an Australian troopship, having survived an attack by bombers of the Regia Aeronautica as his vessel entered the Red Sea. In Egypt, he joined the staff of the then C-in-C, Middle East, General Sir Archibald Wavell, whom he found preparing for Operation COMPASS, an attack on the Italians, which General Sir William Jackson in his account of *The North African Campaign 1940–43* would declare was 'fought with professional standards which were never again achieved by the British in the Western Desert until Montgomery won El Alamein'.

Wavell's plans were inspired by the errors that had been made by his opponents. The Italians had crossed the frontier between Egypt and their North African colony of Libya on 13 September 1940, but after an advance of 75 miles to Sidi Barrani, they had halted and begun to build a line of forts stretching away to the south-west. These contained every available luxury, but Wavell's Intelligence had reported that they were neither properly protected nor mutually supporting, while south of one of them – Nibeiwa – there was a gap, 15 miles wide, which was not even patrolled. Though Wavell's Western Desert Force under the tactical command of Lieutenant General Sir Richard O'Connor was heavily outnumbered, it was decided it should strike through this gap to assault first Nibeiwa, then the other forts in succession, from the rear.

On the night of 8/9 December, Operation COMPASS was launched, complete surprise was achieved, and it was quickly discovered that British tanks, British artillery and the RAF's Hurricane fighters were all vastly superior to anything they had to face. So encouraging was O'Connor's success that Wavell authorized a continuation of the offensive into Cyrenaica, Libya's most easterly province.

Prior to the start of the attack, Harding had been sent to Western Desert Force as Wavell's personal liaison officer, but he also took charge of O'Connor's Tactical HQ. Here his advice and assistance was so highly appreciated that on 20 December, Wavell promoted him to brigadier and made him O'Connor's Chief of Staff, in which role he was always ready to accept responsibility for making quick decisions if O'Connor was not available. His most important contribution to success, however, which was recognized by the award of a CBE, was his ability always to plan one step ahead. This ensured that the speed of the advance never slackened and by 8 February 1941, Western Desert Force had overrun the whole of Cyrenaica and annihilated its Italian defenders.

O'Connor now wished to complete his victory by advancing through the western Italian province of Tripolitania to Libya's capital, Tripoli; but Harding felt some doubts as to whether this would prove feasible. It was a permanent problem in the Desert War that food, water, petrol and ammunition had all to be brought to the front line over immense distances by means of quite inadequate supply lines: only the coastal road was metalled and this was highly vulnerable to attack from the air. As a result, the further an army advanced, the weaker it invariably became, while its retreating enemy became correspondingly more powerful as it fell back towards its supply dumps and any formations that had remained in reserve.

Harding therefore considered that the British should remain on the western border of Cyrenaica, at least for the time being, and concentrate on building up their strength to such an extent that it would render any Axis counter-offensive a very difficult proposition. The need for this was even greater than he had imagined, for Adolf Hitler had decided to come to the aid of his faltering ally and had personally selected General Erwin Rommel to command the German relief force which, on 19 February, was officially named the 'Deutsches Afrika Korps'. Before the effects of Hitler's intervention would become known, however, Churchill, with Wavell's approval, had already dispatched large military and air forces to Greece, a country already at war with Italy and now threatened with a German invasion as well. Harding was horrified: this was, he would insist, 'a great strategic mistake'.

So it would prove and its consequences would be disastrous not only in Greece but in Cyrenaica, where, on 31 March, an Axis counter-offensive did commence. Western Desert Force was then commanded by Lieutenant General Philip Neame VC, but since he lacked experience of desert warfare, Harding suggested to Wavell that O'Connor, who had returned to Egypt suffering from a stomach complaint, should be reinstated. Wavell at first agreed but O'Connor unwisely persuaded him to leave Neame in command while he (O'Connor) acted as adviser.

This was a most unhappy arrangement and was made worse because neither Neame, nor O'Connor, nor indeed Harding appreciated the speed and efficiency of the German onslaught. A series of calamities reached its culmination during the night of 6/7 April 1941, when both Neame and O'Connor were taken prisoner. Their capture left Harding in practical command of the British withdrawal and how well he responded is revealed in the citation for the DSO, which he was awarded that summer:

> The sound decisions which he (Harding) took and the firm control which he exercised in circumstances of the greatest difficulty had great effect upon the stabilization of the enemy advance, and the restoration of control and morale amongst our own forces. His services were invaluable and have had a marked effect upon the subsequent course of the campaign.

Harding withdrew his headquarters staff to Tobruk, to which 9th Australian Division had already retired, and he and its commander, Major General Leslie Morshead, decided they would hold the town, thereby depriving Rommel of a valuable port and posing a permanent threat to his lines of communication. De Guingand, who arrived on 7

April to check the situation, would never forget the sight of 'a tired-eyed John Harding at Tobruk with chaos around him but remaining calm and undaunted'.

On 8 April, Wavell also flew up to meet Harding, receiving from him an assurance that Tobruk could be defended successfully. 'Well, if you think you can hold it, you'd better,' the Commander-in-Chief replied briefly. Harding would be brought out of the fortress on 14 April, but by that time Rommel's preliminary attacks on it had failed, and although his light forces bypassed it to head for the Egyptian frontier, they were brought to an abrupt halt near Sollum by the British 22nd Guards Brigade led by Brigadier William 'Strafer' Gott.

British attempts to relieve Tobruk also failed and on 21 June, the day before Hitler invaded Russia, Churchill transferred Wavell to the post of C-in-C, India. His replacement was the former holder of that office, General Sir Claude Auchinleck, for whom Churchill provided massive reinforcements of men, equipment and aircraft that had been designated for the Far East. This would have ruinous consequences when Japan entered the war at the end of the year,[1] but it enabled Auchinleck to expand his forces into the British Eighth Army and when on 18 November, this began a new offensive, it was superior in numbers and, contrary to myth, in the quality of its tanks, and was backed by a much larger air force.

Operation CRUSADER, as this offensive was code-named, brought about a series of savage, confusing and frankly muddled encounters that by 6 January 1942, had raised the siege of Tobruk and driven Rommel back to El Agheila, the frontier post on the western border of Cyrenaica from which his advance had begun. Harding, who had served as the chief staff officer in Lieutenant General Godwin-Austen's XIII Corps, had earned a bar to his DSO and his commander's tribute that he was 'that invaluable asset: a fighting Staff Officer'. Sadly, his natural pleasure was soon to be soured – as for that matter was Eighth Army's victory as a whole.

By a strange paradox, the most important strategic position in the Desert War lay outside the desert. Supplies were all important and whereas British convoys had to travel some 14,000 miles round the Cape of Good Hope, Axis convoys needed to cross only the 350 miles of sea from Messina in Sicily to Tripoli. Some 60 miles south of Sicily, however, was the island fortress of Malta, and from it aircraft, surface vessels and submarines could and did decimate the enemy's merchantmen. Hitler, whose famous intuition was by no means always wrong, had come to realize this and on 2 December 1941, Fliegerkorps II was transferred from the Moscow front to Sicily, joining with Fliegerkorps X in the Balkans to form Luftflotte (Air Fleet) 2. Its commander, Field Marshal Albert Kesselring, became C-in-C South and was thereby given authority over the Axis warplanes in Libya as well. His orders from Hitler were to 'ensure safe lines of communication to North Africa' by bringing about 'the suppression of Malta'.

Kesselring did his level best and as Malta reeled under an ever-increasing weight of bombs, supplies began to reach Rommel again. Warning of this was received from intercepted enemy signals – the famous 'Ultra' Intelligence – but Auchinleck, who never did appreciate the importance of Malta and as late as August 1942 could declare that the island's retention 'was not absolutely necessary' to his plans, continued to believe that Rommel would be 'hard pressed' even to hold his ground. He was thus taken completely by surprise when, on 21 January 1942, 'Panzerarmee Afrika', as Rommel's command had been renamed, delivered another savage counter-offensive. Once more Harding had to organize a withdrawal at short notice and by 5 February, the British had lost most of the gains made in CRUSADER, particularly the vital Martuba airfield complex near Derna, from which fighter cover was provided for the convoys making for Malta from Alexandria.

Shortly afterwards, Harding, who was badly in need of a rest and whose experience, it was thought, would be of great value to GHQ, Middle East, was transferred to Cairo, first as Director of Military Training and later as Deputy Chief of the General Staff with the rank of major general. It was not therefore his responsibility to arrange the next retreat when, on 26 May, Panzerarmee Afrika began a fresh offensive, which reached a triumphant conclusion on 21 June with the capture of Tobruk, 32,000 prisoners and vast quantities of equipment. Rommel had gained his greatest victory and his field marshal's baton. He can be forgiven for having allowed success to turn his head.

It had been intended that once Tobruk had fallen, Panzerarmee Afrika would pause on the Egyptian frontier until its supply lines had been secured by seaborne and airborne assaults on Malta; Rommel had himself previously warned that 'without Malta the Axis will end by losing control of North Africa'. Yet now, appealing directly to Hitler, he won his Führer's consent to a dash for the Suez Canal, leaving the island fortress still unsubdued. It was a colossal gamble: every mile that he advanced into Egypt, his German troops, who had endured weeks of almost continuous action, became more exhausted, his Italian infantry, most of whom lacked motor transport, fell further behind, his supply situation grew worse and the threat from Britain's Desert Air Force became greater.

By contrast, Eighth Army, even after the fall of Tobruk, still had many more men, tanks, guns and supplies than Rommel, and was also receiving large numbers of fresh, experienced reinforcements. There can be little doubt that if Auchinleck, who had taken personal command of Eighth Army, had made a determined stand at Mersa Matruh, he could have halted Rommel then and there. Unfortunately, he had decided on a delaying action only, his defence was anything but determined and once again Eighth Army retreated, this time to the 40-mile wide 'gap' at El Alamein between the Mediterranean and the huge, impassable quicksand known as the Qattara Depression.

On 1 July, Rommel moved into the 'gap' – and the folly of his gamble became obvious. His forces consisted of just 1,500 weary infantrymen and fifty-five tanks, of which only fifteen were the latest Mark III Specials; he was unsupported by his airmen who took no part in the land battle before 3 July; and he was so short of petrol that he could not manoeuvre but had to attack in the north where the British defences, originally ordered by Wavell, were at their strongest.

It cannot be said that Eighth Army was provided with resolute leadership; even the British Official History[2] complains that Auchinleck gave 'no clear and resolute call' to defend the position to the last: on the contrary he issued warnings of possible future retreats and adopted measures, such as sending formations back to the Nile Delta, which 'seemed to the men in the ranks inconsistent with a firm determination to fight'. Fortunately, Eighth Army's officers and men did remain firm and by the evening of 3 July, Rommel had been forced onto the defensive. The initiative had passed to Eighth Army and all the battles fought during the remainder of the month would be originated by Auchinleck.

There were five of these in all and, despite later claims, they did not make up one 'heroic stand' that halted an enemy advance. Even Horrocks would later believe this – but of course he was not in Egypt at the time. Those who were, like Harding, knew very well that the aim of these operations with their dramatic code-names like EXALTATION and SPLENDOUR was, in the words of Auchinleck's own orders on 4 July: 'to destroy the enemy as far east as possible and not let him get away as a force in being . . . Eighth Army will attack and destroy the enemy in his present position.'

Auchinleck had every reason to be optimistic about his chances of achieving this aim, for the advantages he enjoyed were immense. He had received still further reinforcements, including 9th Australian Division; his tank strength increased to over 200 by 10 July, almost 400 by the 20th, while Rommel's varied from under thirty to about fifty; the Allied dominance in the air was such that the enemy was still having to use Italian CR 42 biplane fighters; and he had a short, easily defended line of communications whereas Rommel's supply situation was 'terribly strained'. Yet five times Auchinleck's offensives failed and by the end of July, the atmosphere in his Army, which was experienced enough to be well aware of the opportunities that had been missed, could only be summed up as one of 'prevailing disappointment'.

Harding certainly shared this view. He was particularly disheartened because he had tried to end that lack of co-operation between the different branches of Eighth Army, which in the later July battles, had resulted in no less than three occasions when British tanks had left infantry formations to face enemy armour unprotected – and he had found it impossible to get any action taken by 'the vast and cumbrous base organization, to which Auchinleck paid little attention'. He accepted that Auchinleck was 'a man of the highest principles and integrity', but he also felt that Auchinleck 'had no real concept of armoured warfare in the desert', his offensives in July were 'far too disjointed', and he had reduced his Army to 'a state of confusion'. Harding held Auchinleck's personal adviser, Major General Eric Dorman-Smith, in even less respect and was appalled to find that Auchinleck 'tended to favour any idea of Dorman-Smith's that appeared unorthodox' in a rather pathetic attempt 'not to appear a blimp'.

Early August saw Harding's anxieties increase. The main concern of Auchinleck and Dorman-Smith at this time was with future retreats.

These took two forms: tactical retirements to rearward strongpoints that were still within the Alamein defences, as part of a plan to meet any new assault by Rommel; and strategic withdrawals to reserve positions far from Alamein and protecting the cities of Egypt. There were three main reserve defences: at Amiriya, south-west of Alexandria, at Khatatba, north-west of Cairo, and at Wadi Natrun, blocking a rough desert road called the 'Barrel Track', which ran towards the Egyptian capital from the southern part of the Alamein Line.

Though Auchinleck would later insist that he had never 'seriously considered' retiring from Alamein, his own official biographer, John Connell, reveals that he had approved 'without material alteration', an 'Appreciation of the situation in the Western Desert' prepared by Dorman-Smith on 27 July. This, as General Jackson points out, emits 'a ring of defeatism' as to whether the Alamein position could be held but finds consolation in the thought that 'the critical period for the preparation and manning of the Delta and Cairo defences is now over' and these 'should be complete, in so far as defences are ever complete by the end of August'. Worse still, Dorman-Smith rejoices that: 'The soft sand areas of the country east of El Alamein, notably the "Barrel Track" axis, the Wadi Natrun, the sand area to its north, are all added difficulties for the enemy's movement' – yet the enemy could only move into these places if he had previously broken through the defences at Alamein.

This attitude is confirmed by a mass of signals that pour out from GHQ Middle East and Eighth Army HQ during this period,[3] dealing with the reserve positions, the troops to be allocated to them, and matters such as the destruction of bridges, the removal of supplies and equipment, and the evacuation of civilians, all of which would only be necessary in the event of an Eighth Army defeat at Alamein. They begin with an urgent query from Eighth Army HQ on 27 July as to 'the progress of the Wadi Natrun defences', and end with a similar query from General Auchinleck personally on 14 August – after which they cease abruptly.

All these enquiries indicated, in Harding's opinion, that the Higher Command doubted whether Eighth Army would be able to resist the new offensive by Rommel that Intelligence reports had indicated was planned for late August. In the prevailing mood of pessimism, he would frankly admit that this was a doubt that he shared. Yet for all the attention paid to the reserve positions, Harding, as he would tell Alexander's biographer Nigel Nicolson, was convinced that, if Rommel had broken through at Alamein, 'the time factor, the topography and the effect on the general political and social situation in the Delta would have been such that nothing could have stopped him entering Cairo . . . there was no other place in which you could fight an effective battle.' Moreover, Harding believed that Auchinleck was himself well aware of this and only 'intended to impose delay on Rommel in the Delta'. He could speak with considerable authority on this point, since it was he who was entrusted with planning a series of holding actions that would give Auchinleck enough time 'to extricate the bulk of his forces south of Cairo, and then over the Suez Canal into Palestine'.

Fortunately, early in August, Churchill and Brooke arrived in Egypt. Auchinleck was relieved of his command – Harding would assure Nigel Nicolson that he was 'absolutely certain' that this decision was a correct one – and Lieutenant General Gott, then leader of XIII Corps, who Churchill wished to command Eighth Army, was tragically killed when the transport aircraft in which he was flying to Cairo was shot down by enemy fighters. And on 12 August, Harding was summoned to a conference with their successors and cross-examined at length on the situation that they would have to face.

Harding's replies were forthright and far from comforting, and perhaps because he had been so closely involved with preparations for retreats, he especially stressed the dangers of these and the harm they were doing to morale. This caused considerable concern to Montgomery in particular because he had previously had an awkward interview with Auchinleck, in which the latter appears to have made no distinction between the tactical retreats to the rearward strongpoints that were definitely intended and the major withdrawals that would be carried out only if they proved necessary. Montgomery, who thought both forms were equally undesirable in any case, had therefore mistakenly concluded that the Alamein position was to be abandoned automatically when Rommel attacked.

Montgomery's own intentions were quite different and having heard Harding's opinions, discussed with him the possibilities of forming a mobile reserve force. This would in due course become X Corps and though its role was not really very different from that of XXX Corps at the time of CRUSADER, Harding was delighted with his new task:

such a contrast to planning the details of possible retreats for General Auchinleck.

Harding's morale was soon to be further lifted by learning that Montgomery, with Alexander's full support, had cancelled preparations for all withdrawals, whether tactical or strategic. The news caused widespread relief throughout Eighth Army but did present tactical difficulties for Major General Bernard Freyberg VC, the huge, heroic commander of 2nd New Zealand Division. His 4th Brigade had had to retire from the battle area after the casualties it had suffered in July and his 5th and 6th Brigades were under-strength. When he met Montgomery on 13 August, he welcomed what he called 'this fresh policy' of making no tactical retreats from the existing forward positions; he pointed out, however, that without reinforcements he simply did not have enough men to hold both his front line and his left flank, which rested on the Alam Nayil Ridge, let alone the high ground further east: Bare Ridge, Point 102 and the ridge officially called Alam el Halfa but plain Alam Halfa to the soldiers.

Since Intelligence reports had already indicated that Rommel's main assault would sweep round the New Zealanders' flank – information confirmed beyond question by 'Ultra' on 17 August – Freyberg's concerns were understandable, but happily, Montgomery's refusal to waste troops guarding the cities of Egypt and Harding's good offices at GHQ, Middle East together solved the problem. Among the formations that Auchinleck had retained in the Delta was 44th (British) Division commanded by Major General Ivor Hughes. In accordance with Auchinleck's usual practice, this had been split up into separate brigade groups, two of which protected Cairo, while the third provided a general reserve still further away to the east of the Nile. Montgomery wished to bring the division up to the front line but his staff's enquiries on the evening of 13 August indicated that this would not be possible before the end of the month.

Montgomery then personally telephoned Harding, who promised he would do everything he could to speed up 44th Division's move forward. He spent the whole of 14 August on this task, and 44th Division arrived in the battle area two days later. Its 132nd Brigade was detached to join Freyberg, though it should be noted that, unlike Auchinleck's brigade groups or smaller battle groups, it did not operate on its own; instead it became 2nd New Zealand Division's third brigade, thereby enjoying the benefit of all that division's facilities. Meanwhile, 44th Division's 131st and 133rd Brigades proceeded to Alam Halfa, where they set to work laying minefields, organizing gun positions and preparing defences for use in the coming conflict.

Harding could now watch with satisfaction as a revitalized Eighth Army smashed Rommel's August offensive. He took no personal part in the Battle of Alam Halfa, but he had already made an invaluable contribution towards the attainment of that victory.

* * *

With his defeat at Alam Halfa, Rommel would later report, 'our last chance of gaining the Suez Canal had gone'. His superior, Kesselring, agreed: 'I realized that the fate of the North African campaign was sealed.' Yet Alam Halfa had really achieved only the first part of Eighth Army's task. It had certainly deprived Rommel of his last as well as his best chance of reaching the Suez Canal while Malta was unsubdued, but if that crucial island could be starved into surrender, victory could still be his.

And Malta's situation remained perilous in the extreme. In August, a large convoy, code-named PEDESTAL, had set out to raise the siege, and four freighters, loaded with a mixture of flour, ammunition and aviation fuel in cans, and the American-built tanker *Ohio*, had broken through to preserve the island for the Allied cause. Yet the relief was only a temporary one. The food and fuel provided would not last beyond the end of November and the loss of nine other merchantmen and several warships, including the aircraft-carrier *Eagle*, gave warning that this costly success was unlikely to be repeated – unless the ships which went to Malta's aid could be provided with strong and continuous fighter protection.

There was only one way in which this could be guaranteed: before mid-November, Eighth Army would have to break through Rommel's positions at Alamein, advance some 480 miles through enemy-held territory and recapture the Martuba airfields. The Army's confidence was high after Alam Halfa, but there must have been many who reflected uneasily that, with every day that passed, their enemies were strengthening the defences and protecting them by laying half a million mines; and that in July when those defences had been almost nonexistent and Eighth Army's superiority in numbers and equipment had been considerably greater, Auchinleck had five times tried to drive back the Axis forces and five times failed miserably.

Montgomery was well aware of both the difficulty and the importance of the task ahead of him and he set about preparing for it with ruthless determination. To assist him he needed reliable subordinates and he had no hesitation in removing those whose ability he doubted – not always correctly, for Montgomery could be hasty in his judgements and was rarely willing to change his mind about anyone who had incurred his displeasure. Among those dismissed was Major General Renton, the head of 7th Armoured Division, who had not been one who had approved of the Army Commander's 'fresh policy'. Montgomery had requested several officers from England to fill key positions but he wisely realized that the 'Desert Rats' would never have accepted the appointment of a newcomer. Luckily, he had a suitable candidate close at hand: 'that little tiger', as he called John Harding.

Harding was still at GHQ, Middle East, where he had gratefully observed the improvements being made to that cumbersome body by General Alexander. Nonetheless, he was delighted to return to an active role and his pleasure was shared by his superiors and subordinates alike. Horrocks, who commanded XIII Corps, of which 7th Armoured formed part, praises Harding's 'calm confidence'; while Roberts, whose 22nd Armoured Brigade was one of its subsidiary formations, describes Harding as 'full of humour, always enthusiastic, always approachable, tremendously alert and quick on the uptake, and of great energy'. Roberts adds that he personally was always spurred on to do his very best for his divisional commander because 'one feels that one cannot let such a chap down'.

7th Armoured Division played only a minor role in the Battle of El Alamein, chiefly because the tanks of 22nd Armoured Brigade, which was its principal striking force were greatly in need of maintenance and overhaul. Detailed to take part in a subsidiary attack by XIII Corps against the southern part of the enemy defences which, it was hoped, would distract attention from Eighth Army's main assault in the north, 7th Armoured went into action at the start of the battle on the night of 23/24 October and withdrew into reserve on the 26th. In the meantime, it had seen much savage fighting and its leader, who was always well forward to check on progress and be available for consultation if needed, and who, incidentally, always refused to wear a steel helmet, had had a number of narrow escapes.

On the morning of 24 October for instance, Harding called a conference of his subordinates, which was held close to the front line in the shelter of a knocked-out tank. Roberts, who was present, complains that: 'it was really quite difficult to concentrate; shells were continually landing close by and we occasionally heard the "ping" of a splinter hitting the tank.' Everyone was relieved when the meeting broke up. That night, Harding had an even narrower escape when a shell burst close beside his jeep, killing his ADC, Captain Cosgrave.

By 4 November, a rested 7th Armoured Division was back in action and, encouraged by the eager Harding, was busily completing the ruin of the crumbling Axis army. Brigadier Mark Roddick's 4th Light Armoured Brigade, which had been one of 7th Armoured's subsidiary formations at the start of the battle, had now been transferred to Freyberg's 2nd New Zealand Division, but 22nd Armoured Brigade had been joined by the motorized infantry of Brigadier Lashmer 'Bolo' Whistler's 131st Brigade, formerly a part of 44th Division. 7th Armoured in turn was now part of Lieutenant General Herbert Lumsden's X Corps, as was 1st Armoured Division under Major General Raymond Briggs and 10th Armoured Division commanded by Major General Alec Gatehouse.

By the late afternoon of 4 November, the Battle of El Alamein had been won. Rommel's Italian infantry, who lacked motor transport, were hopelessly trapped and surrendering in their thousands, among the prisoners being eight Italian generals; while his mobile units were in full retreat with X Corps' three armoured divisions and Freyberg's New Zealanders in pursuit.

Harding would later consider that it would have been better if the pursuit had been left to just one armoured division rather than to three of them 'all competing for petrol'. Certainly it was soon discovered that Eighth Army's new Sherman tanks consumed vast quantities of fuel when crossing open desert, a defect that had been concealed by the static nature of the fighting at Alamein, but this was not the reason why Rommel's mobile forces evaded capture. Roberts was much more accurate in his assessment of the situation. He was all in favour of the armoured divisions being concentrated, but believed that they should have been sent to 'Charing Cross', a road junction just south of Mersa

Matruh, where, he was sure, they 'could have rounded up the remnants of Rommel's army'. As it was, he reports, the British tanks 'tapped in too early'.

So indeed they did, and it may surprise many to learn that the reason for this error was that Montgomery had received singularly misleading information from 'Ultra'. This form of Intelligence was usually valuable and occasionally invaluable but the exaggerated praise bestowed upon it must not be allowed to mask its considerable flaws. In the first place, there was an inevitable delay before the interceptions reached the combat zone. They had to be deciphered and translated; errors or gaps resulting from poor reception had to be corrected; the message had to be re-encoded; and by the time it was received by the appropriate British Intelligence officer in the field, at least one and perhaps as many as three days would have passed, during which the situation might have become completely different. Worse still, since the signal had been intercepted, the intentions it revealed might also have become completely different because its originator had changed his mind, or had been overruled, or, as happened more than once in Rommel's case, had deliberately concealed his true plans from his superiors.

This is what now happened. On 3 November, Montgomery learned from 'Ultra' that, on the previous day, Rommel had warned Hitler that his men were exhausted, his non-motorized units would probably 'fall into the hands of the enemy' – as would shortly prove the case – and even his mobile troops were threatened because 'the shortage of fuel will not allow of a withdrawal to any great distance'. A second signal on the same day added that he proposed to retire fighting 'step by step'. On 4 November, a further 'Ultra' interception revealed that Rommel intended 'to gain some time at the next intermediate position El Daba', some 20 miles west of El Alamein, before retiring a further 30 miles to Fuka.

Since this last report seemed to confirm and elaborate on the previous signals, Montgomery was confident that the Axis remnants were within his grasp. 1st and 7th Armoured Divisions were ordered to attack El Daba, while 10th Armoured Division cut the coast road at Galal, midway between El Daba and Fuka, to block the enemy's escape route. It was an admirable plan with only one defect: the 'Ultra' Intelligence was simply incorrect and Rommel had not made a stand at El Daba after all.[4]

By the time this was realized, Eighth Army had lost its best chance of completing Rommel's destruction. Briggs reached El Daba on the morning of 5 November but took only a miserable 150 prisoners, while Harding halted some 5 miles south of the coast road on learning that his enemy had eluded him. Gatehouse did intercept a straggling Italian armoured column, which he all but annihilated, but the Germans had already escaped and to make matters worse, when 10th Armoured Division followed them down the coast road to Fuka, Gatehouse demanded and received 'full fighter cover' from the Desert Air Force. In consequence very few air attacks were made on the enemy until the afternoon, and then only because Montgomery, on learning of Gatehouse's demands, had overruled them, stating that: 'RAF fighter cover can be dispensed with and all fighters used against the enemy.'

Montgomery had not yet given up hope of cutting off the Axis retreat. He now ordered 1st and 7th Armoured Divisions to make for 'Charing Cross'. Sadly, his intentions were again thwarted, first by difficult going which so increased the Shermans' consumption of fuel that they were compelled to make frequent halts while their supply echelons caught up with them; then, at about 1500 on 6 November, by a rainstorm which Rommel would describe as 'torrential' and which continued for the rest of the day and all night, reducing the desert to a quagmire. Only 10th Armoured Division which, like the Germans, was using the metalled coast road, could continue the pursuit and it was held back by the valiant resistance of Rommel's 90th Light Division which, battered but undaunted, would henceforth act as the German rearguard.

Thereafter Montgomery concentrated the bulk of his available forces in a steady advance along the coast, but he did send 7th Armoured Division on one last outflanking sweep towards the frontier. With his much-used tanks plagued by mechanical defects, Harding could have stood little chance of success even before he was bogged down by more heavy rain on 10 November – but this move and his previous one towards 'Charing Cross' had not been without effect.

Later British accounts would speak very slightingly of Eighth Army's pursuit after Alamein, dismissing it as slow, cautious, unimaginative and, worst of all, dull. This was not the impression it made on the enemy: German sources describe it as unusually rapid, conspicuously bold and relentlessly sustained, allowing them no time for reorganization and forcing them to abandon position after position prematurely as they fell back ever further to the west.

Thus, in Rommel's own words, he had planned to defend Fuka 'long enough for the Italian and German infantry to catch up'. When he was driven out of Fuka late on 5 November, his unmotorized units had no chance of doing anything other than surrender. He had hoped the rainstorm would enable him to 'hold on to Mersa Matruh for a few more days' while defences were constructed in the frontier area – but the threat of being cut off by Harding and Briggs soon changed his mind. Late on 7 November, he retired to Sidi Barrani, where he intended to make a stand at least until the evening of the 10th – but the main body of Eighth Army was close behind him and Harding was again moving round his flank, so in fact he withdrew on the evening of the 9th. And on the night of 10/11 November, a brilliant attack by Brigadier Howard Kippenberger's 5th New Zealand Brigade captured Halfaya Pass and compelled Rommel to abandon his frontier defences, yet again 'earlier than anticipated'.

With the frontier passed, Montgomery faced those supply problems that affected every advancing army in the Desert. He therefore halted most of his forces, entrusting the pursuit to 7th Armoured Division which had now regained control of Roddick's 4th Light Armoured Brigade. Harding, as usual, rose to the occasion. The Germans had been assured that Tobruk would not fall 'without a struggle' but by the evening of 13 November, Rommel was hastily saying that the town 'possessed only symbolic value' and the next day it was occupied without resistance. On 15 November, 4th Light Armoured Brigade seized the greatest strategic prize of the victory at El Alamein and the Martuba airfields were made ready to receive Allied fighters just in time to provide protection for a convoy, code-named STONEAGE, heading for Malta. In the early hours of the 20th, its four merchantmen reached the island, finally raised the siege and ended the last chance of the Axis dominating the Mediterranean. In his diary, Brooke noted a simple 'Thank God!'

On 23 November, Harding moved up to the 'bottleneck' at El Agheila and Eighth Army came to a temporary halt. After CRUSADER, Eighth Army had reached El Agheila from Tobruk, a distance of 470 miles by the coast road, in thirty days. The advance from El Alamein to El Agheila, 'slow and cautious' though we are assured it was, had covered the 840 miles by the coast road in just nineteen days. Montgomery was delighted with Harding's performance. He wrote personally to congratulate 7th Armoured on the way it had 'shown the whole Army how to fight the pursuit battle' and ensured that Harding was awarded a rare third DSO.

The citation for this mentioned that Harding's 'personal gallantry in dangerous situations was an inspiration to his whole Division'. Harding had certainly experienced his fair share of such situations since Alamein – on 6 November, for example, he had come under shellfire though it had left him unhurt and outwardly unmoved – and the pursuit had scarcely ended when, on 25 November, an attack by Junkers Ju 87 Stuka dive-bombers forced him to seek shelter under a tank. Furthermore, when Eighth Army began its attack on the El Agheila defences on the night of 13/14 December, Harding was again in action leading 7th Armoured Division – which now contained Whistler's 131st Brigade, 153rd Brigade temporarily transferred from 51st Highland Division and 8th Armoured Brigade, which had replaced the exhausted men and machines of 22nd Armoured – and, as usual, leading from the front. The enemy was in full flight by 16 December and Harding headed another pursuit as far as Rommel's next defensive position at Buerat. There must have been some who wondered how long his luck could continue.

It ran out during the course of the well-named Operation FIRE-EATER, which began on 15 January 1943. Eighth Army's task was a threefold one: to break through the Buerat defences; to storm the huge escarpment which, beginning at Homs on the coast and curving in a great arc through Tarhuna and Garian, protected Tripoli from the east, south-east and south; and finally, to capture the Libyan capital itself. Harding was again in command of 7th Armoured Division and on 19 January, its 8th Armoured Brigade and 131st Brigade were attacking the pass at Tarhuna, a narrow defile between two high ridges.

Harding was, of course, well forward, standing on top of a tank to direct operations. A shell burst just in front of this, killing one of the crew and knocking Harding to the ground with severe wounds to chest, leg and particularly left arm and hand, from which he lost three fingers. He managed to crawl under the tank, where he lapsed into unconsciousness.

So serious were Harding's injuries that it was feared he would not survive a journey by ambulance back over the dreadful terrain through which his division had passed. Fortunately, his chief staff officer, Lieutenant Colonel Michael Carver – later Field Marshal Lord Carver, Chief of the Defence Staff – was able to arrange the preparation of an improvised landing-strip by a combined Army and RAF party, working all the next night. On the following day a light aircraft, escorted by fighters, flew to the strip and carried Harding to a Casualty Clearing Station, from which he was later moved to Cairo. Before his departure, he was visited by Colonel Charles Turner, 7th Armoured's principal Administrative Officer, who told him 'how much we would miss him and what an example he had been to us'. 'I was only doing my duty Charles,' Harding replied quietly.

* * *

    During the three months that Harding spent in hospital in Cairo, he was deeply troubled by the knowledge that 'the doctors had written off my chances of further active duty'. At the same time he was immensely heartened by the genuine concern and interest shown by Montgomery, who in a number of hand-written letters, expressed his sorrow at Harding's misfortune, his regret that Harding was no longer serving under him, and his good wishes for Harding's future. 'Keep up a stout heart,' he urged, 'and do not worry. So long as I have any influence in the Army, you can rest assured that you will always be looked after.'
    Finally, shortly before Harding left hospital, Montgomery, who was in Cairo to discuss plans for the invasion of Sicily, came to see him. 'I knew he must be very busy,' says Harding, 'and I expected a short visit. Not a bit of it. He pulled up a chair by my bed, sent his ADC away and spent an hour or more telling me all that had happened since I was wounded, particularly the exploits of my old division, and of his plans for my future.' Harding would 'always remember with deep gratitude that act of kindness and compassion'.
    In early May 1943, Harding was sufficiently recovered to be able to return by flying boat to England, where he set about regaining his full fitness with immense determination. Aided by an operation on the nerves of his injured left arm that successfully restored its movements, he had managed to do so by early October. He wrote delightedly to Montgomery with the good news, and learned from the reply that

Montgomery had immediately recommended to Brooke that he be given command of a corps. On 11 November, Lieutenant General Harding took over VIII Corps, one of its subsidiary formations being 11th Armoured Division which, at the beginning of December, also received a new leader. Major General 'Pip' Roberts found Harding 'in very good form and quite recovered from his very nasty wounds', but their service together this time was destined to be brief. On 1 January 1944, Harding was again in the air, on his way back to the Mediterranean theatre, having been selected by Brooke for the post of Chief of Staff to General Alexander in Italy.

Alexander was then in charge of Fifteenth Army Group. This had originally controlled the Seventh US and Eighth (British) Armies but the former had later been replaced by the Fifth US Army of Lieutenant General Mark Wayne Clark. In the previous six months, Alexander's men had conquered Sicily and southern Italy, caused the downfall of Mussolini, and persuaded his successor, Marshal Pietro Badoglio, to renounce the Axis Pact and join the Allies. They had also forced Hitler to pour troops into Italy rather than sending them to or keeping them in Russia or North-West Europe, where the great invasion of Normandy, code-named Operation OVERLORD, had been provisionally planned for 1 May 1944.

Unfortunately, their reinforcements had enabled the Germans to crush the feeble Italian resistance and on 4 October, Hitler had ordered his soldiers to stand firm south of Rome, He entrusted the defence of the Italian capital to the redoubtable Field Marshal Kesselring, who, on 21 November, became C-in-C, South West and head of Army Group 'C' with control over two German Armies: the Tenth led by General Heinrich-Gottfried von Vietinghoff and the Fourteenth under General Eberhard von Mackensen. Fourteenth Army remained north of Rome but could provide reserves when needed, while Tenth Army fell back slowly before Alexander, who at this inopportune moment was deprived of four British divisions, including 7th Armoured, and four American ones, all destined for ultimate use in North-West Europe.

Behind the retreating Tenth Army, Kesselring's engineers were working furiously on a major defensive position. Across the narrowest part of the Italian peninsula, where the Apennine mountains provided formidable natural obstacles, the Gustav Line, a maze of interconnected strongpoints, stretched from the mouth of the Garigliano

River on Italy's Mediterranean coast to the mouth of the Sangro River in the east. As the men of Fifteenth Army Group fought their way towards this, they encountered a foe more relentless than any human one. Every day the rain became heavier and more persistent, grounding the Allied airmen. Rivers became raging torrents that drowned men and swept away the temporary bridges that the sappers had erected to replace those destroyed by the enemy. The ground became a sea of thick, clinging mud, where motor vehicles could only move with difficulty on roads the Germans had deliberately wrecked and could not move at all off them, and where essential equipment had to be carried to the front line by mules or by the soldiers themselves. Snow, sleet and biting winds added to the appalling conditions and during December five men from 78th (British) Division froze to death and there were 113 cases of exposure. By the end of the year the Allied advance had come to a halt.

It was at this point that Harding joined Fifteenth Army Group. Montgomery, who had been chosen to command the OVERLORD land forces, had left Italy on 30 December, handing over Eighth Army to Leese, but as early as 31 October he had declared in a letter to Harding that it was a pity that the Allies could not follow the example of the warriors of classical times and refrain from warfare during the winter. Harding entirely agreed, but of course if Alexander was to fulfill the Allies' main aim, that of preventing German reinforcements being sent from Italy to more vital areas, he would, as he warned Churchill, have to 'keep the Germans on their heels' by continuing his assaults. On the other hand, if he could break through to Rome, its capture would probably compel Hitler to send more divisions to Italy and quite certainly have an immense morale effect on both sides.

Accordingly, Harding learned that the Allies were already preparing for an assault on the Gustav Line. In the Adriatic sector, spurs of the Apennines, with rivers between them, ran down to the sea, giving the Germans a whole series of perfect defences. At the western end of the Line, Route 7, the famous Via Appia, was hemmed in between the coast and the Aurunci Mountains. The best 'road to Rome' seemed to be Route 6, the Via Casilina, which passed through the little town of Cassino and then followed the valleys of the Liri River and its tributary the Sacco north-westward straight for the Italian capital. It was decided that II US Corps under Major General Geoffrey Keyes should cross the southward-flowing Rapido River, which joined the Liri south of Cassino,[5] and then advance on Rome through the Liri Valley. Meanwhile, VI US Corps led by Major General John Lucas would land at Anzio, south of Rome but behind the enemy lines, threatening Tenth Army's communications.

Harding was not at all happy about these proposals. He believed that Clark did not have sufficient resources for both the thrust into the Liri Valley and the Anzio landing and that the latter in particular had been planned too hastily and without regard for the risks posed by the inevitable German counter-attacks. Churchill, however, was strongly in favour of Operation SHINGLE, as the Anzio mission had been code-named, and Allied Intelligence offered reassuring predictions that the Germans were exhausted and low in morale and the frontal attack, combined with the threat from Anzio, would undoubtedly cause them to withdraw from their southern defences.

It was a woefully inaccurate assessment. In reality, the Germans were comparatively fresh and justly confident in the Gustav Line's fortifications, the strength of which the Allies had greatly underestimated. The II US Corps' attack began in the evening of 20 January 1944; two days later it had been thrown back over the Rapido with ruinous losses.

On the evening of 24 January, Clark tried again. On the northern edge of the Liri Valley, Monte Cassino, 1,700 feet high and topped by an enormous monastery founded by Saint Benedict in AD 529, towered almost vertically over Route 6, giving the Germans a superb observation post. The Americans now determined to eliminate this by crossing the Rapido north of Cassino and taking the town, the mountain and the monastery from behind. They kept up their efforts in increasingly vile weather until 11 February but their objectives remained in enemy hands.

Meanwhile on 22 January, VI US Corps had gone ashore at Anzio against negligible resistance. Some of Kesselring's staff urged him to pull back from his southern front but he refused to panic, as indeed might have been anticipated from his previous record. By the end of the month, the bridgehead was surrounded by elements of eight German divisions and though much criticism has been directed against the uninspiring leadership of Major General Lucas, the fact was that SHINGLE had been intended only as a subsidiary move in support of an advance by Clark into the Liri Valley. His failure to do so placed the troops at Anzio in great danger: 'Ultra' was recording blood-curdling demands by Hitler that they be slaughtered or driven into the sea and drowned.

A successful advance down the Liri Valley seemed the only quick way to help the beleagured bridgehead, and it was therefore decided to make another attempt to seize Cassino town and its mountain. To carry out this task, Harding made arrangements for both 2nd New Zealand Division and 4th Indian Division to be transferred from Eighth to Fifth Army and formed into a new corps under the command of Freyberg. He in turn intended that his New Zealanders should attack the town from the south-east, while 4th Indian renewed the assault on Monte Cassino from the north. This was not an order welcomed by 4th Indian's able but acerbic leader, Major General Francis Tuker, who was greatly alarmed by the losses his soldiers were likely to suffer. He could 'never understand' he would later complain, the 'extraordinary obsession in British commanders' minds that they must challenge the enemy strength rather than play on his weakness'.

It was scarcely a sensible comment: the intention of the British commanders was to challenge the enemy at a point where success would be most decisive and it was inevitable that this would be strongly defended. Tuker suggested that his division should instead make a wide turning movement to isolate the defenders of Cassino and so force their retirement, but this was not considered an acceptable alternative because of the inevitable delay it would impose even if it succeeded. And many had (justifiable) doubts that it would succeed. It would fall on defenders of a less high calibre but it would have to cross a whole series of high ridges, be at the risk of attacks from the rear, and necessitate a long supply line which Clark, for one, believed could not possibly be maintained because there were simply not enough mules available.

Tuker was not pleased by the rejection of his plan and his anger would later find vent in caustic denunciations of his superiors: Alexander was 'quite the least intelligent commander I have ever met in a high position'; Clark was 'a flashy ignoramus'; Freyberg 'should never have been put in command of a corps'. Tuker did concede that General Alphonse Juin, head of the newly-arrived French Expeditionary Corps, was 'probably the finest tactical commander in Italy' – but then Juin had supported Tuker's proposed turning movement and offered French troops to take part in it.

Thwarted in one direction, Tuker set in motion the train of events that would lead to the most controversial incident of the Italian campaign. He had a genuine and attractive empathy with his soldiers and, almost without exception, the Allied troops regarded the great Monte Cassino monastery with fear and hatred, certain that it housed German observers at the very least. In fact it did not, less out of respect for its sacred character than because the shape of the hill restricted the view from it and positions elsewhere had a better field of vision. Similar considerations ensured that there were no German soldiers in the building: it was an obvious target and they were much safer in their shell-proof bunkers outside.

Tuker, however, shared his men's misconceptions and regarded it as irrelevant whether the monastery held a German garrison or not: they could always retire into it if they wished. Confusing the building with the mountain on which it stood, he described it as a 'fortress' and a 'thorn in our side', and demanded that his division should not deliver its planned assault until the monastery had been 'so demolished' by aerial bombing 'as to prevent its effective occupation' – though how he thought that bombing could completely destroy such an immensely strong building, it is difficult to discover.

No senior Allied commander was prepared to accept Tuker's extreme views. To them it was a very relevant question whether the monastery contained enemy troops or not. If it did not, then bombing it would do no harm to military personnel or military installations, would give the Germans a splendid propaganda weapon, and would allow them to take over the ruins with a clear conscience, in which case it would make a far finer stronghold, since there would be no roof to fall in on its defenders. Unfortunately, Allied Intelligence could give no answer to the question and it appears that an 'Ultra' interception, which might have revealed the truth, was mistranslated. Clark and, interestingly enough, Juin were sure that the monastery was not being used for military purposes. Harding and Freyberg were sure that it was.

In these hideously difficult circumstances, Alexander, despite his own fears that bombing might do more harm than good, decided that in the last resort the morale of his troops must take priority over 'purely material reasons'. As Harding notified an unhappy Clark: 'General

Alexander has made his position quite clear on this point. He regrets very much that the monastery should be destroyed, but he sees no other choice.' On the morning of 15 February, which for once provided clear visibility, two major air strikes were delivered. These brought about all the evil consequences against which Clark and Juin had warned and, in addition, killed at least 100 civilian refugees. The Germans did not lose a man and by 18 February had defeated every effort to break through their defences.

As a result, VI US Corps in Anzio was left unsupported to face the full fury of the German onslaught. Mercifully, though forced right back to its original bridgehead area, it remained firm and the enemy assaults were finally abandoned on 4 March. On the 15th, the New Zealand Corps made another attempt to take Cassino but by the 20th this had clearly failed also, and it was Harding who persuaded Alexander to call off the battle and postpone any further operations until the spring.

Harding, as a true pupil of Montgomery, regarded it as vital to retain the initiative and was therefore very unhappy at the way the threat to Anzio and the need to 'keep the Germans on their heels' had meant that, in practice, Fifteenth Army Group had been compelled to respond to events rather than dictating them. On 22 February 1944, the staff, under Harding's guidance, accordingly produced an Appreciation designed to show how the initiative could be recovered. It would form the basis for Operation DIADEM, Fifteenth Army Group's final triumphant Battle for Rome, the details of which were worked out over the next couple of months.

Whereas Montgomery had always given clear, decisive instructions for his subordinates to follow, Alexander preferred to seek opinions and reach decisions by consent if possible. Fortunately, Harding both liked and admired Alexander, though he never really got to know him, while Alexander, for his part, had the utmost respect for the abilities of his Chief of Staff. They therefore acted in happy accord when discussing the proposals for DIADEM and each of them could claim high credit for the plan that finally emerged.

Alexander and Harding were as one in their belief that DIADEM's main aim, as Harding stated in his Appreciation, must be 'to force the enemy to commit the maximum number of divisions in Italy at the time OVERLORD is launched'. Alexander had always regarded the capture of Rome as the best means to this end, but Harding now convinced him that a surer way of achieving the desired result would be not just to capture Rome but, in the process, to maul the German formations defending it so badly that Hitler would have to send reinforcements to prevent the whole Italian front from collapsing.

To achieve their objective, Harding estimated that the Allies would need a superiority of at least three to one in infantry at the main point of attack, which would once more be the crucial Liri Valley, supported by a subsidiary advance on the Mediterranean coast and a breakout from Anzio. So large an operation could only take place in the spring, since it had already been shown that only a limited number of attackers could be supplied and supported during an Italian winter; moreover, the Allied superiority in armour, artillery and aircraft would not become apparent until weather conditions improved. The bulk of Eighth Army would have to be moved from the Adriatic coast to the site of the intended assault, and sizeable reinforcements sent from other parts of the Mediterranean. Finally, if DIADEM proceeded, there would not be enough troops or shipping available for ANVIL, a landing in the south of France intended to assist Operation OVERLORD.

These proposals, particularly Harding's recommended cancellation of ANVIL, aroused strong misgivings in Washington, but Harding, again following Montgomery's teaching and example, was quite prepared to put forward views that he knew would be unpopular but believed to be right. He persisted with his list of requirements and eventually on 24 March 1944, after long and surprisingly bitter arguments, DIADEM was approved. So important was Harding's influence that some have claimed he was the 'brains' of Fifteenth Army Group and Alexander not much more than a figurehead.

In reality, this opinion, while a deserved compliment to Harding, was very unfair to Alexander, whose views were almost certainly behind many of the DIADEM plans and preparations – such as the roles the Allied airmen would play and the major adjustment made to the command structure so that, on the Gustav Line at least, all American troops, or those equipped by the Americans such as Juin's Frenchmen, came under Fifth Army control, while all units with British equipment formed part of Eighth Army. And we know that in at least one instance, Alexander overruled his Chief of Staff. Harding had intended that DIADEM's opening assault should be made by VI US Corps in Anzio. Alexander, knowing from 'Ultra' that the Germans considered such an attack more likely than one against the Gustav Line, and believing that it would in any case be more effective if delivered after the enemy had already come under maximum pressure on his southern front, decreed otherwise.

Even with the main plan settled, Harding still had many duties. He supervised the transfer of the Eighth Army formations to the Cassino area. He devoted much time to deception measures such as false wireless signals and deliberately 'leaked' information, intended to suggest that the Allies were planning a new amphibious assault north of Rome and that no action of any sort would be taken before the end of May. Since this would coincide with the anticipated Russian 1944 summer offensive, the Germans swallowed the bait and when DIADEM in fact began on 11 May, a number of important enemy commanders were on leave or attending an indoctrination course in Berlin, to which they had been summoned by Hitler.

It was also Harding who translated the ideas that had been agreed into practical instructions. One of these deserves particular notice. At a Fifth Army conference held on 5 May, Harding emphasized that the assault from the Anzio bridgehead, the timing of which would be decided by Alexander, was 'a most important weapon of opportunity to be launched when the situation is fluid, and which may well be decisive in cutting off the supply and preventing the withdrawal of the enemy force then opposing the advance of the main armies on the main front'.

Unfortunately, Lieutenant General Mark Clark had other ideas. On 23 May, VI US Corps broke out of the Anzio bridgehead and two days later it had linked up with II US Corps and its advanced units seemed on the point of reaching the town of Valmontone on Route 6, the capture of which would have blocked the principal German supply line to their troops further south. Instead, to the dismay of most of his own subordinates, Clark turned the main body of VI US Corps down the coastal Route 7 towards Rome, the capture of which he desired above all else. Harding would later accept that it would never have been possible for Clark to have cut off all Kesselring's forces, but he stated bluntly that had Clark captured Valmontone, as 'was expected of him, it would in my opinion have made the German retreat more difficult, have inflicted greater casualties from air and ground attacks, increased their losses of material by forcing their retreating columns eastwards on to the more difficult mountain roads and tracks and possibly have made it impossible for them to reform a cohesive front between Rome and Florence'.

The Allied achievement was still immense; while DIADEM was in progress Hitler had sent four more divisions as well as other independent formations to Italy, and he would go on dispatching reinforcements afterwards. Rome fell on 4 June, perfectly timed to prepare the way for OVERLORD on the 6th. Nonetheless, Fifteenth Army Group's victory had been impaired just at the moment when it had seemed on the verge of a triumphant conclusion – and worse was to follow.

Despite his defeat and the loss of Rome, the resilient Kesselring remained undaunted. He had prepared another typically efficient defensive position, the Gothic Line, 200 miles long and up to 10 miles wide, running across the Apennines from north of Pisa to south of Rimini. His intention was to fall back slowly to this, delaying his pursuers as long as he could by a series of advanced positions. Fifteenth Army Group's morale was so high after DIADEM, however, that Alexander and Harding were both confident that they could reach the Gothic Line by the end of July, assault it on 15 August and break through to the valley of the River Po. This would deprive the Germans of the northern Italian industrial centres, bring Allied ground and air forces dangerously close to southern Germany, maul Kesselring's battered divisions and divert German attention and German troops to Italy from Russia and North-West Europe.

It was not to be. Operation ANVIL, the proposed landing in the south of France, had not been cancelled as Harding had advised but merely postponed. The Americans now demanded that it be revived and, after a month of wrangling, the British Chiefs of Staff agreed. On 5 July, Alexander was notified that Fifteenth Army Group would have to give up three-fifths of Clark's command, including Juin's French Expeditionary Corps, 70 per cent of Clark's supporting air forces, and so many landing-craft that future amphibious operations in Italy were ruled out for a long time to come. Much of Fifteenth Army Group's enthusiasm vanished as well: Juin for instance, formerly so staunch, abandoned all pressure on the enemy opposing him, citing the need to prepare for operations elsewhere.

Morale was partly restored by the visits to Italy of Churchill, Brooke and King George VI, and Harding was naturally delighted and honoured to be knighted in the field by the King on 25 July. Nothing, however, could restore the Allies' lost momentum. Harding had planned for both Fifth and Eighth Armies to attack the centre of the Gothic Line together, aiming at Bologna, but neither Clark nor Leese were happy with this. They can scarcely be blamed, for it had been learned that the defences in this area were being strengthened and they would be without the help of the French who, as mountain-warfare specialists, had been expected to play the crucial role in the operation.

It was therefore decided that Eighth Army should attack on the Adriatic coast and only after the enemy's attention had been diverted would Fifth Army advance on Bologna. The battles for the Gothic Line began on 25 August, but in early September, the well-remembered and much-hated rain and mud of an Italian winter returned. Fifth Army had to abandon its bid for Bologna by the end of October and though Eighth Army captured Rimini on 21 September, its subsequent progress was desperately slow and costly.

At the end of the year, Alexander called off all offensive action until the spring. It was high time for the winter conditions, and the departure of still more ground and air forces to other fronts had thoroughly disheartened the troops. Harding appears to have shared their attitude and matters were made worse when, on 12 December, Alexander – who had been promoted to field marshal on 27 November – was appointed Supreme Commander, Mediterranean. The change made little practical difference to Alexander's control of the armies in Italy, but added the problems of a civil war in Greece between the pro-Royalist government and Communist guerillas to the burdens that he and Harding carried. Harding indeed appears to have felt increasingly under strain at this period. He was unreasonably upset by disputes between Clark and Leese over the boundaries allotted to their respective armies and greatly exaggerated the ill-feeling this caused. His description of the diversion of forces to Greece as 'the biggest disaster since Tobruk' was scarcely a balanced judgement. It became clear to his colleagues that he was longing to resume the post of corps commander, which he had sacrificed on his transfer to Italy.

On 6 March 1945, Harding's wish was granted when the illness of its commander allowed him to take over XIII Corps. His departure was a great loss to Alexander and the latter's Australian ADC, Major Sir Rupert Clarke, reports in his memoirs, *With Alex at War*, that it proved 'a sad time for many of us, for the Headquarters had been a very happy place under his (Harding's) jurisdiction and we were all devoted to him'. Harding, though, was delighted and his pleasure was only marred by the fact that when Alexander's final offensive, Operation GRAPESHOT, began on 19 April, XIII Corps contained only 10th Indian Division and was stationed in the mountains between the bulk of Eighth Army attacking Bologna from the south-east and Fifth Army attacking it from the south-west.

Happily, Harding was not to be left on the sidelines for long. On 14 April, XIII Corps joined in the great pincer movement on Bologna, which fell on the 21st. General von Vietinghoff, who had commanded the Axis armies since 8 March when Kesselring was recalled to Germany, had already ordered a retreat to the Po – but it was too late. In addition to its offensive towards Bologna, Eighth Army had secured bridgeheads over the River Reno on its northern flank. From these 6th (British) Armoured Division pushed north-west, while 6th South African Armoured Division, which was then under the command of II US Corps, struck north-east from Bologna. On 23 April, the two met at the aptly-named village of Finale. Most of von Vietinghoff's best troops were trapped and forced to surrender. The remainder retired in disorder to the Po, where they found that the Allied Air Forces had destroyed all the bridges and ferries. Those who escaped did so at the cost of leaving behind their tanks, guns, transport and equipment.

Resistance was virtually at an end and Harding, as at Alamein, was in the forefront of the pursuit. XIII Corps had already taken over 2nd New Zealand Division and was now given 6th (British) Armoured Division as well. With Harding personally urging on his divisional commanders, a pontoon bridge was erected over the Po; XIII Corps crossed it early on 25 April and advanced to the River Adige, which was also crossed two days later. On 2 May, Harding accompanied Freyberg's New Zealanders on their entry into Trieste. It was his final contribution to the Allied victory in Italy, which he had already done so much to help bring about. On the same day, the German forces in Italy, almost a million men, laid down their arms: a fitting overture to the greater surrender that many of Harding's former colleagues would witness two days later at a place called Lüneburg Heath.

Notes:

1. So much was this the case that Captain B.H. Liddell Hart in his *History of the Second World War* has suggested that the fall of Singapore was indirectly brought about by Rommel.
2. *The Mediterranean and Middle East* Volume III (September 1941 to September 1942), appropriately entitled 'British Fortunes reach their Lowest Ebb' by Major General I.S.O. Playfair with Captain F.C. Flynn RN, Brigadier C.J.C. Molony and Group Captain T.P. Gleave.
3. These are duly recorded in their *War Diaries* which, together with all others mentioned hereafter, may be found at the Public Records Office, Kew.
4. The 'Ultra' signals quoted appear in *British Intelligence in the Second World War: Its Influence on Strategy and Operations* Volume II by Professor F.H. Hinsley and others. Montgomery was not, of course, the only commander to be badly served by 'Ultra'. In February 1943, for instance, II US Corps in Tunisia was warned by 'Ultra' of a pending German attack through the Fondouk Pass. When this was in fact launched through the Faid Pass, not only did it achieve complete surprise but reinforcements were held back in the belief that it was a diversion only and the major blow would be delivered at Fondouk later.
5. Strictly speaking, the Rapido River was only correctly so named north of Cassino. Thereafter until its junction with the Liri, its official name was the Gari. However, the soldiers always continued to call it the Rapido, which was a good description of its fast-flowing waters. To confuse matters still further, after joining the Liri, the 'Rapido' became known as the River Garigliano.

Chapter 3

The Guardsman

As Fifteenth Army Group's Chief of Staff, Harding had worked closely with Eighth Army's Commander, Lieutenant General Sir Oliver Leese, Baronet. Like Harding, Leese had also fought in North Africa under Montgomery, but his service record included a much larger number of theatres. He had returned to England in March 1940 and on 10 May, the day that Churchill became Prime Minister, he also received a new appointment – as Deputy Chief of Staff to General Lord Gort VC, Commander-in-Chief of the British Expeditionary Force.

Leese did not arrive under auspicious circumstances, for on that same 10 May, Germany's Army Group B under General Fedor von Bock had invaded the Low Countries. As previously planned, the BEF and the northern French Armies wheeled into Belgium to oppose it, only to find that they had walked into a trap. Behind them, on 13 May, the infantry units of General Gerd von Rundstedt's Army Group A, supported by some 200 Stukas, thrust over the Meuse near Sedan. By nightfall on the 15th, von Rundstedt's tanks were racing towards the Channel coast, which they reached near Abbeville on the 21st.

It seems that Leese realized sooner than anyone else at General Headquarters that it would become necessary to evacuate the northern Allied armies by sea. As early as 18 May, he drew up an outline plan for the retirement of the BEF to Dunkirk. Unfortunately, Gort was unable to act on this, for the orders of the French High Command, to which he was officially subordinate, were that he should strike southwards so as to cut off and isolate the outflanking German formations. Nonetheless, on the 21st, he did allow Leese to commence a preliminary evacuation of communications troops, Royal Army Pay Corps personnel and the sick and wounded, which five days later had resulted in the safe departure of 28,000 men.

By that time, Gort had accepted that the southward attack could not succeed – Leese had never thought it had the slightest chance – and the only course open to him was to get his men to Dunkirk as soon as possible and thence away by sea. As the creator of the original withdrawal plan, Leese was entrusted with overseeing the organization of the beachhead, clearing the roads to it and directing the Headquarters Staff to the perimeter. His tireless energy in this role, for which he would later be awarded a CBE, so impressed Gort that when the majority of his officers, including the Chief of Staff, Lieutenant General Sir Henry Pownall, returned home, the Commander-in-Chief who was determined not to leave his troops, asked Leese to stay on as Pownall's successor.

Leese would later describe this as 'a proud moment' but the compliment was a dangerous one that might well have led to his death or capture. Luckily, Churchill sent express orders that once Gort's effective fighting strength had been reduced to three divisions, he should appoint a successor and leave for England. On the morning of 31 May, Gort entrusted the completion of the evacuation to the imperturbable Alexander and he and his acting Chief of Staff were carried away from the beaches on a motor boat. In the course of transferring to this, Leese got thoroughly soaked and on arrival at Dover, he was clad in blue pyjamas and a naval duffel coat. There was no time to find alternative clothing before he was summoned to accompany his chief to London, where they reported to the Secretary of State for War, Mr Anthony Eden. Leese, who as a Guards officer was used to a smart turn-out, noted with some envy that Gort, unlike himself, 'was really very well dressed'.

Leese left Gort on 12 July to take over 29th Infantry Brigade. Just before Christmas he was promoted to major general and thereafter he held increasingly responsible posts. They culminated in 'a marvellous command', the Guards Armoured Division, with which he was serving when, in late 1942, he received further promotion. Montgomery, now preparing for Alamein, had requested a number of officers be sent from England to assist him. One of these was Lieutenant General Sir Oliver Leese who arrived in Cairo on 14 September to take command of XXX Corps.

Leese had not had an easy journey, having spent it in the bomb-bay of a Liberator which was the only spare space available – but he quickly recovered his spirits. Montgomery was 'charming', and Leese for his part was full of praise for both the Eighth Army and its current commander. He shrewdly noted the beneficial effects of the recent victory at Alam Halfa and would later tell Lucas Phillips that: 'Relations between officers and men, tested in battle, were extremely good and there was a strong sense of comradeship everywhere.'

Montgomery's intention was that while XIII Corps under Horrocks carried out a diversionary attack in the south, Eighth Army's main thrust would be made in the north by Leese's XXX Corps and Lumsden's X Corps – an infantry and an armoured formation respectively – acting in unison. Even as Alam Halfa was being fought, Montgomery had issued instructions calling for 'a co-operation of all arms', and now for the first time infantry and armour trained together and in some cases were partially merged. 2nd New Zealand Division, for instance, returned 132nd Brigade to 44th Division and received instead 9th Armoured Brigade. 44th Division did, however, lose 133rd Brigade, which was hastily equipped with lorries and joined Gatehouse's 10th Armoured Division.

The task of both X and XXX Corps was to break into, but not at first through, the enemy lines. In July, Auchinleck had found that if his tanks tried to penetrate Rommel's defences, the Germans' matchless 88mm anti-tank guns would take a merciless toll of them; if his armour was 'husbanded', his infantry would be savaged by the panzer divisions. Montgomery's solution to the problem was that after XXX Corps had seized preliminary positions, X Corps would clear two large gaps, known as 'corridors', through the enemy minefields and pass its tanks through these to take up station on 'ground of its own choosing', threatening Rommel's supply lines. The enemy armour would naturally try to regain the vital positions lost and be confronted by British armour and anti-tank guns, paradoxically fighting defensively in the middle of an offensive battle.

While these tactics were new to Eighth Army, they did follow its traditional principle that the Axis armour should be destroyed first and the Axis infantry 'mopped up' at leisure. On 6 October, however, alarmed by the doubts being expressed by his armoured commanders, particularly Lumsden and Gatehouse, and beginning to wonder if Eighth Army was yet sufficiently well trained to carry out his original intentions, Montgomery changed his mind. He decided to destroy the enemy non-motorized units first by a protracted process of attrition, which he called 'crumbling', carried out by XXX Corps. X Corps meanwhile, still standing on the defensive, would thwart the counter-attacks of the Axis tanks as they tried to come to the aid of their embattled infantry.

This, as General Jackson points out, was a 'radical change of policy', though, happily, not one that necessitated 'a major revision of existing plans', and it demonstrated one of Montgomery's greatest virtues – though one that has too often been overlooked: he could be and often was extremely flexible.[1] It did, however, place a very great burden on Leese, for, as Montgomery made clear, the battle would be 'a killing match' involving 'bitter fighting' for as much as twelve days, with no 'spectacular results' to be expected quickly. Even the code-name chosen for the offensive had a grimly appropriate implication for a conflict among minefields: Operation LIGHTFOOT.

Despite the occasional 'flare-up' already discussed, Leese quickly established a good relationship with the staff of XXX Corps but, potentially at least, he faced greater problems with the leaders of his five infantry divisions. We have already met Major General Tuker of 4th Indian. He had had little respect for the Auchinleck regime but apparently resented the arrival of fresh commanders from England as well. He certainly resented their decision to omit 4th Indian from Eighth Army's initial advance, transfer its vehicles to Leese's other formations and restrict it to making diversionary raids.

The reason for this attitude was probably that it was the general opinion in the Middle East, as recorded by Colonel Ian Jacob, Military Assistant Secretary to the War Cabinet, on the occasion of Churchill's and Brooke's visit, that 4th Indian was not at that time of a high quality, having too many 'newly trained units with officers who had not had the long experience of their own men which is so essential with Indian troops'. This, though, was not a verdict that Tuker was prepared to accept. In his indignation, he would claim that Montgomery and his new subordinates had contributed nothing fresh to Eighth Army except firm leadership – which as we have already seen was not true in respect of El Alamein and will see later was still less true in respect of Alam Halfa – and indulged in other more specific complaints as often as possible.

As far as Leese was concerned, Tuker's particular criticisms related mainly to the start and the end of the battle. Leese's inital break-in was made on a front of 6 miles but Tuker believed that a narrower, concentrated attack would have been more effective. It seems unlikely, for the soldiers, hemmed in among minefields, would have had no 'elbow room' and the resulting congestion and traffic problems would have been horrific. When the enemy finally broke, Tuker felt that two of his brigades that had seen comparatively little action should have headed the pursuit. He seems to have forgotten that, apart from being well back among the minefields, they were short of transport – a matter about which he had previously so loudly complained. Leese was perhaps lucky that 4th Indian's minor role meant that he need not be too concerned about its leader's carpings.

Major General Douglas Wimberley, Commander of 51st Highland Division, presented a different problem. The original division had been forced to surrender at St Valéry in June 1940 – to Rommel, as had not been forgotten. Its successors were desperately anxious to see action and bitterly disappointed that, despite Montgomery's wishes, Alexander had refused to allow them to take part in Alam Halfa, believing, rightly, that they were not yet ready for this. Montgomery was very eager that 51st Highland should be on hand for Alamein since it was his only fresh infantry formation and the only one at full strength. Yet Alamein would be a brutal introduction to combat and Wimberley's justifiable pride in his men was tempered by anxieties over the casualties they were liable to suffer – an attitude that called for Leese to display understanding and firmness in about equal proportions.

Leese's approach to his other three chief subordinates, Morshead, Freyberg and Major General Dan Pienaar, commanding 9th Australian, 2nd New Zealand and 1st South African Divisions respectively, had also to be considered carefully. The officers from the Dominions, as the self-governing parts of the British Commonwealth were then called, were independent by nature, had lost all confidence in the Higher Command under the Auchinleck regime and had to bear in mind their responsibilities to their own countries. These characteristics had led to what General Sir Ian Fraser in *And We Shall Shock Them: The British Army in the Second World War* calls 'indiscipline at the top', whereby 'orders were received, doubted, questioned, discussed'. Happily, Leese, by a tactful display of faith in their abilities, mixed with an easy informality, quickly won them over, enjoying an especially close relationship with the often 'difficult'

Freyberg. Throughout the battle, the Australians, New Zealanders, South Africans and indeed the Highlanders acted as a team and competed with each other to ensure the success of the corps to which they all belonged.

The battle began late on 23 October and by the early morning of the 24th Leese's men had taken 80 per cent of their objectives, including almost the whole of the Miteirya Ridge; during the rest of the day, they would secure most of the remaining ones. Unfortunately, the British armour made little progress on either the first night or the first day and when on the night of the 24th/25th, Gatehouse's 10th Armoured Division pushed south-westward from the Miteirya Ridge as planned, it was attacked by enemy bombers, which set twenty-two petrol or ammunition lorries ablaze. Gatehouse and his Corps Commander, Lumsden, were much disheartened and the latter telephoned de Guingand, the Eighth Army Chief of Staff, with a very pessimistic report. De Guingand then contacted Leese and learned from him that XXX Corps' divisional commanders, particularly Freyberg, also had serious doubts of X Corps' ability to make further progress.

Greatly concerned, de Guingand arranged for both Leese and Lumsden to attend a conference at Eighth Army's Tactical HQ at 0350 on 25 October. Here, to a background of what de Guingand calls 'a positive inferno caused by enemy aircraft', 'both the corps commanders', in the words of General Jackson, declared their belief 'that the battle had gone so wrong that it should be broken off to avoid further profitless expenditure of life and resources'.

While no one questions that this was Lumsden's attitude, it has been suggested that Leese did not agree with him. This seems most unlikely, however. Both in his *Diary* and in his *Memoirs*, Montgomery states that he instructed Leese as well as Lumsden that his orders were unchanged, and no suggestion that Leese ever contradicted Lumsden appears in the accounts of the conference by de Guingand, by Lucas Phillips, who got a great deal of his information from Leese, and by Leese's own admirable and thorough biographer, Rowland Ryder. Not that Leese could be blamed for his doubts: his infantry could scarcely be expected to win the battle on their own and in a letter to his wife written shortly after the conference he dutifully states that he thought and hoped the battle was 'going well', but he still reflects uneasily that the armour seemed to have 'no stomach for a fight'.

Having by his firmness prevented the battle being abandoned prematurely, Montgomery now showed his adaptability. Gatehouse's south-westward advance was cancelled but Briggs pushed due west with his 1st Armoured Division, while Morshead was ordered to attack to the north. On the night of 25/26 October, a brilliant assault by the Australians captured Point 29, the most prominent feature on a spur just north of Morshead's position, and this inspired Montgomery to make a more substantial change of plan. Next day, he discussed his intentions with Leese, and that night, the XXX Corps Commander called a conference of his own to pass on the new orders: the Australians would thrust north from Point 29 to the coast; 2nd New Zealand Division, including 9th Armoured Brigade, would withdraw into reserve and prepare for a major attack down the coast road, to be codenamed Operation SUPERCHARGE; the Highlanders, the South Africans and 4th Indian Division would extend their fronts to cover the gaps these moves would create.

Leese would later tell Lucas Phillips that the atmosphere of this conference was 'tense, almost electric', but the mutual respect he had established now paid dividends. His subordinates enthusiastically set to work to carry out the new plan. The Australians tied down large numbers of Rommel's best troops and severely mauled them in the process. SUPERCHARGE, for reasons to be discussed later, was in fact launched further south than originally intended and was carried out by X Corps as well as XXX Corps, but its initial assault, at 0105 on 2 November was still made by the New Zealanders, reinforced by two extra infantry brigades, one of them from 51st Highland Division; and the rest of Wimberley's men and a brigade from 4th Indian Division took their part in the operation later. Both 9th Armoured Brigade and the Highlanders suffered severe losses but by the late afternoon of 4 November, the Axis forces were in full retreat.

There can be no doubt that Leese, who was now made a Companion of the Bath had proved, as Lucas Phillips puts it, 'one of the great successes of Alamein'. Montgomery, reporting on his Corps Commanders to Brooke, considered Leese 'the best of the lot' and 'quite first class'.[2] Nonetheless, Leese must have relished the relaxation from responsibilities that followed Alamein. He was not put in charge of the pursuit and his delightful letters home read like those of a happy tourist. He described Derna as 'a lovely little place – a small white township nestling in the side of the hills, the houses mingled with palm trees, all backed by a small harbour and the bright blue of the seas'; and he made no mention of the vital Martuba airfields nearby. And he was less impressed by the modern towns Eighth Army had taken than by the noble ruins of Roman Cyrene: 'the most wonderful sight I've seen – a vast ruined city of reddish brown.'

Leese's 'holiday' was of brief duration, however, for XXX Corps was now detailed to take the El Agheila position. Alexander, in his Official Despatch, would call this the strongest in Libya. It was almost entirely surrounded by salt marshes, soft sand and broken ground, which could only be outflanked by a wide move over very difficult country; and it was guarded by strongpoints, an anti-tank ditch and a profusion of mines. Moreover, the lengthening Allied supply lines meant that Leese had only one armoured and two infantry divisions under command. The Axis defenders, particularly 90th Light Division, could be relied on to offer resolute resistance and XXX Corps' task would have been formidable had not Rommel's nerve been shattered by Alamein – as Kesselring unkindly notes, 'he wanted to get back to Tunis; if possible still further away to Italy and the Alps'.

Leese's plan was that 51st Highland Division should advance down the coast road – the Via Balbia as it was known – while 7th Armoured Division attacked at Bir es Suera, about 15 miles to the south, and 2nd New Zealand Division made a lengthy flanking move south of the salt marshes, supported by the forty-five tanks of 4th Light Armoured Brigade. Leese had wanted every available tank and gun transferred to Freyberg but, as de Guingand points out, the size of his force had to be limited by 'administrative conditions': a larger one would have experienced great delays and at best the enemy would have been given plenty of time to escape. At worst Leese's main force, deprived of its armour, might have been unable to break through the strong El Agheila defences, leaving Freyberg isolated and, if spotted from the air as was almost certain to happen, very vulnerable to one of those brilliant counter-attacks with which Rommel had so often turned the tables in the past.

Freyberg set out on the night of 12/13 December, and was duly spotted by Axis airmen at 1700 on the 14th. Luckily, on the previous night Leese's main offensive had begun. Rommel would later suggest it would have been better if this had been delayed until Freyberg had reached the coast road and could mount a simultaneous attack from the rear. Even ignoring the fact that the New Zealanders could never have got that far without being sighted, however, they would surely in that case have been assaulted by the German armour. Rommel's officers in fact urged him to do just that anyway, but the threat from the main XXX Corps attack was such that he dared not take the risk. By 16 December, he had begun another retreat of 250 miles to Buerat, hindering his pursuers by what Leese described as a 'never-ending' series of mines, the clearing of which proved 'one of the most trying operations that I have ever carried out'.

Eighth Army was still 230 miles away from Tripoli, but Montgomery intended to cover them in one move. This was scarcely the decision of a cautious commander for a fierce gale had struck his advanced base at Benghazi, sunk four supply ships, one of which carried 2,000 tons of ammunition, and so damaged the harbour that it could no longer provide the tonnage his Army would need. As a result, Montgomery would have to take Tripoli within ten days of the start of his offensive or shortage of supplies would force him to break off the action. Moreover, while Buerat was not a particularly formidable obstacle, the difficulties beyond it were immense. An attack along the Via Balbia would be hemmed in by rough country and salt marshes and the road itself was obstructed by 177 craters, ten destroyed bridges and six anti-tank ditches. If the advance was made over the desert, it would have to cross the roughest terrain Eighth Army's veterans had yet experienced. And whichever route was followed, it would lead Eighth Army to that seemingly impregnable barrier, the Homs-Tarhuna escarpment.

Montgomery determined to use both possible lines of advance in order to divide his enemy's strength. Since he considered the distance between them too great for effective control by one corps commander, he took personal command of the coastal thrust towards Homs, using 51st Highland Division, supported by 23rd Armoured Brigade, and with 22nd Armoured Brigade in reserve. Leese was ordered to carry out the flanking movement aimed at Tarhuna with 2nd New Zealand and 7th Armoured Divisions.

Operation FIRE-EATER began at 0715 on 15 January 1943. Resistance was fierce but by dawn on the 16th, the Buerat position was in Eighth Army's hands and Montgomery was urging Wimberley to follow up his success with resolution and determination. Leese, meanwhile, was earning praise even from Rommel for the energy with which he was advancing over dreadful 'going', consisting in Leese's own words of 'miles of soft sand – then large fields of high hummocks – then steep wadis and cliffs, full of great boulders'.

By 19 January, Leese was attacking Tarhuna and had so alarmed Rommel that he transferred all his German troops except 90th Light Division to meet the threat. Whereupon Montgomery, as at Alamein, switched the direction of his main thrust, reinforcing 51st Highland Division with 22nd Armoured Brigade and sternly commanding Wimberley to attack day and night until victory had been achieved. The Highlanders captured Homs on the afternoon of 20 January and continued down the Via Balbia in the face of bitter resistance from 90th Light. On the night of the 21st/22nd, Rommel, realizing that he could not hold Montgomery's coastal advance, abandoned the Tarhuna Pass and Leese's men also pressed forward. The two thrusts converged at Tripoli on 23 January; Montgomery and Leese met and shook hands; then, says the latter, 'we made a triumphal progress round Tripoli', ate a sandwich lunch in a garden, and finally, in a delightful contrast to the conditions they had recently experienced, set up their caravans in 'a lovely almond blossom orchard'.

It was a fitting culmination to all that Leese had achieved since his arrival in the Desert, and it is sad to reflect that he would never enjoy such a wonderful moment again. His later career would be marred by setbacks for which he was not to blame, disappointments that were not within his control and unpleasantness that was not of his making. But at this moment, for Leese as for Eighth Army as a whole, the capture of Tripoli was reward enough.

* * *

The first setback came on the night of 16/17 March. Shortly after Alamein, Operation TORCH, an Anglo-American landing in Vichy French North Africa, had secured Morocco and Algeria, but Tunisia was firmly held by Fifth Panzer Army, led by General Jurgen von Arnim, under the overall control of Kesselring. It was joined by Rommel's men as they fell back from Tripolitania, and Alexander, who on 18 February had taken command of Eighteenth Army Group, set up in Algiers to co-ordinate all Allied forces in Tunisia, quickly realized that his main thrust must come from the south. Already on 6 March, Eighth Army had won a brilliant little defensive battle at Medenine, but it now had to overcome another daunting obstacle: the defences of the Mareth Line.

Ironically, this maze of mutually supporting strongholds, blocking a 22-mile-wide passage between the Mediterranean and the Matmata Hills, had been constructed by the French to protect Tunisia from the Italians but was now defended by the First Italian Army. Despite its name, though, this contained a strong German contingent, being in fact Rommel's former command, re-named and led by General Giovanni Messe, who as an Italian Corps Commander on the Russian front had been awarded a Knight's Cross by Hitler. On the night of 16/17 March, at an advanced strongpoint at Sidi el Guelaa – 'Horseshoe Hill' to the British for obvious reasons – his men gave notice that whatever their title, they were still redoubtable opponents.

Leese's XXX Corps had been carrying out a series of probes and preliminary attacks but the one at Horseshoe Hill found both the extent of the minefields and the strength of the defenders, a detachment of 90th Light, much greater than anticipated, and 201st Guards Brigade lost thirty-eight officers and 484 other ranks killed, wounded or captured. Leese was distraught, declaring: 'I blame myself very much.' Montgomery also accepted responsibility, writing to Brigadier Julian Gascoigne to apologize for having underestimated the difficulties the Guards would have to face.

In reality, the main cause of the tragedy was the earlier capture of a British artillery officer who was carrying a map showing full details of the Guards' supporting fire-plan. Neither Montgomery nor Leese could be blamed for this, but it seems not unfair to suggest that they were at fault in not realizing the full implications of the Horseshoe Hill action.

Just as Eighth Army's attack on the Buerat position had not stopped until Tripoli was reached, so Montgomery's planned offensive against the Mareth Line, Operation PUGILIST, was intended to continue well beyond its immediate objective. With the Line secured, Eighth Army would race forward to take the next 'bottleneck', the Gabes Gap, 15 miles wide between the sea and the vast, trackless salt-marsh called the Chott el Fedjadj, 'on the run'; then advance to capture the ports of Sfax and Sousse, perhaps even Tunis. It was a daring scheme but it seemed within Eighth Army's capability, for 'Ultra' had revealed that both Rommel and von Arnim had favoured a withdrawal from Mareth to at least the Gabes Gap and possibly to Enfidaville at the northern end of the central Tunisian plains.

Unhappily, 'Ultra' had again served Eighth Army badly. Neither Hitler, nor Kesselring, nor Messe had any intention of abandoning the Mareth Line without a struggle, and perhaps the defeat of 201st Guards Brigade should have given warning of this. As it was, both Montgomery and Leese remained dangerously over-optimistic, paying far more attention to the actions to be taken after the Line was overrun than to the need to capture it in the first place. The main attack was entrusted to XXX Corps but Leese, with three infantry divisions under his command, left 51st Highland and 4th Indian in reserve to follow up the initial breakthrough, and X Corps under Horrocks was similarly held back to exploit success.

The assault on the Mareth Line was therefore made solely by 50th (British) Division, which contained only two brigades, had seen little action since Alamein and was supported by just fifty-one Valentines of 50th Royal Tanks. Moreover, despite the division's lack of experience, its commander, Major General Nichols, received little guidance from his superiors. It says much for his soldiers that when they attacked at 2345 on 20 March, following a typical artillery barrage, they forced their way over the Wadi Zigzaou, which formed the Mareth Line's outer 'moat', and captured five major strongholds and a large number of prisoners.

Thereafter, everything went wrong. The Wadi Zigzaou was an impressive obstacle at any time, being 20 feet deep, from 60 to 200 feet wide and with artificially steepened sides, and it had been made worse by heavy rain, which had left its floor soft and treacherous and covered with up to 8 feet of water. It was not until the early hours of 22 March that the selfless efforts of the Royal Engineers, working under heavy fire, had prepared a suitable crossing over it, and then, despite repeated enquiries from Montgomery, who was now becoming anxious, as to whether 50th Division was ready 'to receive a counter-attack with 6-pounder guns', tanks, not anti-tank guns were brought forward. In the process, they so damaged the crossing that it could not be used again.

At 1340 on 22 March, Axis armour and infantry launched the

inevitable counter-attack and Leese's bridgehead had been all but eliminated by 0200 on the 23rd. It was not the end of the Battle of the Mareth Line, for Montgomery once more showed his flexibility by switching his line of attack, but the victory would be achieved by other officers than Leese – chiefly Horrocks, to whom, it may be noted, Leese offered charming and generous words of encouragement. XXX Corps would subsequently play its part in the successful passage of the Gabes Gap, but Leese's role as Montgomery's chief subordinate in the field had come to an end – though only temporarily.

It would be revived in Sicily, the conquest of which crucial island, Operation HUSKY, was the responsibility of Alexander, who in turn was answerable to the Supreme Commander, Mediterranean, the American General Dwight Eisenhower. Alexander's command, now designated Fifteenth Army Group, controlled both Montgomery's Eighth Army and the Seventh US Army of Lieutenant General George Patton. At the time of the HUSKY landings, the latter contained three divisions, two forming the II US Corps led by Major General Omar Bradley, the third under Patton's direct control. Eighth Army had four divisions, divided equally between the XIII Corps of Lieutenant General Miles Dempsey and XXX Corps, still under Leese.

The initial landings in the early hours of 10 July achieved tactical surprise. A fierce storm resulted in subsidiary airborne operations suffering heavy losses but greatly assisted the main seaborne assaults by causing the defenders, commanded nominally by the 66-year-old General Alfredo Guzzoni but in reality by Kesselring, to relax their vigilance at the crucial moment. Eighth Army came ashore on the Pachino Peninsula in the south-east of Sicily and by 12 July, had captured the ports of Syracuse and Augusta. The way seemed clear for the next phase of Montgomery's plan: an advance up the island's east coast through Catania to the main enemy base at Messina.

It did not take place – because, ironically enough, Montgomery now showed too much flexibility. Patton's Seventh Army, which had landed over open beaches in the Gulf of Gela west of the Pachino Peninsula, had met with determined resistance and Montgomery decided to leave the advance on Catania to XIII Corps while XXX Corps wheeled inland to take the towns of Leonforte and Enna, in which case, he assured Alexander, 'the enemy opposing the Americans will never get away'.

Unfortunately, the enemy did get away because, by a still more unkind irony, the Americans recovered so swiftly that they drove the defenders out of the trap before it could close. By the time this was realized, airborne reinforcements had already enabled Kesselring to block Dempsey's push towards Catania. Montgomery therefore ordered Leese to continue his move to Leonforte and Enna; then swing eastward to Adrano and thence north of Mount Etna to take the forces facing XIII Corps from the rear. Meanwhile he wanted Bradley's II US Corps to advance on Leese's left to guard against any attack from the west.

This was another clever tactic but, as so often, Montgomery, in Leese's restrained words, proved 'a bit impatient and hasty with others'. The only good road northward was Route 124 and Montgomery directed XXX Corps onto this, regardless of the fact that Alexander had allotted it to the Americans. Bradley, thus forced to mount his own offensive further to the west, was rightly displeased and Leese who was 'very fond of Bradley, who is a very nice man and a good soldier', had to smooth over a difficult situation. More trouble was soon to follow. XXX Corps captured Leonforte late on 21 July, but in the process passed to the east of Enna, an Eighth Army responsibility after the change of the inter-army boundary, and thereby exposed the flank of II US Corps, which was left to clear the town itself. Bradley was again indignant but Leese mollified him with prompt apologies and a gift, variously described as two bottles of whisky and a crate of champagne.

Leese went on to visit Patton with the intention of further improving good relations between the armies. He believed that he 'got on well' with Patton, which was apparently true on a personal basis, but he was far too late to prevent the volatile commander of Seventh US Army from taking an extraordinary decision. Bradley had always believed that when II US Corps had reached the north coast, it should turn eastward towards Messina, and by 21 July, Montgomery had come to agree with him. Already on the 17th, however, Patton had insisted on directing his main effort against Palermo in the north-west of Sicily. This fell on 22 July, but unfortunately it was useless as a port since the enemy had effectively blocked its harbour and none of Patton's field commanders believed that its capture was of the slightest value.

Three days later, Montgomery invited Patton to visit him and urged that the full strength of Seventh Army should be sent against Messina, offering it the use of both the main east-west roads in northern Sicily for the purpose; meanwhile Leese would continue his advance on

Adrano over more difficult tracks. Though convinced that this must be some crafty 'Limey' trick, Patton agreed, but he needed some time to reorganize his forces before bringing them back from western Sicily, so his assault had to be postponed until 1 August. Leese, on the other hand, began XXX Corps' attack on the night of 29/30 July, using as his spearhead the fresh 78th (British) Division, sent from North Africa as a reinforcement. On 3 August, it stormed the key position of Centuripe – a brilliant achievement since the only approach was over a steep winding mountain road with deep ravines on either side – and moved on to capture Adrano after dark on the 6th.

Kesselring now ordered a withdrawal from Sicily – to commence as soon as possible. He was aided in this task by a number of varied factors: north-eastern Sicily tapers to a point in the vicinity of the intended embarkation area around Messina, so the further his soldiers retired, the shorter the front they would have to defend; the Straits of Messina between the island and the Italian mainland were protected by a massive array of AA guns; and regrettably the Allied Navies had made no plans to interrupt any evacuation.

The first Axis troops left on the night of 11/12 August and thereafter the end came quickly. XIII and XXX Corps met north of Mount Etna and Leese took command of both of them for the final advance on Messina. His men captured Taormina on the east coast on 15 August and that night made a seaborne landing at Scaletta, 8 miles south of Messina. They found that the area had already been abandoned but followed up the retreating enemy and early on the 17th entered Messina – unopposed, for the town had been taken by the Americans on the previous evening.

Montgomery had put Leese rather than Dempsey in control of the final British advance because he wanted the latter to plan for a campaign on mainland Italy, in which Leese was not to take part. Instead, Montgomery, who always kept a close watch on his chosen subordinates, arranged for Leese to have a lengthy rest in England, which would give him a chance to recover from the strain caused by his almost continuous responsibilities. Leese would arrive in Italy only at the end of the year, but then it would be not as a corps commander but as the leader of Eighth Army.

It was not a good time at which to have attained this high honour. Mr Harold Macmillan, the future Prime Minister who was then

Alexander's political adviser, would later tell Leese that succeeding 'a very distinguished and successful man' like Montgomery was in itself a 'traditionally difficult situation'. It was made no easier by Montgomery having taken a number of valuable staff officers with him and continuing to demand both staff and field officers – Dempsey for example – to serve in his Twenty-First Army Group preparing for the Normandy landings. It was made infinitely more difficult because Fifteenth Army Group had been halted by Kesselring's Gustav Line and the first months of Leese's command saw only the fierce but disappointing actions at Cassino and Anzio and the continuous ordeal imposed by the vicious winter weather.

In these circumstances, it was probably inevitable that Leese's attempts to follow Montgomery's example and raise his men's morale by personal contact and inspiring addresses were not particularly successful and seemed to many rather artificial. Nor could Leese copy Montgomery's dogmatic and immensely forceful attitude; though he demanded high standards, he was normally easy-going with a keen sense of humour. Even when his Tactical HQ was bombed by American aircraft on 15 March 1944, luckily with only four men slightly wounded, his rebuke merely took the form of a mild enquiry as to whether Eighth Army had done something to offend its allies.

On the other hand, by the time that DIADEM opened, Leese had once more won the liking, respect and co-operation of subordinate commanders who represented a wide variety of nationalities. Eighth Army's old station on the Adriatic side of Italy had now been left to the two divisions of V (British) Corps, while the rest of Leese's command prepared to move on Rome through the Liri Valley, supported by II US Corps and Juin's French Expeditionary Corps advancing along the Mediterranean coast. As at Alamein, Leese would be faced by strong defences, manned by very able troops, and he was well aware that even if the French and Americans made rapid progress, this would not prevent desperate resistance in the Cassino area, the retention of which had become of immense significance as a matter of morale.

Leese intended that the two divisions of II Polish Corps, commanded by Lieutenant General Wladyslaw Anders, should assault Monte Cassino from the north, while X (British) Corps, which contained only 2nd New Zealand Division and some independent brigades, guarded the Poles' right flank. The one armoured and three infantry divisions of XIII (British) Corps under Lieutenant General Sidney Kirkman, once Eighth Army's senior artillery officer, would cross the Rapido River, outflank Cassino town and link up with the Poles. Then both Anders and Kirkman would move down the Liri Valley where, supported if necessary by an armoured and an infantry division of I Canadian Corps and by the Army Reserve, 6th South African Armoured Division, they would break through the Hitler Line, a further defensive position prepared by Kesselring some 8 miles to the rear.

DIADEM began at 2300 on 11 May with an artillery bombardment by 2,000 guns – but not well for Eighth Army at first. Intelligence reports had badly underestimated the strength of the defences facing XIII Corps and the fast flow of the river it would have to cross; by first light, 8th Indian and 4th (British) Divisions had only been able to secure two shallow bridgeheads. The Poles had fared still less successfully and by 1400 on the 12th, they were back on their original start-line. Leese's response, however, was splendid. He consoled Anders, praised the Poles' courage and their value in holding down crack German troops who could otherwise have been used elsewhere, and predicted that when the time came for a renewed attack, it would certainly succeed.

Leese's staunch reaction proved justified. During 13 May, Kirkman secured and united his bridgeheads and part of 6th (British) Armoured Division crossed the Rapido; Leese sent XIII Corps' reserve infantry division, 78th (British) over the river on the 14th and I Canadian Corps on the following day. At 0700 on the 17th, XIII Corps pushed northwards towards Route 6, while Anders embarked on a fresh attempt to take Monte Cassino. That night the gallant defenders of both Cassino town and its mountain at last began a reluctant retirement. At 1020 on the 18th, a patrol from the 12th Podolski Lancers hoisted the Polish flag over the shattered remains of the monastery. Leese hastened to congratulate them and share a bottle of champagne with their commander.

Eighth Army had broken through the Gustav Line and on 19 May reached the Hitler Line[3] – where it found that its Intelligence had again underestimated the task before it. The Line included a number of tank turrets set on concrete bases; their high-velocity 75mm guns came as an unpleasant surprise, inflicted heavy casualties on Leese's armour, and ended his hopes of taking the Line 'on the run'. He therefore made careful and thorough preparations for a full-scale assault by I Canadian Corps on 23 May, when it would coincide with VI US Corps' breakout from Anzio.

Both attacks proved successful in the face of the usual fierce resistance, and while VI US Corps pushed across the coastal Route 7 towards Route 6, the Canadians continued their advance through the Liri Valley. They secured a small bridgehead over the Liri's tributary the Melfa River on the 24th, and both they and XIII Corps crossed it in force the next day. Eighth Army then proceeded along a Route 6 choked with mines and demolitions to capture an important road junction, Frosinone, south-east of Valmontone, on 31 May. Valmontone had still not been taken by the Americans, but on the same day they broke through the last line of German defences at Monte Artemisio near Velletri, and the capture of Rome became only a matter of time.

Leese's achievements during DIADEM have received little praise and a good deal of undeserved criticism. He has been attacked, for instance, for not having used XIII Corps as well as I Canadian Corps to assault the Hitler Line. Yet XIII Corps would have had to conduct its operations in full view of German observation posts on nearby Monte Cairo and Leese ensured that the Canadians were supported by XIII Corps' artillery in addition to their own – a factor that proved crucial. He has been rebuked for having crowded too many tanks and transport into the Liri Valley after his capture of Cassino. Yet the blame for this should really be attributed to Intelligence: the Liri Valley had been endlessly called the 'Gateway to Rome' and no mention had been made of the numerous steep-sided streams or ditches that had to be bridged. Leese must, however, be considered at fault when, despite warnings, he repeated his action in the later stages of the battle after crossing the Melfa River.

Criticisms were also heard of Leese's rate of progress; Juin in particular taking pleasure in pointing out that he had moved faster than Leese during both the early attacks on the Gustav Line and the later advances to link up with the forces from Anzio. In the first of these instances, however, Eighth Army, unlike the French, was hampered by the presence of superbly placed enemy observation posts, and opposed by far better enemy units and far stronger fixed defences. In the second instance, the advances of Eighth Army on Frosinone and VI US Corps on Valmontone formed the jaws of a trap, so naturally met with vigorous resistance, whereas Juin was confronted only by troops withdrawing as fast as possible to avoid being cut off. Moreover, on the one occasion in the battle when the French had met strong opposition, they had been brought to a halt and failed to outflank the Hitler Line from the south, leaving it to Leese to have to take this by direct assault.

Even at the time, Eighth Army's part in the fall of Rome was largely ignored and Leese was very hurt when both Clark and Juin cold-shouldered him at a victory celebration. Yet he endured this stoically, as he did the subsequent departure of Fifth Army forces to strengthen Operation ANVIL, as previously described. And nothing could deprive him of one satisfaction: like Harding, he was knighted in the field by King George VI.

The diversion of troops to southern France was particularly disheartening since Alexander, Harding, Clark and Leese had all previously entertained visions of reaching the valley of the Po and perhaps continuing through Austria to capture Vienna. These hopes were never entirely abandoned, though, as we saw earlier, it was decided that the major attack originally planned against the centre of the next great German defensive position, the Gothic Line, was no longer practicable. It was determined therefore to transfer the bulk of Eighth Army to the Adriatic coast, where it would deliver the first and main assault on the Line, code-named Operation OLIVE.

This move was first suggested by Kirkman, and after Leese had studied the ground ahead from an observation post in a church tower, he agreed and in turn won over Alexander. Harding was less convinced and would later suggest that the main motive of Leese and Kirkman had been to put distance between themselves and Clark, whom they disliked. Since it was also agreed that Kirkman's XIII Corps, the Eighth Army formation nearest to the Americans, should be placed under Clark's command to strengthen a follow-up thrust by Fifth Army against Bologna, and Kirkman's diary confirms that he knew of this possibility, Harding's belief seems unlikely in his case at least. As for Leese, his first impressions of Clark had been good – 'Young and alive and very friendly' – and although he had been disgusted by Clark's conduct at the time of the capture of Rome, his private correspondence shows that this had soon been forgiven and he very much sympathized with Clark over the weakening of Fifth Army. Equally, Clark would later praise Leese as 'a magnificent soldier', 'a fine officer' and 'a good strategist', adding that 'we got along beautifully' – as, incidentally, they continued to do after the war.

Leese was surely much more influenced by the memory of how the rapid transfer of Eighth Army from the Adriatic coast had helped break through the Gustav Line. He now hoped the same move in reverse would help break through the Gothic Line. Amazingly, his soldiers, together with 1,000 guns, 1,200 tanks and about 60,000 other vehicles, were brought over the Italian peninsula secretly at night in transport that could show no lights, and when Operation OLIVE began an hour before midnight on 25 August 1944, the Germans were taken completely unawares. It was a great achievement, of which Leese was rightly proud.

As usual, Kesselring's troops fought savagely but by the evening of 2 September they had fallen back, leaving some 20 miles of the Gothic Line in Leese's hands. The next major obstacle in his path was the Coriano Ridge, which 1st (British) Armoured Division intended to seize on 4 September. Unfortunately, the tracks leading to this were rapidly deteriorating and a large proportion of 1st Armoured's tanks suffered mechanical failure. As a result, no real progress had been made before, on 6 September, the advance was most effectively bogged down by heavy rain, which continued for two full days.

Leese was therefore compelled to pause while preparations were made for a fresh assault. This began on the night of 12/13 September, and next day the British tanks, with Gurkha infantrymen riding on them, cleared the Coriano Ridge. For Kesselring, this was 'terrible news', but his ally, the weather, had not deserted him. As Eighth Army moved forward, it was constantly hampered by once trivial watercourses that had become raging torrents. Yet it struggled on until 21 September, when it captured Rimini, beyond which, Leese had been assured by Intelligence reports, an area of low, level ground known as the Romagna Plain, would provide good 'tank going'. Sadly, in practice it proved to be covered by deep rivers and irrigation ditches and, having been reclaimed from marshland, it quickly became waterlogged after rain.

This was a crushing disappointment and the optimism and enthusiasm that Leese had generated prior to Operation OLIVE now became subjected to a good deal of adverse comment. Long afterwards, it would be said that he had promised that Eighth Army would reach Bologna in two days, Venice in four and Vienna in seven. Since Leese's advance on Bologna was to be supported by a subsidiary converging offensive by Fifth Army that was not even planned to start for some days, and since in an address to senior officers on 23 August, Leese had specifically warned that the coming battle would not be an easy one, it is difficult to accept the reliability of this particular story. It is true, though, that Leese had made unwise and exaggerated comments such as: 'Gentlemen, we march on Vienna!' In consequence, when he left Eighth Army on 1 October, his period as its commander did seem to have ended in a definite anti-climax.

It was not seen as such by those who knew the obstacles Leese had overcome. Macmillan assured him that he had 'carried on and strengthened' the work of Montgomery. His successor, Lieutenant General Sir Richard McCreery, thanked him 'for having left me such a splendid machine'. And Leese had departed only because he had been given greater responsibilities; as he wrote home exultantly: 'I am to be an Army Group Commander – a Commander-in-Chief – with a Union Jack'. He little knew that this would lead to his cruellest and most unjust disappointment.

* * *

Leese's new title, to be exact, was Commander-in-Chief, Allied Land Forces, South East Asia and Commander, Eleventh Army Group, under the theatre's Supreme Commander, Admiral Lord Louis Mountbatten. He was delighted to find the outlook was vastly more encouraging than when he had taken over Eighth Army just as the Allied advance had ground to a halt. In South-East Asia – which in practice meant on the India-Burma frontier – long weary months of stalemate had ended during the previous spring and early summer with decisive victories at the twin battles of Kohima and Imphal, when Lieutenant General Sir William Slim's Fourteenth Army had inflicted 53,000 casualties on the Japanese, at the cost of less than 17,000 of its own, and when Leese officially assumed control on 12 November 1944, an Allied advance was in progress.

Nor had the Japanese any reasonable prospect of doing more than impose delay on this. During the Kohima-Imphal campaign, Slim had already enjoyed a preponderance in manpower, artillery and armour, superior tanks and a total command of the air, and since then the enemy had suffered far greater disasters elsewhere. In October, the titanic Battle of Leyte Gulf, the largest naval battle in history, had all but annihilated the Japanese fleet and thereby ensured the loss of the Philippines; this in turn would cut off the Japanese from the natural resources for which they had gone to war in the first place. In these circumstances, the Japanese High Command could not possibly strengthen their Army in Burma; on the contrary, they were compelled to weaken it in order to provide the reinforcements needed in more vital areas.

Leese had been called 'the finest fighting soldier in the British Army' in a charming letter of congratulation sent to him by Mountbatten at the time of his appointment, and he certainly lived up to his name in his desire to engage his latest enemy as quickly and decisively as possible. When he met Mountbatten at the latter's Headquarters in Kandy, Ceylon, he was told that 'our task is to deny Burma to the Japanese'. 'Surely Supremo,' retorted Leese (most unwisely), 'our task is to destroy the Japanese Army in the Field.'

On 14 November, Leese left Ceylon to set up his Headquarters at Flagstaff House, Barrackpore, a town some 20 miles from Calcutta. Nearby was the HQ of Major General George Stratemeyer, the American officer responsible for Allied air force operations over Burma. Stratemeyer would assure Leese after the war that 'I never, throughout my military career, have had more pleasant associations than I had with you' – and he co-operated with Leese completely. Some indeed have suggested that he allowed Leese too much control over air operations but in any case his provision of Dakota transport aircraft on an unprecedented scale would constitute a decisive factor in subsequent Allied successes.

Under Leese came three main military formations. In northern Burma, Chinese forces under the American Lieutenant General Sultan, concentrated on reopening the Burma Road to their homeland. West of the Chindwin River were the IV and XXXIII Corps of Slim's Fourteenth Army, preparing to engage the enemy in the area between the Chindwin and the mightier Irrawaddy River, a task code-named Operation CAPITAL. In the Arakan, the coastal area of Burma, was Fourteenth Army's XV Corps under Lieutenant General Philip Christison. Because of the distances involved, this in practice operated independently, and was making ready to assist Slim's move by an advance of its own, code-named Operation ROMULUS.

Leese had requested Slim and Christison to meet him in Barrackpore on 15 November – though on subsequent occasions he would always fly out to their respective Headquarters. He knew Christison well and found him 'in great heart' but it seems clear that he never really got on with Slim, describing him in letters home as a grumbler – 'He can never stop crabbing' – and 'traditionally difficult with his higher HQs', though he did add with disarming candour that: 'I have been the same!'

In one respect, however, Slim was an ideal subordinate for Leese at this time. He was an aggressive, determined fighter who could count on receiving the maximum support from his soldiers, of whom he was rightly proud and to whose interests he was completely and sincerely devoted. Having served in Burma almost from the moment of the Japanese invasion, commanding first Burma Corps, then XV Corps and finally since 15 October 1943, Fourteenth Army, he had shared his men's defeats, frustrations and successes, their fears, anxieties and hopes, and had come to appear almost synonymous with them and their cause, winning their respect, their loyalty and the affectionate nickname of 'Uncle Bill'.

These qualities naturally appealed to Leese. Even after the imbroglio that will be described later, he would reiterate his belief that Slim was 'a good soldier, inspires his men with confidence, and above all wins battles' and had 'put up a magnificent show'. Despite their different characters – 'we have very little in common', Leese recorded – they were as one in their determination to defeat the enemy, and both could take pride in the parts they played in attaining this result.

One of Leese's most important contributions was made before the campaign was properly underway. Prior to his arrival, the ultimate aim of both Mountbatten and Slim, as the former confirmed in a letter to Leese dated 23 December 1944, was that of 'reaching Mandalay before the monsoon' – which would come by the end of May. On 7 December, however, Leese had dined with the Governor of Bengal and former Minister of State, Middle East, Sir Richard Casey, who had expressed a strong opinion that this was far too limited an objective. Inspired by Casey's advocacy and Stratemeyer's promises to supply the vital air transport, Leese began to consider the possibility of taking not just Mandalay but Rangoon also before the monsoon broke. 'This,' as he would later write home with justifiable satisfaction, 'would be a wonderful triumph, as when I came out here it was never even thought of.'

While Leese was reassessing Allied strategy, Slim was rethinking Allied tactics. On 4 December, Fourteenth Army had crossed the Chindwin but the Japanese wisely declined to fight in an area ideally suitable for the vastly superior Allied armour and air forces, and made a hasty withdrawal behind the Irrawaddy. Slim therefore recast his plans with admirable speed and on the 17th, he submitted to Leese his initial proposals for Operation EXTENDED CAPITAL, the capture of Mandalay. Leese accepted them with enthusiasm, while Slim for his part proved equally supportive of Leese's desire that success at Mandalay should be followed closely by an attempt to take Rangoon as well.

For either move to succeed, though, the services of the Dakota transport aircraft would be essential and both Leese and Slim protested strongly when in December three squadrons of these were diverted to China. Accordingly, on 16 January 1945, Mountbatten's Chief of Staff, Lieutenant General Sir Frederick 'Boy' Browning, previously commander of the British Airborne Corps, arrived in London, asking Brooke to provide 'additional aircraft for Burma'. Happily, the request was granted, probably because of the promise that this would make the speedy capture of Rangoon a distinct possibility.

The offensive could now proceed. As a preliminary, Leese had already ordered Christison to press on down the coast with the principal object of taking the islands of Akyab and Ramree as bases from which air transports could keep Slim supplied. Reconnaissance Hurricanes reported on 2 January that Akyab had been abandoned and it was promptly occupied without resistance. Though the detailed arrangements for its capture thus proved unnecessary, they provided useful guides for later amphibious landings by XV Corps, chiefly at Myebon some 40 miles to the south-east on the Burmese mainland on 12 January, and at Ramree on the 21st.

Then on 12 February, 20th Indian Division from Lieutenant General Stopford's XXXIII Corps crossed the Irrawaddy at Myinmu, to threaten Mandalay. The Japanese Commander-in-Chief, Lieutenant General Kimura ordered his pitifully few armoured vehicles against the bridgehead, only for the rocket-firing Hurricanes of 20 Squadron to justify Slim's description of them as 'our most successful anti-tank weapon'. And while Japanese attention was directed towards Myinmu, Lieutenant General Messervy's IV Corps also crossed the Irrawaddy at Nyaungu, over 100 miles south of Mandalay, and on 21 February made a dramatic dash for the Japanese supply centre at Meiktila, the loss of which would cripple Kimura's Army.

It seemed that the battle was as good as won, but as usual the Japanese proved unbelievably tenacious. Major General Kasuya, the energetic commander at Meiktila, threw every available man, including patients from the hospital, into its defence, and by the time they had been wiped out on 3 March, reinforcements from the Mandalay area had arrived to block any further Allied move northward. By this time also, Slim was showing the inevitable ill-effects of his long and tireless efforts; Christison, who visited him, reported that 'he was about played out. We were great friends, yet he was rude, crotchety and off-hand.' Browning had reached a similar conclusion and on 16 March he visited Leese to discuss the situation. On the previous day, Leese had reflected anxiously that 'these battles take a long time and time is short before the monsoon', and he quickly decided to move forward, setting up his Tactical Headquarters close to the HQ of Fourteenth Army.

It would later be claimed by some of Leese's loyal staff that he had taken control of the fighting, prevented it lapsing into a stalemate, and brought about the capture of Mandalay, which had been completed by the evening of 20 March. While this view was surely exaggerated, it is clear from the *War Diary* of Leese's HQ that he 'was fully occupied with the battle of Mandalay'; his letters home show that he followed its course very closely; and his presence must at least have been an encouragement and a spur to his subordinates. Yet most later commentators have not only ignored Leese's part in the battle, but have accused him of delaying the subsequent move against Rangoon. This is probably because the main drive south did not begin before the end of March but Slim in his memoirs, *Defeat into Victory*, states that he had 'issued detailed orders for the advance on Rangoon' as early as the 18th, before the final fall of Mandalay. Since, however, we learn from the C-in-C's *War Diary* that Leese had been 'planning for the assault on Rangoon' from at least 17 March and was engaged in conferences or discussions regarding the administrative requirements of the operation every day from the 21st to the 31st, it would seem that he has, yet again, received less than his due.

Certainly Leese personally felt that he was entitled to some credit for Fourteenth Army's spectacular race to Rangoon. This was occupied on 3 May – though, rather sadly, not by Slim's men but by Christison's XV Corps, which had landed at the mouth of the Rangoon River south of the Burmese capital on the previous day. In a letter to his wife on 4 May, Leese declared: 'We are all very excited – El Alamein, Tripoli, Mareth, Sicily, Cassino, Rome, Florence, Rimini, Mandalay – and now Rangoon.'

Unfortunately, the background to the last two successes differed from that of the earlier ones. In those, Leese had usually enjoyed happy relationships with superiors, colleagues and subordinates alike – as indeed he had during the Burma campaign with characters as diverse as Browning, Christison and Stratemeyer. It is difficult therefore to believe that his inability to do so in two other instances was by any means all his own fault, though his approach in both cases may well be considered ill-advised.

Leese had met Mountbatten at the time of the Sicily landings and had assessed him as 'forceful' but 'overbearingly conceited'. He should therefore have realized that Mountbatten – who had dismissed the previous C-in-C Allied Land Forces, South East Asia, General Sir George Giffard, for daring to disagree with him – had to be handled tactfully. Instead, Leese raised his eyebrows far too obviously over some of the 'comic opera' aspects of Mountbatten's Kandy HQ, made it far too clear that it was he who in practice was directing overall strategy, and finally, fatally, shortly before the capture of Rangoon, told Mountbatten that the 'repeated enquiries calling for detailed replies' that the Supreme Commander persisted in making, merely wasted 'valuable time which my staffs cannot afford with operations in their present state'. If Leese should ever have problems elsewhere, he would not get much support from Mountbatten – and those problems were just about to arrive.

In later years, Slim would be greatly and rightly admired for his unstinting service in Burma, but perhaps receive even more credit for *Defeat into Victory* which, it was said, revealed his 'noble humility'. Certainly Slim was always generous in praise of his soldiers, gracious in accepting formal responsibility for the mistakes of subordinates, and prepared to admit errors of his own. Or at least some of them. Major

General James Lunt in his account of the original retreat from Burma, *A Hell of a Licking*, reveals that soon after Slim had taken command of Burma Corps in March 1942, he declared his 'intention to recapture Rangoon before the monsoon broke in mid-May'. This was absolute folly in the light of his corps' strength and condition, its lack of any air support and the fact that it could always be outflanked by the main Japanese offensive that was directed against the Chinese forces stationed further east, and it led to a whole series of futile and near-fatal counter-attacks. In *Defeat into Victory*, Slim makes no mention of either his 'intention' or the underestimation of his enemy that had brought it about.

For a book of 550 pages, *Defeat into Victory* indeed omits a surprising number of important facts. We are not told that in July 1944, Fourteenth Army was temporarily commanded by Lieutenant General Sir Geoffrey Scoones while Slim recovered from a prostate operation. We are not told that the enemy offensive against the Imphal plain was a strictly limited one, designed to seize a better defensive position than the Chindwin River, which the first 'Chindit' mission had shown was not the secure barrier previously believed. We are not told that Slim's major base, Dimapur, was always safe from any Japanese attack because that would have pushed more deeply into India than the enemy wished – or that Slim was well aware of this from 'Ultra' interceptions.

Of course, Slim was unable to mention 'Ultra' specifically in his memoirs as it was then still a closely guarded secret, but he could surely have given some praise to Intelligence in general. We learn from Michael Smith's *The Emperor's Codes* that throughout his later campaigns, 'Ultra' provided Slim with 'a wealth of information' including 'a complete order of battle of the Japanese forces', both Army and Air Force, but his only response was to complain that: 'I had not at my disposal the sources of information of the enemy's intentions that some more fortunate commanders in other theatres were able to invoke. We depended almost entirely on the Intelligence gathered by our fighting patrols.'

This was not only unjust, it was untrue, and it is far from the only example of the unreliability of *Defeat into Victory*. Slim pictures the purely 'preventative' move against the Imphal plain as designed to seize the 'glittering prize' of India – a 'March on Delhi'; it was nothing of the kind. Slim announces that Chindit operations during this offensive did no more than 'delay for a couple of months two infantry and one artillery battalions of the Japanese 15th Division'; Lieutenant General Mutaguchi who commanded the offensive declares that the Chindits had 'a decisive effect' as they 'drew off the whole of 53rd Division and parts of 15th Division, one regiment of which would have turned the scale at Kohima'. Slim constantly refers to the activities of the famous Japanese Mitsubishi Zero fighters; the Zero, being an Imperial Navy aircraft, took no part in the Burma campaigns, which were conducted by less efficient Japanese Army Air Force machines.

Slim's disinformation becomes most noticeable in his references to those he resented for any reason, and for all his 'noble humility' the reason was usually because they had drawn attention away from his own achievements. It had been generally accepted that morale had begun to be restored in Burma at the time of Brigadier (later Major General) Orde Wingate's first Chindit raid behind enemy lines in February 1943. This, if at high cost, had shown that British and Indian soldiers could outfight and outwit the Japanese in the jungle and, by using air transport for their supplies, could outmatch the superior Japanese manoeuvrability. Slim not only dismisses these benefits as 'somewhat phoney propaganda', but later belittles Wingate personally. He assures us that when one of the proposed landing-grounds for the second Chindit mission was found to be blocked by treetrunks, Wingate became 'very emotional' and wanted to call off the whole operation. Wingate, in an official report written immediately afterwards, states that, on the contrary, he wished the raid to continue and persuaded Slim to agree. Five witnesses who were present, two of them RAF officers who may be considered reasonably impartial, all confirm Wingate's version of events and call Slim's 'decidedly inaccurate'.[4]

Slim was equally displeased that Alexander had been given the main credit for saving the remains of the Burma Army at the time of the Japanese invasion, while his own part in this had remained largely unknown. He would later declare that Alexander had not had 'the faintest idea of what was going on' and in *Defeat into Victory* he mentions Alexander only briefly and slightingly, largely ignores Alexander's immense contribution to the maintenance of morale that is stressed by all other first-hand accounts, and even sneers at Alexander's legendary personal courage, which he prefers to call 'foolhardy'.

These points have been detailed so that the ultimate cause of Leese's problems with Slim may be appreciated – Slim resented him also – and the reliability or otherwise of Slim's version of their final clash may be assessed. Slim's initial resentment, shared by others, was the perhaps inevitable reaction by members of a fine army to the appointment of a superior who was not one of their number. To make matters worse, Leese, like Montgomery earlier, had taken many of his staff with him when he left Italy. They 'replaced most of our old friends at General Giffard's headquarters,' notes Slim sourly. Sarcastic comments about 'the dash of the Eighth Army to the rescue of South East Asia Command' made the rounds.

Leese had done his best to overcome this prejudice. On his first meeting with Slim he had expressed his pleasure at having come to Slim's 'great Fourteenth Army' – though, as he wrote home ruefully, Slim 'showed no signs of wanting to see me!' Unhappily, Slim's resentment went deeper than Leese realized. In *Defeat into Victory*, Slim revealingly refers to Leese's staff as having 'a good deal of desert sand in its shoes'. It had far more Italian mud, but what irked Slim were the desert victories that had made Eighth Army a household name, while his own command remained 'The Forgotten Army'. In these circumstances, it was most unwise of Leese and his staff to quote Eighth Army's way of working when discussing any problems to be faced or actions to be taken: Slim regarded this as a desire 'to thrust Eighth Army down our throats'.

This then was the background when, after the fall of Rangoon, Leese turned his attention to his next task: planning a seaborne invasion of Malaya, code-named Operation ZIPPER. For this he wished Christison to command Fourteenth Army, partly because of Christison's experience of amphibious operations in the Arakan, partly because Slim had previously asked to go home for a four months' rest once Rangoon had been secured; Leese agreed that he richly deserved this but if the planning for ZIPPER was to begin forthwith, it would have to be done by an officer in the Far East, not one on leave in England. When Slim returned, Leese wished him to take control of a new Twelfth Army, which would administer Burma and complete the 'mopping up' of the numerous Japanese troops who had been cut off by Fourteenth Army's race to Rangoon.

To Leese these proposals seemed eminently sensible and though he rightly sought the approval of Brooke and Mountbatten, he did not anticipate any objections. Mountbatten raised none and suggested that

Leese explain his intentions to Slim, but since Leese was eager to get everything settled and preparations for ZIPPER started, he did not wait to hear from Brooke. This, as it transpired, was a mistake, but Leese had already made a bigger one. He had never expected that his actions would hurt or offend Slim, nor had he any wish to do so; in his letter to Brooke – on 5 May – he had urged that Slim be 'built up as the conqueror of Burma' and was 'the right man to set Burma on a sound footing for the future', and he would even request Lady Leese to 'do everything you possibly can to help' Slim and his wife when they reached England. Considering Slim's request for a long leave, his constant complaints that he was tired, and the possibility that he had not fully recovered from his prostate operation, Leese had never doubted that he would be happy with the new arrangements. He saw Slim on 7 May and afterwards informed Browning that his proposals had been accepted.

Whether Leese had deceived himself, or whether Slim did agree at first but later allowed his resentment of Leese to suggest that this was an attempt at a further 'take-over' by Eighth Army is not known. What is clear is that the next day Slim was 'leaking' the news to trusted subordinates and claiming that he had been unfairly removed from his command. On the 9th, he called together his staff and, making no mention of his desire to go on a lengthy leave, he declared that his 'one ambition' was to continue to lead Fourteenth Army 'until the Jap is finally beaten flat', but it was 'not to be', because he had just been dismissed.

This was nonsense: Slim had no more been dismissed than Leese himself had been dismissed when Montgomery had decided he needed a long rest after the Sicily campaign. But the tale that '"Uncle Bill" has been sacked' spread like wildfire. Fourteenth Army seethed with protests, and staff and field officers alike offered their resignations. Alarmed by the furore, Mountbatten hastily withdrew his support for Leese's proposals and asked Leese to confirm Slim as head of Fourteenth Army. Then, either because he had not forgiven Leese for having wounded his vanity in the past, or because he wished to appease the protesters, whom he knew to be as angry with him as they were with Leese, he sent a series of complaints about Leese's conduct to the CIGS. Brooke, thousands of miles away, could not possibly judge the situation for himself, and, somewhat hesitantly for he had an uneasy feeling that Leese, like Giffard before him, had been given 'a raw deal', he agreed that Mountbatten might remove him.

It may be added that, on reflection, Slim made no mention in *Defeat into Victory* of his mythical 'sacking'. True to form, he made no mention either of Leese having been the first to consider the possibility of taking Rangoon before the monsoon, or of Leese having gone forward to Fourteenth Army during the struggle for Mandalay, but he did grant that Leese was 'easy to serve under' and that Leese's 'military judgement was eminently sound'. It was perhaps the nearest Slim could get to an apology. Mountbatten expressed formal regrets at the time that he dismissed Leese but it is permissible to doubt his sincerity, considering that in later years he would frequently denigrate his former Land Commander-in-Chief, especially after Leese was safely dead. Yet even Mountbatten felt compelled to acknowledge his 'appreciation' of the results Leese had 'achieved in the last six or seven months of the Burma campaign'.

For these, Leese received no promotion, no awards and precious little recognition. It is a sad and rather sordid story with only one redeeming feature: 'the wonderful, manly way,' as Brooke described it, 'in which Oliver faced up to the blow that had hit him.'

Notes:

1. Ironically, Montgomery was himself responsible for the failure to appreciate this aspect of his generalship: it tended to be masked by his notorious reluctance ever to admit that events had not gone entirely according to plan.
2. Horrocks he considered 'very good'– but Lumsden 'poor'. This last verdict was by no means fair but Montgomery believed that Lumsden did not realize the need for co-ordination of the different branches of the Army, which for the Army Commander was an article of faith.
3. Though Allied accounts would continue to refer to the reserve defences in the Liri Valley as the 'Hitler Line', Kesselring had in fact prudently renamed them the 'Dora Line'.
4. Full details of Slim's attitude may be found in *Wingate and the Chindits* by David Rooney, a former senior lecturer at Sandhurst. That most of Wingate's subordinates felt that after their leader's death, the Chindits had been very badly handled, a situation for which Slim bore the ultimate responsibility, probably did nothing to soften that officer's asperity.

Chapter 4

'Berthier'

It was not only Leese who had occasion to complain of callous treatment by a superior: so did 'Freddie' de Guingand – but only after the war was over. During it, Montgomery, the superior with whom he was most closely associated, was kindness itself, even advising him of what hot drinks he should take when he was ill and sending him little presents of these. Admittedly, this consideration was not entirely altruistic, for Montgomery was well aware of the value of a subordinate whom he would later compare with Marshal Louis Alexandre Berthier, Prince of Neuchâtel and Wagram and, in the opinion of most authorities, prince of all staff officers as well.

Of course if de Guingand was Berthier, that would make Montgomery Napoleon, and no doubt he was very conscious of this when he made the comparison, for noble humility was never one of Montgomery's virtues. Equally though, no other field commander would ever acknowledge his indebtedness to a subordinate with anything approaching the honesty that Montgomery showed in his *Memoirs*. Of his North African campaigns he declared: 'Without de Guingand, I doubt if I could have done my part of the overall task.' Of the invasion of North-West Europe, he had no doubt at all: 'I could not possibly have handled the gigantic task that lay ahead without the trusted Chief of Staff who had been at my side since Alamein.'

De Guingand had proved his value long before his crucial service to Montgomery. He began the war as a staff officer of the Secretary of State for War – though his time as Military Assistant was brief. On 4 January 1940, Mr Hore-Belisha, who had incurred the enmity of too many senior generals, was forced to resign, and a month later, de Guingand journeyed through France and a still-peaceful Mediterranean to take up a different duty as Chief Instructor of the new Middle East Staff College at Haifa, Palestine.

In August, de Guingand was joined as an instructor by Richardson, who considered him 'highly intelligent, humourous and articulate' but 'without a trace of pomposity', and who quickly became a firm friend. Among their pupils were Roberts, who also arrived in August and who agreed that de Guingand had 'a brilliant brain, a great sense of humour and a charming manner', and the future Field Marshal Lord Carver, then a young captain.

In December, however, de Guingand reverted to his natural role, this time on the Joint Planning Staff in Cairo. He quickly gained a high reputation, not least for independence of thought. When the transfer of forces to Greece was mooted, he repeatedly warned against this and when his advice was ignored, drew up plans for the evacuation he was sure would inevitably follow; they would prove of immense value in due course. This attitude did not at first meet with the approval of General Wavell, but he later relented and sent de Guingand to Greece to check on its defences. It was not a happy visit, for de Guingand was first arrested as a spy and then, when staying in a hotel at the town of Larissa, was almost killed by an earthquake – twice, since he unwisely returned to his room to recover his belongings and was caught by the aftershock.

Despite having proved his abilities, de Guingand never did establish a close rapport with Wavell, but he enjoyed at first a happier relationship with Auchinleck who, in late February 1942, appointed him Director of Military Intelligence with the rank of brigadier. De Guingand, for his part, was 'very fond' of his new chief but this did not prevent his experiencing a mounting uneasiness as time passed and he observed Auchinleck's mishandling of the situation in the Middle East, about which, in his role of Intelligence head, he was exceptionally well informed.

De Guingand was particularly unhappy about the way in which, as he puts it, 'Auchinleck had a lot to say regarding the major decisions in Eighth Army.' This constant interference caused immense difficulties and rarely served any useful purpose, since by the time instructions from Cairo reached the front, the situation in the mobile, fast-moving desert battles had usually changed completely.

Yet despite all his interferences with Eighth Army, Auchinleck, in de Guingand's opinion, did not really know what to do for the best. Conferences called to determine courses of action 'used to go on sometimes for hours'. When the question arose whether Tobruk should be abandoned, after Eighth Army's defeat at Gazala, or held as it had been in the previous year and as Churchill was demanding, it seemed to de Guingand that Auchinleck would never give an answer. De Guingand had strongly advised against defending the fortress, but when Auchinleck finally ordered otherwise, he confesses that: 'Although, not happy, I remember going to bed with a certain relief – at last a definite decision had been made.'

After Auchinleck had taken personal command of Eighth Army, de Guingand became still less happy. In July, at Auchinleck's request, he spent ten days at Army HQ and he returned there towards the end of the month, having been appointed, much to his own disquiet, Eighth Army's Brigadier General Staff. The Headquarters was sufficiently depressing on its own account. It was situated in an unpleasant, unhealthy part of the Ruweisat Ridge, surrounded by camel dung and swarming with flies. More to the point, it was dangerously far forward, with poor communications. From such a base, Auchinleck and his staff, mockingly known in Eighth Army as 'The Short Range Desert Group' were no more able to provide rapid, flexible control over the battlefield than when they had attempted to do so from Cairo.

As if that were not enough, the move to the Ruweisat Ridge had ended the previous close contact between Eighth Army and the Desert Air Force. The HQ of the latter had remained on the coast, over 40 miles distant, which, as de Guingand laments, 'alone produced great difficulties in the laying-on of the best air support'. As a result, during July when the supremacy of the Allied airmen was most marked, it was the Luftwaffe which intervened more effectively in the land battles.

It might just have been possible to overcome these disadvantages, for de Guingand quickly found that Eighth Army was blessed with a remarkable group of staff officers. There were the brigadiers, Brian Robertson, the Senior Administrative Officer and Frederick Kisch, the Jewish Chief Engineer. There were the lieutenant colonels, de Guingand's old colleague Richardson, in charge of Plans, Hugh Mainwaring, in charge of Operations, Miles Graham, Robertson's Deputy, and R.F.K. 'David' Belchem, who would later become in effect de Guingand's own deputy. There was also Captain – soon to be Major – Edgar Williams, then responsible for the 'Ultra' interceptions but subsequently made Intelligence chief by Montgomery.

All these officers in fact would be valued by and perform vital services for Montgomery but Auchinleck made little use of their talents, preferring to rely on his personal adviser, Dorman-Smith. De Guingand had always liked 'Chink', as Dorman-Smith was known from his prominent teeth, but doubted his ability, recalling that: 'His quick brain and fertile mind produced appreciations and plans at a quicker rate than anyone I have ever met; he was perhaps too clever to be wise . . . At first I sat up all night conscientiously working on these projects, but soon I found they took up too much of my time and, I regret to say, wasted a lot of it as well.'

De Guingand deplored Auchinleck's reliance on his silver-tongued but shallow adviser. A particularly unfortunate consequence of this, de Guingand believed, was that it became the fashion for Eighth Army to operate 'in battle groups . . . and not in divisions, as the Army had been trained to fight'.

This tendency had begun shortly before the Battle of Gazala, when Auchinleck had divided the British infantry divisions into brigade groups. These operated independently, which meant that they were deprived of the divisional resources such as field artillery, anti-tank guns, engineers, medical staff, signals staff etc, and was one of the reasons for the 'indiscipline' of the commanders of the Dominion divisions who strongly resisted the practice. Undeterred, Auchinleck on taking direct control of Eighth Army, followed Dorman-Smith's advice and brought the process on a stage further. In General Jackson's words, he 'ordered the creation of mobile battle groups within each brigade based on the available artillery and transport. No more infantry than was needed to protect the guns and could be kept mobile was to be retained in the forward area' – the remaining 'surplus infantry' being sent to the rear.

It was intended that the battle groups would come to each other's assistance if the need arose but this frequently proved impossible in actual combat conditions. Their vulnerability was increased by the current lack of co-operation between infantry and armour and Auchinleck's determination, again under Dorman-Smith's influence, to 'husband' the latter. It became a cynical saying in Eighth Army that the definition of a battle group was 'a brigade group which has been twice overrun by tanks'.

Intelligence reports had warned that Rommel would soon renew his offensive and de Guingand regarded with considerable anxiety the prospect of meeting this with battle groups, without effective support from the air and at a time when considerable doubts existed whether the present defences would be held at all. He knew all about Dorman-Smith's pessimistic reliance on reserve positions. He knew that, among his own subordinates, Richardson had been ordered to plan a possible Eighth Army withdrawal to Khartoum and Graham was arranging the administrative details of this. He knew that 'a new site for the Headquarters had been selected on the Nile, 60 miles south of Cairo.' 'I don't say it is not prudent to be prepared for the worst,' de Guingand declares, 'but on the other hand if there is too much of this sort of thing it is most unlikely that the troops will fight their best in their existing positions. The wrong outlook is likely to be encouraged – one of hesitation.'

But Churchill and Brooke came and Auchinleck went – de Guingand 'felt intensely sorry for my Chief' but adds that: 'I'm sure the decision was right.' And early on 13 August, Eighth Army's Brigadier General Staff met that Army's new commander at a crossroads outside Alexandria. To Montgomery, de Guingand 'looked thin and worried; he was obviously carrying a heavy burden.' Montgomery greeted him with a wave, asked him into his car and, as they drove on to the Ruweisat Ridge, listened to de Guingand's detailed review of the present situation and his account of the numerous maladies affecting Eighth Army that required urgent attention.

Since the first of these was 'the dangerous "looking over the shoulder" defensive policy', de Guingand's report confirmed the one Montgomery had previously received from Harding. It must have caused him much disquiet, as Rommel's offensive was then anticipated as early as 26 August at the period of the full moon. Yet Auchinleck – presumably as a sop to his wounded vanity, since no other explanation has ever been forthcoming – had earlier persuaded the good-hearted and generous Alexander to agree that he might retain his command until 15 August and had ordered Montgomery not to take over Eighth Army until then but only 'get the feel of his responsibilities and his opportunities'.

Fortunately, Montgomery was unequalled in his ability to assess a military situation and on their car journey he had astonished de Guingand by the way he had already 'spotted most of the weaknesses' of the present one. The sight of Eighth Army's dismal, fly-encrusted Headquarters decided him: he was not prepared to 'kick his heels' in such conditions for two more precious days. At 1400, he assumed command of Eighth Army and countermanded all existing plans for retreat, whether tactical or strategical.

Since this action automatically ended 'the dangerous "looking over the shoulder" defensive policy', de Guingand was naturally delighted. His delight was increased when at 1830, Montgomery addressed his staff officers as a whole[1] and with ruthless realism ended all doubts as to the course of action that would be followed in the immediate future:

> The defence of Egypt lies here at Alamein and on the Ruweisat Ridge. What is the use of digging trenches in the Delta? It is quite useless; if we lose this position we lose Egypt; all the fighting troops now in the Delta must come here at once, and will. *Here* we will stand and fight; there will be no further withdrawal. I have ordered that all plans and instructions dealing with further withdrawal are to be burnt, and at once. We will stand and fight *here*. If we can't stay here alive, then let us stay here dead.

With this one gesture, Montgomery united all the various formations and the different branches of the Army behind him in relieved approval; and in his speech he also dealt with de Guingand's other major concerns. There must, he declared, be 'a complete change in the layout of our dispositions', and later he confirmed that this would mean the end of battle groups – de Guingand tells us that he ordered that 'the expression ceased to exist' – and that henceforth 'divisions would fight as divisions, and be allowed to develop their great strength'. He announced that 'the first thing to do' was to get away from the present depressing and unhealthy Headquarters and back to the coast 'side by side with the HQ of the Desert Air Force'.

De Guingand had also had a private anxiety. Though he had been 'delighted that Montgomery had been selected to lead Eighth Army', he had not expected to 'remain long in office', believing that Montgomery would want to choose his own chief staff officer. Now he heard Montgomery not only confirm his appointment but increase his powers and responsibilities: he was to be not just the Brigadier General Staff but a Chief of Staff through whom Montgomery would issue all orders and whose own orders were to be treated as those of the Army Commander and acted upon at once. No wonder he reports that:

> We all felt that a cool and refreshing breeze had come to relieve the oppressive and stagnant atmosphere. The effect of the address was electric – it was terrific! And we all went to bed that night with a new hope in our hearts, and a great confidence in the future of our Army.

* * *

From then until the night of 30/31 August when the Battle of Alam Halfa began, de Guingand was constantly in close touch with Montgomery as he visited unit after unit, impressing his personality on his men and winning their trust and confidence, and at the same time put into effect that 'complete change in the layout of our dispositions', which would ensure that he and they could meet Rommel's assault effectively. De Guingand's admiration was increased by his commander's own obvious confidence in a successful outcome. When the battle began, Montgomery was asleep in his caravan. De Guingand woke him to report the news but 'all he said was "Excellent, excellent", then turned over and went to sleep, breakfasting at his usual hour in the morning'.

That same morning, Montgomery gave a different example of coolness that de Guingand would never forget. The enemy had received reinforcements of men, armour, anti-tank guns – and aircraft, which were very active before and at the start of the battle. De Guingand was talking to Montgomery at Eighth Army HQ when, he tells us:

> Suddenly the air became alive with enemy planes. They were bombing and strafing a nearby airfield, and shooting up anything they could see. We were getting a little attention . . . When the attack commenced, I immediately pressed Montgomery to take cover – feeling the urge pretty strongly myself! He took not the slightest notice and merely went on talking, quite unmoved. I remember the feeling of self-confidence this small incident gave. It set an example for the future.

Another example of Montgomery's coolness and one of the trademarks of his generalship was his ability to look beyond his immediate problems. On his arrival in the Desert, he astonished Williams by asking for all available information not only about Rommel's coming attack but also about the enemy defences that he would have to attack himself later on. De Guingand reports that preparations for both the battles that would be known as Alam Halfa and El Alamein 'went on concurrently at a terrific speed' and once the former had been won, all efforts were naturally directed towards the latter.

It was Montgomery who prepared the general plan for Alamein, made his basic intentions and basic tactics clear to everyone, and then concentrated on his men's morale and training. He left it to the members of his staff to work out the details of the operation, each so far as it concerned his particular field; all their efforts being co-ordinated by de Guingand. This lifted a great weight from the Army Commander's shoulders and allowed him that time for quiet reflection, which he rightly valued so highly.

By the same token, of course, this system imposed a tremendous burden on the Chief of Staff, and as the day of battle approached, it had taken such a toll that he was finding it difficult to get to sleep. Montgomery, who as he recounts in his *Memoirs*, was well aware that de Guingand 'lived on his nerves and was highly strung', wisely sent him for a short break in Alexandria. De Guingand spent two nights as guest of the Naval C-in-C, Mediterranean, Admiral Sir Henry Harwood, victor of the Battle of the River Plate. 'I was allowed breakfast in bed,' he recalls, 'and slept better than I had done for many weeks.'

Returning to Eighth Army, rested and refreshed, de Guingand showed a similar consideration for his own subordinates and on 23 October, took Richardson, Belchem and Williams for an excellent lunch in Cairo. All, however, were back at El Alamein when at 2140, a tremendous artillery bombardment opened the battle. De Guingand and Richardson set up a forward base in an old pillbox close behind the front line, from which they watched the barrage and rejoiced as they saw the 'occasional deep red glow light up the western sky', showing that 'another Axis gun position had gone up'.

It should be added that at this time Montgomery always discussed his ideas with de Guingand and often followed his Chief of Staff's advice. It was de Guingand who persuaded Montgomery that his armoured formations were unable and perhaps unwilling to carry out the role originally allotted to them, and that the main burden must be placed on Leese's XXX Corps. It was de Guingand who arranged the conference with the corps commanders in which Montgomery prevented the battle being broken off prematurely. Towards the end of the fighting, however, it seems that de Guingand's advice may have had more questionable consequences.

It may be recalled that Montgomery had originally intended his final penetration of the Axis positions – Operation SUPERCHARGE – should be made along the coast road. De Guingand and Williams had urged him to deliver it further south where Intelligence reports had indicated it should encounter only Italian units, but Montgomery had rejected their suggestions. Then on 29 October, a delegation headed by General Alexander arrived at Eighth Army Headquarters, urgently enquiring how the conflict was progressing. Montgomery, according to de Guingand, 'radiated confidence' but it is easy to understand Alexander's concerns. He accepted that overcoming Rommel's lethal defences must be a lengthy affair but he could not afford its being too lengthy, partly because the Martuba airfields had to be secured to provide fighter cover for the convoy to Malta, and partly because it was felt with good reason that the reception of the TORCH landings, which were planned for 8 November, would depend very much on whether Eighth Army had previously gained a decisive victory.

Alexander agreed with de Guingand that SUPERCHARGE would probably achieve victory more rapidly if launched further south and he brought with him a telegram from Churchill promising that TORCH would have momentous consequences if only Eighth Army had won its battle first. Armed with this information, de Guingand renewed his arguments and this time Montgomery allowed himself to be persuaded. Since the revised SUPERCHARGE did break through the last enemy defences, all but destroyed the remnants of Rommel's panzer divisions and captured their leader, General Wilhelm Ritter von Thoma, it might seem that he had been right to do so.

Yet the change was by no means an unmixed blessing. It is possible that it did not in fact win the battle more quickly, for the need to recast his plans caused Freyberg to postpone the attack, originally scheduled for the night of 30/31 October, to the early hours of 2 November; and it met mainly German opposition since their dispositions extended further south than Williams had believed. It certainly ensured that the victory was less complete, because to speed up success the British armour, formerly kept back to follow up an enemy retreat, took part in SUPERCHARGE and suffered casualties, which reduced its effectiveness as a pursuit force. And when it did pursue, it was unable to use the metalled coast road and turn the enemy's seaward flank as Montgomery had wished but instead had to cross the open desert, thereby giving Rommel a priceless advantage even before the heavy rains turned the ground into a quagmire. It may therefore be that in this instance de Guingand's influence did not prove beneficial.

Of course, as we have already seen, the main reason for the escape of the remnant of the Axis army was the inaccurate information given by 'Ultra'. In any case, this particular incident was at most a minor flaw in the overall brilliance with which de Guingand had discharged his responsibilities – for which he was awarded an immediate DSO. Those responsibilities did not cease with the victory at Alamein, however; in some ways they were increased, if only by the admirable yet somewhat dangerous conduct of Montgomery – now a full general and a Knight Commander of the Bath – who led the pursuit of the retreating enemy very much from the front.

Montgomery, as de Guingand notes resignedly, 'was always to be seen in the danger area of the battlefield, being quite unmoved by any unpleasant incident'. 'I rarely accompanied him on these expeditions,' de Guingand notes with charming modesty, but he and the rest of the staff had little choice in the matter at this period: for a time Montgomery's Tactical HQ was nearer to the front line than the headquarters of any corps or divisional commander. Indeed, on 7 November Mainwaring and some of his Operations staff, including Montgomery's stepson, Major Richard Carver, went too far forward and were captured by an enemy rearguard near Mersa Matruh.

De Guingand's natural concern for his colleagues was mingled with the fear of a possible breach of security, as Mainwaring always carried a small notebook, which might have yielded valuable information. Fortunately, he had managed to conceal and subsequently destroy this but the incident may help to explain de Guingand's very terse reaction when the Air Officer Commanding-in-Chief, Middle East, Air Chief Marshal Sir Arthur Tedder, urged that after taking Tobruk, Eighth Army should leave the coast and strike through open desert across the base of the Cyrenaican 'Bulge' towards El Agheila, cutting off the enemy in Benghazi. Montgomery was right to reject this move, since not only would it have been very vulnerable to air attack but he wanted to make quite sure that his coastal thrust reached the Martuba airfields in time – which it only just did. Nonetheless, Tedder's suggestion was not unreasonable in itself and de Guingand's subsequent complaint about interfering people 'sitting back in Cairo and not in possession of all the facts' seems very different from his usual good-natured tolerance.

De Guingand's attitude may also have been caused by his being far from well. Towards the end of November, he had to be rushed to hospital in Cairo, suffering from a gallstone; his place being taken by Erskine, the former Brigadier General Staff of XIII Corps. A lengthy period of recovery in South Africa was recommended but this was not at all to de Guingand's taste and when Montgomery visited him on 8 December, he gladly agreed with the Army Commander's opinion that a few weeks' leave would restore him sufficiently; he tells us that the visit itself 'seemed to put new strength in me'.

Perhaps de Guingand had additional reasons for feeling strengthened. The confirmed bachelor had finally succumbed and, on 17 December, he married Mrs Arlie Stewart, a close friend of long-standing whose husband had been killed in action the year before and who was then serving in an Intelligence organization in Cairo. Montgomery offered encouragement and support, while typically warning de Guingand that: 'You must be quiet and not rush about to parties etc.'

His illness caused de Guingand to miss the El Agheila action and though he was back with Eighth Army just in time for its final push to Tripoli, Montgomery, who as described earlier, took personal control of the coastal thrust, kept Erskine as Chief of Staff at his Tactical Headquarters with de Guingand in charge of Main HQ.

Montgomery was in fact wondering whether it might perhaps be best for de Guingand's health if he did leave Eighth Army after all, and had written to Brooke, arranging that de Guingand be awarded a CBE, but also strongly recommending that de Guingand be given the post of Director of Military Intelligence at the War Office with the rank of major general. This was a generous action for, as he frankly admitted to Brooke, if de Guingand did go home, 'I do not know what I should do without him.'

Brooke, who never seems to have shared Montgomery's high opinion of de Guingand, rejected the proposal. His lack of faith would have sad consequences at a later date but for the moment it greatly benefited Eighth Army since, after the fall of Tripoli, de Guingand resumed his old role as its Chief of Staff. He assisted in preparing the defences that won the Battle of Medenine; he reassured and encouraged Montgomery after the defeat of XXX Corps at Mareth and then helped to organize the flank attack which would regain the initiative; he was involved with the plans for the assault on the Gabes Gap, including Montgomery's decision to strike on a moonless night which was contrary to his usual practice and consequently caught his enemy completely by surprise.

By this time, Montgomery's confidence in his 'trusted Chief of Staff' was total and in mid-April 1943 he gave a further demonstration of this. As usual he was looking well beyond current operations and was anxious to ensure that planning for the proposed invasion of Sicily – Operation HUSKY – should proceed as a matter of urgency. At the same time, he did not want to leave Tunisia before the final defeat of the Axis armies there. His solution was to appoint de Guingand as his deputy and send him to Cairo to get to work on HUSKY and co-ordinate matters with the appropriate Navy and Air Force authorities. 'It was agreed,' de Guingand reports, 'that in view of my new status and responsibility I should be given the rank of major general.' Typically, he celebrated his promotion with a considerable quantity of champagne.

De Guingand arrived in Cairo on 15 April and two days later set about solving the many problems of amphibious warfare. These were new to most of the planners but de Guingand's experience of the evacuation from Greece had given him a good deal of insight into most of them and not only were they resolved but the techniques used for dealing with them would be employed again in later and still greater invasions.

Unfortunately, however, this lengthy series of responsibilities again took its toll, as did some unpleasant events that occurred during this same period. Shortly before the Battle of Medenine for instance, Montgomery, Leese and members of their staff were inspecting the small, steep hill of Tadjera Khir which Leese calls 'the pivot of the defence', when, de Guingand tells us, a German artillery shell 'landed very close to our path'. It had 'no visible effect' on Montgomery or Leese, who calmly carried on with their conversation, but de Guingand was well aware that the incident could so easily have had tragic consequences.

On 28 April, de Guingand had a still narrower escape. Montgomery, who was in bed with influenza, tonsillitis and a high temperature, asked his deputy to fly to Algiers to represent him at a conference on HUSKY. The Hudson aircraft in which de Guingand was making the journey crashed while taking off in poor weather and de Guingand suffered concussion and was unconscious for several hours. He was told by his doctors to take a fortnight's sick leave, which was extended for a further fortnight by Montgomery, who ordered him to 'have a thorough good rest' as he was 'far too valuable to be wasted'.

De Guingand therefore spent a delightful holiday with his wife in Palestine and Syria, but he was back wrestling with his detailed problems on 1 June and at his chief's side during the campaign in Sicily, where he again had his share of dangerous experiences. The landings took place on 10 July and Montgomery established his tactical HQ at Pachino airfield next day. De Guingand joined him on the 12th and that night a series of raids were made on the landing-ground or on the assault shipping on nearby beaches by enemy bombers, one of which was shot down, says de Guingand, 'nearly in our camp – quite a spectacular party'. On 28 July, he was again fortunate to avoid injury when Montgomery's notorious Flying Fortress[2] was 'written off' by a crash-landing at Palermo. The Army Commander, incidentally, was said by onlookers to have showed no concern whatever.

Three days earlier, the entire political and strategic situation had taken a dramatic new turn. King Victor Emmanuel III had demanded Mussolini's resignation, ordered him taken into custody, officially for his own protection, and appointed as his successor his long-time critic, Marshal Pietro Badoglio. Desperate to extract Italy from a ruinous war but aware that if he simply surrendered, his country would be taken over by the Germans, Badoglio made secret approaches to the Western Allies with a view to joining them as a co-belligerent.

Clearly a successful occupation of Italy would bear rich fruit and de Guingand was soon deeply involved in planning for this. The trouble was that his staff had not been told of Badoglio's 'feelers' and even those exalted personages who were 'in the know' had no idea if, when or with what effect Italy really would change sides: at the Casablanca Conference in January, Churchill and President Franklin Roosevelt had demanded the 'unconditional surrender' of the Axis powers, which idiotic slogan theoretically made any negotiations impossible. A month passed in hypocritical manoeuvres designed to reassure Badoglio that he could surrender 'unconditionally' on favourable conditions, and Italy only capitulated on 3 September and even then this was not officially announced for a further five days.

These uncertainties, declares de Guingand, made the task of drawing up plans 'as difficult as possible' and resulted in the hasty preparation of a whole series of them, many mutually contradictory and some wholly unrealistic. Eventually it was decided to make three landings on the Italian mainland. The first, on 3 September, would be a strike, officially by Eighth Army but in reality by Dempsey's XIII Corps, across the Straits of Messina to the 'toe' of Italy; this was code-named Operation BAYTOWN. The main one would take place in the Gulf of Salerno on 9 September, the day after the official Italian surrender; this was Operation AVALANCHE and would be carried out by Mark Clark's Fifth US Army, to which the British X Corps had been added. On the same day, the hastily-arranged Operation SLAPSTICK would set the men of 1st (British) Airborne Division ashore at Taranto on the 'heel' of Italy; this would be a seaborne landing as 1st Airborne had no troop-carrying aircraft available – or tanks, artillery or transport vehicles either, apart from a few jeeps, which meant that it could not possibly advance very far to the north.

Neither Montgomery nor de Guingand was happy with these arrangements. Both felt that BAYTOWN would not assist AVALANCHE by diverting enemy forces as was hoped, because the Germans could rely on Eighth Army being delayed by rearguards and the dreadful terrain it would have to face. And both regarded optimistic forecasts that the Italians would turn on the Germans and assist the Allies to drive them from the country as being purely fanciful.

Nonetheless, on 3 September, Eighth Army's XIII Corps did cross the Straits of Messina as planned under cover of a massive artillery bombardment. This was in fact unnecessary because the enemy had prudently retired from the area. Intelligence reports had suggested that opposition would be weak but small units landed secretly to confirm this had not done so and, remembering the false information that had been circulated in the past, Montgomery preferred to risk wasting metal rather than risk sacrificing men's lives. A relieved XIII Corps captured the port of Reggio almost undamaged and took 3,000 Italian prisoners;

after which 5th (British) Division pushed northward over the Calabrian Peninsula's western coast road and 1st Canadian Division over its eastern one.

Now the problems began. 'Never,' declares de Guingand, 'was a country more suited to delaying action.' The roads were the only means of advance and they twisted and turned over innumerable hairpin bends, hemmed in by steep cliffs, which the Germans brought down onto them, and crossing deep ravines, the bridges over which the Germans blew up. Even so, by 10 September, after a journey of 100 miles as the crow flies but as much as 250 miles by road, Eighth Army had reached Catanzaro on the narrowest part of the Calabrian Peninsula, known with scant regard for anatomical accuracy, as the 'neck' of the 'toe'.

Any satisfaction that Eighth Army had gained from this achievement, which in view of the difficulties it had experienced was not inconsiderable, was marred that evening when a signal was received from Alexander, asking Montgomery to put maximum pressure on the enemy opposing him so as to reduce the build-up of German strength at Salerno where the situation was starting to cause concern. Montgomery, says de Guingand, responded 'wholeheartedly and with speed'. The port of Crotone and its nearby airfields were captured intact next day and Kittyhawk fighter-bombers from the Desert Air Force – which had retained its former title despite its change of location – began attacks on the forces menacing Clark.

Alexander also summoned every other available aircraft to Clark's assistance, as well as strong naval forces to provide supporting fire for the AVALANCHE beachhead. It was these moves that prevented the destruction of the landing forces, as both Montgomery and de Guingand later accepted, though German records do show that the advance of Eighth Army, which came up on Clark's right flank on 16 September, was a contributory cause of the enemy's decision to withdraw. Thereafter, Fifth and Eighth Armies proceeded separately on either side of the Apennine Mountains; the former followed the west coast, while Eighth Army changed its base from Reggio to the ports on the Italian 'heel' – a 'very complex and expensive business' according to de Guingand – before advancing on the Adriatic side.

By this time, XIII Corps had been joined by Lieutenant General Charles Allfrey's V Corps and other reinforcements would soon be arriving, including Freyberg's 2nd New Zealand Division. On 27 September, Eighth Army captured the strategically vital airfield complex at Foggia, from which Allied heavy bombers could attack targets in southern Germany, Eastern Europe and the Balkans, previously out of range. On the night of 2/3 October, a commando raid seized the port of Termoli just north of the Biferno River and, aided by reinforcements from 78th (British) Division, held it in the face of heavy counter-attacks, urged on personally by Kesselring. On the night of 2/3 November, the river Trigno was also crossed and by the 19th, Eighth Army had secured the southern bank of the River Sangro and had reached the edge of Kesselring's Gustav Line.

These continuous combats had once more had an adverse effect on de Guingand's health, but a number of events combined to sustain him. One was the news that he had been made a Commander of the Bath on 14th October; another was a happy three-day visit to Augusta, Sicily, where he temporarily rejoined his wife, then on her way from Egypt to England by sea; a third was the arrival of an unshaven and rather dirty 'Italian peasant' wearing an old straw hat – he turned out to be Lieutenant Colonel Hugh Mainwaring who had come all the way through Italy from a prisoner of war camp south of Milan. De Guingand was of course prominent at the spectacular reunion party which was held that evening.[3]

De Guingand needed such cheering incidents, for his last few weeks in Italy proved very disappointing. Montgomery's intention was to cross first the Sangro, then the River Moro and gain the port of Pescara and the inland town of Chieti some 10 miles to the south-west. Both stood on Route 5, the main road over the Apennines, which Montgomery proposed to follow to Rome. Once more this was hardly the plan of a cautious commander and it greatly worried de Guingand, who felt success was only possible if the weather remained kind – and for an operation that was to commence on 20 November, there was a strong likelihood that it might not.

Nor did it. The latter part of November brought continuous heavy rains, which caused the rivers to rise dramatically and reduced the whole area to a sea of mud. This ruined the elaborate deceptions that had been employed to suggest that the main assault would come in the mountains on Eighth Army's left flank; Kesselring knew that the existing conditions would make movement literally impossible except on the coast road to Pescara and the parallel Route 81 to Chieti. Since these were naturally heavily guarded, progress was painfully slow and Montgomery has been roundly condemned for using them – though it is difficult to see what other choice he had. Eighth Army had taken the Li Colli Ridge, the main German defensive position beyond the Sangro, by nightfall on 30 November and the Moro was crossed on 8 December, but Pescara and Chieti remained out of reach and before the month was over, Montgomery had advised Alexander that the offensive should be discontinued.

There would, however, be ample consolation for Montgomery and de Guingand in the news that they then received; they were to leave for England to participate in Operation OVERLORD, the invasion of North-West Europe. Montgomery would be Commander-in-Chief of the land forces in the initial assault and until direct control was assumed by the Supreme Commander, General Eisenhower; he would also be permanent head of Twenty-First Army Group, which then consisted of First US Army under Bradley and Second British Army under Dempsey. De Guingand, of course, would be Montgomery's Chief of Staff.

De Guingand performed one last service for Montgomery in Italy: organizing his farewell address to a large gathering of Eighth Army personnel in the Opera House of a small town called Vasto. Afterwards they drove together to Main Headquarters, de Guingand 'feeling very uncomfortable, for I had tears on my cheeks and we were riding in an open car'. At the Headquarters, senior commanders had come to say their farewells and offer their best wishes. 'Later,' de Guingand continues, 'Freyberg, Dempsey, Allfrey and the others departed, and I had the feeling that something rather terrible was happening – I was leaving this great family. But then again I remembered that I was leaving in company with the one who had given us that inspiration, and that guidance, and so although sad I felt content with fate.'

*   *   *

On arriving at the Headquarters of Twenty-First Army Group, de Guingand was at first somewhat daunted by the number of 'entirely new faces, the majority of whom had not had much practical experience of war'. His band of trusted colleagues and subordinates had been dispersed over the course of time. The Germans had deprived him of Mainwaring and of his 'very dear friend' Kisch, who had been killed by a mine while examining the defences of the Gabes Gap. Others had been transferred or left behind in Italy. De Guingand did, however, have the nucleus of what he calls 'the old firm' in key positions. Robertson had been promoted to major general and become GOC Tripoli and later an indispensable Chief Administrative Officer to Alexander, but his deputy and successor Graham had accompanied de Guingand to England, as had Williams. Moreover, they would soon be joined by Belchem as head of Operations and Richardson as head of Plans.

Montgomery of course laid down the basic guidelines for the invasion of and subsequent strategy in Normandy. Having done so, he concentrated on visiting and encouraging the formations that would take part. In accordance with his usual practice, he left it to his staff – which now included a small but extremely able team of US Army officers led by Colonel Bonesteel – to work out the details under the supervision of de Guingand, acting more than ever as Montgomery's deputy.

'The work involved was terrific,' Montgomery would record in his *Memoirs*, and the responsibilities shouldered by de Guingand equally so. Among the matters that he and his subordinates had to consider were: the movement of the troops to their embarkation areas; their build-up in the beachhead and their progress out of it; their equipment, particularly that needed for a seaborne invasion such as the DD (Duplex Drive) amphibious tanks; their logistic support including the 'Mulberry' artificial harbours and 'Pluto', an oil 'pipeline under the ocean'; security, Intelligence and Operation FORTITUDE, the deception plan that succeeded beyond expectation in convincing the enemy first that the assault would come in the Pas de Calais and later that the Normandy landing was only a subsidiary move preceding a main one further to the north-east; and the co-ordination of all these items with the Americans and the Allied Naval and Air Force authorities.

Naturally, many of these problems had been considered by de Guingand's predecessors but their solutions had been dismissed as 'impracticable' and drastically amended by Montgomery. He decreed that the frontage of attack must be widened and the strength of his initial seaborne assault force increased from three to five divisions, landing on beaches stretching from the base of the Cotentin (or Cherbourg) Peninsula in the west to the River Orne in the east.

In the far west, Bradley's First American Army would put 4th US Infantry Division from VII US Corps ashore on 'Utah' beach, and 1st US Infantry Division from V US Corps east of it on 'Omaha'. On Bradley's left, Second British Army under Dempsey would direct 50th Division from XXX Corps to 'Gold' and 3rd Canadian and 3rd (British) Divisions both from I Corps to 'Juno' and 'Sword', still further east, respectively. In addition, 82nd and 101st US Airborne Divisions would be dropped beyond 'Utah' beach and 6th (British) Airborne Division would seize bridges across the Orne.

Montgomery had also altered the strategy to be adopted once a secure bridgehead had been established. On 7 April, in a Presentation of Plans held in the lecture hall of St Paul's School, Hammersmith, he explained this to Churchill, Brooke, Eisenhower and senior officers from the Allied land, naval and air forces. De Guingand, who of course was well acquainted with all the details, would later describe the tasks that were allotted to each of the four armies that would participate in the Battle of Normandy.[4]

On the left of the bridgehead, Second British Army was ordered to secure important positions to the south and south-east, chiefly Caen, which was a major road and rail junction, the Carpiquet aerodrome 2 miles west of the city, and the wide plain south of it, which was ideal for the construction of further airfields. These moves, though, were not made to prepare for a breakthrough to Paris as some critics have averred, but to ensure that this part of the Allied line was firmly held. Dempsey's main role was defensive: the Presentation states it as being 'to protect the eastern flank of First US Army', which in turn was directed against the port of Cherbourg. At the Presentation, a 'Phase Line Map' was exhibited, showing the maximum progress likely to have been made at any given time. Even this 'best possible case' forecast indicates that after its initial gains, Second Army was intended to advance no further to the east for nearly three weeks and only some 10 miles eastward for another fortnight after that. Instead it would 'pivot on its left and offer a strong front against enemy movement towards the lodgement area from the east', in which task it would be joined in due course – on 23 July, as it transpired – by the First Canadian Army of

Lieutenant General Henry Crerar.

There was ample reason for this attitude. Though we have been told that Montgomery failed to foresee that the Germans would send their panzer divisions against the British and Canadians in the Caen area, he had required Dempsey to 'offer a strong front' precisely because this was just what he did foresee. The German Commander-in-Chief, West was Field Marshal von Rundstedt but he would later complain without undue exaggeration that 'my only authority was to change the guard in front of my gate'. Hitler had given operational control of the forces in France to his favourite field marshal, Rommel, who commanded Army Group 'B', consisting of the German Seventh Army south of the River Seine and Fifteenth Army north of it. At his Presentation, Montgomery warned that Rommel was 'a determined character' who 'likes to hurl his armour into the battle' and would probably have two armoured divisions available with which to do so as early as the evening of D-Day and six by D + 5. Since Allied Intelligence had reported that the three panzer divisions already in Normandy were all stationed south-east of Caen and the others would have to come from north of the Seine, it was obvious that their initial blows would fall on Second British Army.

Whatever may have been stated by critics outside Twenty-First Army Group at the time or later, all Montgomery's subordinates were well aware of his intentions. De Guingand declares bluntly: 'Remember this – the original conception was followed and worked . . . the enemy concentrated the build-up of his armour against the Caen hinge, and we held him there whilst Cherbourg was captured and the lodgement area was seized.' Bradley also never doubted the value of Second British Army's role; he believed that 'Monty's success should have been measured' not in the territorial gains made on the eastern flank but 'in the panzer divisions the enemy rushed against him'.

Bradley further acknowledges that when Montgomery 'bossed the US First Army as part of his Twenty-First Army Group, he exercised his Allied authority with wisdom, forbearance and restraint'. 'I could not have wanted a more tolerant or judicious commander,' Bradley adds, and he for his part, relates de Guingand, was 'co-operative and charming' and did everything in his power to ensure that Montgomery's strategy would succeed.

Bradley's own role in that strategy was as vital as Dempsey's but more dramatic. After securing Cherbourg, he was to turn south to capture another crucial road centre at St Lô, from which he would advance to the port of Avranches at the north-east of the Brittany (or Brest) Peninsula. At this stage, Bradley would hand over First US Army to Lieutenant General Courtney Hodges, becoming instead head of Twelfth US Army Group, controlling both First and Third US Armies. The latter under Patton would capture the Brittany ports, while Hodges moved on to the River Loire. Finally, with Patton covering its southern flank, First US Army would head north-east for Paris, the capture of which was thus expressly made an American, not a British objective.

It will be noted that Third US Army and hence Twelfth US Army Group would only become active after Avranches had fallen. Patton personally arrived in Normandy on 7 July, eager for action, and was most disappointed to learn that Bradley had no intention of altering this programme. Uncharitable critics have declared that Montgomery wished to postpone Bradley's appointment as an Army Group Commander because Bradley would then be 'independent' of Twenty-First Army Group. As with so many of the attacks on Montgomery during this period, however, the charge has absolutely no justification.

In the first place, there is no indication whatever that Montgomery ever did want to delay bringing Third US Army into the fight. His 'Phase Line Map' shows that it was his hope that the Americans would reach Avranches and so enable Patton to break into Brittany as early as D + 20. That this proved impossible to achieve was certainly not Montgomery's desire. On 27 June, he wrote to Brooke that he had 'tried very hard to get First US Army to develop its thrust southward' without waiting for the capture of Cherbourg; it was Bradley who, perhaps rightly, 'didn't want to take the risk'.

Moreover, by 7 July, Montgomery already knew that the formation of Twelfth US Army Group would not result in Bradley becoming 'independent'. As Montgomery wrote to Brooke on that date, Eisenhower had decided that when the new Army Group was formed – which it would eventually be on 1 August – Montgomery would retain 'operational control' of it and be responsible for the 'tactical co-ordination' of both it and Twenty-First Army Group until such time as the Supreme Commander assumed direct control, which would only happen after the Battle for Normandy was over. It may be added that this situation was unhesitatingly accepted by the ever-loyal Bradley.

A more reasonable complaint could be made that Montgomery, far from being the cautious commander of legend, was over-optimistic about the rapidity with which initial successes would be gained. He never disguised his hopes that by the end of D-Day or immediately afterwards, on the left of the British bridgehead Caen would have fallen and on its right formations would be pushing towards the important high ground at Villers-Bocage, some 20 miles from the sea. Nor did he ever deny his wish to capture the airfield sites beyond Caen as early as possible and in any case before the end of June. These ambitions were not unreasonable at the time of Montgomery's Presentation but in the weeks that followed, Hitler's 'intuition' had told him that Normandy might be threatened and the Germans had greatly increased both its defenders and its fixed defences. Some prudent officers were therefore sounding notes of warning. Bradley felt that specific dates should not be attached to the phase lines as they might then be considered not general indications of intention but guarantees, while de Guingand repeatedly stated that no promises could be made of the progress that would be achieved by any particular day.

De Guingand especially emphasized that 'it would be very dangerous to assume that the capture of Caen would be easy'. Lieutenant General John Crocker, whose I Corps was given this task, agreed, issuing an Operation Order which specifically indicated that by nightfall on D-Day, Caen should be captured *or* 'effectively masked' by brigades stationed to its north-east and north-west. Their doubts were understandable as Intelligence reports had revealed that the defences in the Caen area were extremely strong and that 21st Panzer Division was stationed in its vicinity. Moreover, although I Corps' 3rd Canadian Division had been detailed to secure the road from Caen to Bayeux, which would threaten the former from the west, the direct assault on it would be left to 3rd (British) Division and this was handicapped by an unlucky but inescapable feature of geography.

On maps of the D-Day landings, the impression is usually given that 'Sword' beach, on which 3rd (British) Division came ashore, directly adjoined the neighbouring I Corps beach of 'Juno'. In reality, outcrops of rock ensured that there was a 5-mile gap between them. They also so restricted the width of 'Sword' that the division's three brigades had to land in turn, one behind the other. Even so, suggestions that the assault on Caen had been made the responsibility of one infantry brigade supported by the tanks of the Staffordshire Yeomanry and the 'DDs' of 13th/18th Hussars, and that the planners should have provided a stronger force, are most misleading. The assault was the responsibility of the whole of 3rd (British) Division and its supporting armour, its 8th Brigade being directed to seize preliminary positions, through which 185th Brigade could pass and strike onwards to Caen, while 9th Brigade acted as a reserve. The trouble was that the narrowness of the beach caused appalling congestion, which was made worse by heavy enemy artillery fire – and could only have been made worse still had larger numbers attempted to land on it. As it was, 9th Brigade could not come ashore until mid-afternoon and the forward move of the other formations, particularly the tanks, was considerably delayed. Since the probability of such difficulties had been foreseen, it might well appear that Montgomery was indeed unwise not to have echoed his subordinates' doubts and stressed the problems the capture of Caen would present.

Nonetheless, Montgomery had two very good reasons for refusing to alter the timetable laid down in his Presentation. Though he personally had performed wonders in inspiring and heartening his troops, his efforts had taken place against a background of general depression and anxiety; even Churchill, haunted by a nightmare vision of the English Channel awash with bodies, seemed to have lost his fire and vitality. For the sake of morale, Montgomery was not prepared to make the slightest gesture that might weaken his men's confidence. There was also a tactical consideration: Montgomery realized that after a successful invasion there would be an automatic relaxation of effort; he insisted on the retention of his original bold and optimistic objectives, says the War Correspondent Chester Wilmot in *The Struggle for Europe*, so that 'his troops should have a star to strive for, and would not miss opportunities of exploitation for lack of orders'.

That Montgomery was right to pursue this policy seems confirmed when we observe that despite his own strongly-expressed instructions to the contrary, many formations did pause to consolidate after their successful landings and then moved forward in a somewhat leisurely fashion. 50th (British) Division captured Bayeux – which had been a D-Day objective – on 7 June, but made little further progress towards Villers-Bocage against negligible opposition. And the advance of 3rd (British) Division was hampered, says Wilmot, not only by the 'traffic jam' on the beach but by 'an absence of drive' – though it seems unlikely that it could have taken Caen in any case in view of the enemy strength in this area.

Indeed, on the afternoon of D-Day, 3rd (British) Division was subjected to the first German counter-attack by 21st Panzer Division. Fortunately, harried by airstrikes from rocket-firing Typhoons and opposed by wellsited anti-tank guns, this assault failed with heavy losses; as did a similar one by 12th SS Panzer Division against 3rd Canadian on the following day. Panzer Lehr Division arrived on 8 June and 2nd Panzer Division five days after that – and the pattern of operations over the next few weeks was thus established.

On the one hand, the German armour was concentrating against Dempsey, whose men acted as a shield for the rest of the bridgehead, precisely as Montgomery had anticipated and desired. This was just as well because further west the Americans had gained only a perilously narrow foothold at 'Omaha' on D-Day, and the 'Utah' beach was 10 miles away from the main invasion area and separated from it by land that had been extensively flooded. Full-scale assaults on them might have proved catastrophic, as it was the Americans were given a chance to recover, which they took with splendid courage and resilience. On 8 June, 'Omaha' was joined to the British and Canadian beaches to form one continuous front and Bradley then pushed steadily forward, taking Caumont, some 20 miles inland, on the 12th. Elsewhere, on the same day, the Americans had captured the road-junction at Carentan, thereby joining hands with their compatriots at 'Utah'. By the 17th, they had cut across the base of the Cotentin Peninsula and they secured Cherbourg ten days later.

On the other hand, there was now no possibility of an early seizure of Caen, leaving the bridgehead in the Second British Army area cramped, restricted and dangerous. Nonetheless, having crossed the Channel on 7 June to confer with Bradley and Dempsey in their command ships moored just off the beaches, Montgomery went ashore on the following day and set up his Tactical Headquarters in the grounds of a château to the east of Bayeux. This was only some 3 miles from the front line, so perhaps not an ideal location for the C-in-C of the Allied Land Forces. On 9 June, as he cheerfully informed de Guingand, a bombing raid scored 'a very near miss' but luckily this did no damage, and his presence, sharing at least to some extent the dangers of his soldiers, provided a great stimulus to morale.

De Guingand had remained in England in charge of Twenty-First Army Group's Main HQ. Montgomery kept him well informed of the situation and when they needed to discuss future moves, de Guingand flew to the bridgehead in a Dakota provided by the generosity of Eisenhower. On doing so, he was quickly reminded of the dangers at Tac HQ. This was well within range of enemy artillery and, de Guingand reports:

> A shell burst about 100 yards short, followed by another about 200 yards over. Being rather imaginative I was finding it very hard to concentrate, expecting the result of this 'straddle' at any moment. Before long, one landed sufficiently near to scatter mud against the caravan. The only remark my Chief made was: 'That must have been quite near.' But other than that it had no effect upon him.

The efforts of Second British Army to extend its bridgehead and deal with the increasing array of German tanks facing it can be dealt with most conveniently elsewhere. Suffice for the moment to say that for many weeks visible results were extremely disappointing and naturally this caused concern, particularly at Eisenhower's Headquarters, where it was feared that the vaunted 'Second Front' might end in stalemate. As a result, de Guingand spent much of his time forwarding Montgomery's reassurances of ultimate success to the Supreme Commander, while also protecting his Chief from uninformed criticism. His diplomatic charm made him ideally suited for this task but it became increasingly taxing and he welcomed the call for more difficult but more constructive duties, which would come in early August.

On 18 July, the Americans finally took the shattered remains of St Lô. Seven days later, the long-planned, long-awaited break-out – Operation COBRA – began. Avranches fell to First US Army on 30 July, and next day, Patton's Third US Army began to pour through it to fan out westward and southward. Captain Liddell Hart has complained that the Allies should have disregarded the 'outdated pre-invasion programme' of liberating Brittany first, but in fact Montgomery again showed his flexibility, giving orders to Bradley at 1030 on 1 August that only Patton's VIII Corps should go into

Brittany, while XV and XX Corps made for the Loire. It was not until 3 August that Bradley passed on his instructions but on the following day, the bulk of Third US Army began a huge sweep south and east, to reach Le Mans on the 8th. North-east of Avranches, First US and Second British Armies pushed southwards, and on 7 August, on the eastern side of the bridgehead, First Canadian Army delivered a thrust towards Falaise which, however, advanced only 9 miles before it was called off three days later.

An organized withdrawal was now the only reasonable option for the German forces in Normandy, but Hitler would not hear of this. Instead, on 4 August, he ordered that all his available armour should advance through Mortain, which First US Army had taken on the 2nd, to Avranches, cutting off the outflanking Americans. The attempt began in the early hours of 7 August but even on paper the strike force contained only 185 tanks or mobile guns and many of these were unable to reach the start-line on time. Allied Intelligence had given warning of the attack; Bradley, Hodges and their men met it with admirable coolness and courage, and it was fiercely assaulted from the air by the rocket-firing Typhoons. By nightfall, it had already been halted, having gained only 7 miles. Yet Hitler continued to insist that the offensive be renewed, and not until late on 11 August would he accept that it was no longer feasible.

Hitler's attempt to control the battle from a distance had left great numbers of his soldiers in a gigantic salient, later called the 'Falaise Pocket', which was under pressure from all sides. It had originally been the Allied intention that the Americans should reach the Seine in the Paris area and then swing north along the river in a 'long hook' to engage the Germans as they tried to retreat from Normandy. On 8 August, however, Bradley urged that Third US Army should instead make a 'short hook', which would take first Alençon, the enemy's main supply centre, and then Argentan, where it would link up with the Canadians advancing through Falaise, and trap the formations in the 'Pocket'.

It seems that Montgomery had doubts at first, but de Guingand strongly supported Bradley and his advice won the day. Montgomery did approve Bradley's plan and on reflection decided, unfortunately but surely not unreasonably, that the 'short hook', by threatening Alençon, the loss of which would deprive the Germans of vital stocks of fuel and ammunition, would have the further advantage of reducing the resistance offered to the Canadians. This in turn should enable them to break through to Argentan before the Americans could reach it. He therefore fixed the boundary between the two Army Groups at just south of Argentan.

For his part, de Guingand was less confident about the Canadians' chances and unfortunately his more pessimistic appreciation would prove correct. The SS troops defending Falaise offered fanatical resistance and its ruined remains were only finally secured on 17 August. Meanwhile, Patton's XV Corps under Major General Wade Haislip had taken Alençon on the 12th, and next day it was only just short of Argentan when it was prevented by Bradley from proceeding any further.

It has been surmised that as Montgomery was still the Allied Land Forces Commander, Bradley did not feel it proper to request him to alter the inter-Army Group boundary. Bradley was certainly sensitive about such matters after his unfortunate experiences in Sicily, but had he asked for a change, he would have been supported by de Guingand for one and it seems most unlikely that Montgomery would have refused him. Probably, though, Bradley was more concerned about the dangers inherent in a further advance. He feared that the retreating Germans, who had three armoured divisions in the vicinity, all admittedly considerably under strength, might overwhelm Haislip's men and much preferred, as he put it, that these present 'a solid shoulder at Argentan' rather than suffer 'a broken neck at Falaise'. Eisenhower, who was visiting Bradley at the time, approved his decision, but by an unintentional oversight Montgomery was not consulted – though this has not prevented some later commentators from following Patton's example and blaming him for Bradley's attitude.

In fact, neither Montgomery nor Bradley deserves blame. The failure was that of Allied Intelligence, which had informed Bradley that the German retreat was already underway, whereas it really only began on 14 August. A further erroneous report then stated that the bulk of the forces in the salient had already passed beyond Falaise and Argentan by the 16th. Montgomery therefore directed that the 'Pocket' should be sealed off further to the east, and also urged Bradley to continue the 'long hook' to the Seine to catch those Germans who had either already escaped from it or had never been in it in the first place.

The point of junction for the Allied pincers was now fixed at the village of Chambois. This and the neighbouring village of St Lambert soon became scenes of blood-soaked chaos as 4th Canadian Armoured and 1st Polish Armoured Divisions from the north and 90th US Infantry and 2nd French Armoured Divisions from the south closed in on the Germans struggling to break out of the 'Pocket', and 9th and 10th SS Panzer Divisions, which had been withdrawn from the salient earlier, attacked from the east to help keep the escape routes open.

On 18 August, the Poles captured a ridge which, from its shape, they called 'The Mace'. Shellfire from this and missiles from Allied aircraft poured onto the wretched German soldiers, and by the following evening, the jaws of the trap had met. On the 20th, the remnants of 2nd Panzer Division smashed its way out past the Canadians, but the gap was then closed again and all further attempts to escape ceased on the 21st. It is believed that 20,000 men in all did avoid being cut off in the salient, including, disappointingly, most of the senior officers, though the head of Seventh Army, SS General Paul Hausser, was carried out unconscious on the back of a tank, having lost an eye and most of his lower jaw, and LXXXIV Corps' Commander, Lieutenant General Otto Elfeldt, was taken prisoner by the Poles.

Behind them, however, they left 10,000 of their men dead, 50,000 in captivity, and some 1,200 guns, 500 tanks and 7,700 other vehicles destroyed or abandoned. De Guingand, who twice flew over the area in a light aircraft, reports that he could never even have imagined 'such a scene of desolation'. Many more men and vehicles were lost before they could cross the Seine, either to Allied airmen or to American soldiers whom Bradley had started on Montgomery's wide enveloping movement on 20 August – though this was not as strong as Montgomery had hoped, since Patton had diverted many of his formations to the Seine south of Paris. Even so, by 29 August when the last German soldiers crossed the Seine, enemy sources confirm that the equipment abandoned on its western bank almost equalled that lost in the 'Pocket'. The total number of German tanks lost in Normandy rose to some 2,200, the total number of prisoners to 210,000, and the total German casualties to half a million, nearly twice the number of those incurred in the fighting at Stalingrad.

De Guingand was now Sir Francis, having been recommended for a KBE by Montgomery in recognition of his 'great and outstanding services', but from now onwards his influence rapidly declined. This was partly because Montgomery's own influence had been reduced. Eisenhower took direct control of his armies on 1 September, and increasing numbers of American soldiers were pouring into North-West Europe, while at the same time a shortage of manpower was leading to the break-up of some British formations and the dispersal of their men to provide reinforcements for others. It was thus inevitable that the British voice, however clear and forceful, would be heeded less and less; in addition to which de Guingand's relationship with Montgomery was itself in the process of changing.

After the war, de Guingand would state that he had not been in favour of the concentrated thrust to the Ruhr urged by Montgomery but considered the 'broad front' strategy of Eisenhower had been correct. When Montgomery read this, he protested, surprisingly mildly, that: 'I cannot remember that you ever told me that you disagreed; I cannot remember that you ever argued the matter with me.' This was probably correct, for Richardson, who as Twenty-First Army Group's head of Plans was in the best position to know, declares that de Guingand had originally 'reached the same conclusion as his chief' and only changed his mind later after learning that Eisenhower would not give Montgomery the logistical support that his thrust would need. Yet the fact was that de Guingand's opportunities for argument had in any case been greatly restricted.

Already during the Battle for Normandy, Montgomery had detached himself from his Main Headquarters, spending all his time in his Tac HQ, close behind the front line, with a small hand-picked group of brilliant young liaison officers of comparatively junior rank whom he used to obtain first-hand information of events in all parts of the battlefield. In general, de Guingand approved of this arrangement, which saved Montgomery from unnecessary distractions and enabled him to 'exercise such intimate tactical command over his forces'. Yet it also meant that he lost the benefit of the free and frank opinions of trusted members of his staff, which he had previously welcomed. There was little occasion for this during de Guingand's brief visits, while the differences of age, experience and rank naturally inhibited the liaison officers from querying their leader's ideas.

In consequence, de Guingand notes, Montgomery 'became more dictatorial and uncompromising as time went on'. As his dissatisfaction with the conduct of the campaign mounted – being in no way assuaged by his own promotion to field marshal on 1 September – he showered the long-suffering Eisenhower with demands, thinly veiled as suggestions, which displayed a growing lack of respect and even of good manners.

All this meant that de Guingand became ever less an adviser and ever more an advocate, putting over Montgomery's case to the Supreme Commander but also trying to reduce the friction caused by Montgomery's constant criticisms. A culmination was reached on 30 December 1944, when de Guingand brought to Eisenhower a very forceful letter from Montgomery, dated the previous day, in which he urged, not for the first time, that 'all available offensive power' be given to the northern line of advance and that a ground forces commander be appointed to carry this out with control over both Twenty-First Army Group and Twelfth US Army Group. Eisenhower's patience was exhausted; he drafted a reply, warning that if Montgomery persisted in his demands, there would be no alternative but to refer their differences to the Combined Chiefs of Staff.

Bearing in mind the vastly greater contribution that the United States was making to the war effort in North-West Europe, the result of such a step must have been Montgomery's resignation. De Guingand, realizing this, persuaded Eisenhower, who had a high regard for him, to take no action until he had had a chance to talk to his chief. His report stunned Montgomery who, on 31 December, sent an apologetic signal, expressing regret that he had upset his superior, whose authority he acknowledged without reservation. Eisenhower, as might have been expected, responded with grace and generosity, but there can be no doubt that de Guingand's intervention had rescued Montgomery from a very dangerous situation. There can also be no doubt that these continuous clashes had placed more strain on de Guingand at a time when he was least able to endure it.

The final reason for the decline of de Guingand's influence was that he was suffering from bouts of ill-health, which often seemed to occur at the most inconvenient moments. On 7 September, he had to go to England for medical treatment and did not return until the 17th, thereby taking little part in the preparations for the airborne assaults that attempted to seize a bridgehead over the Rhine. On 15 December, he again went home for a rest and so missed the start of Hitler's

Ardennes offensive, which began next day. On 7 January 1945, Montgomery reported to Brooke that his Chief of Staff was once more 'not very well' and 'really needs three or four weeks' rest'. De Guingand duly left for England but he resumed his post after only a short break – most unwisely, for he had to have drugs to make him sleep, his memory was becoming unreliable and his colleagues, Richardson reports, were all 'appalled at his condition'.

De Guingand's devotion to duty had cost him dear. It is sad to learn that the news of the German surrender left him with no feeling of elation or satisfaction; merely 'rather tired and deflated'. By the end of May, his health was so poor that he was compelled to quit Twenty-First Army Group and take six months' sick leave. He says that he did so 'with a heavy heart', which was undoubtedly the case, but his regrets must have been tempered with an overwhelming sense of relief that his 'long journey from the Nile to the Baltic' had ended and he was finally free from the crushing responsibilities which that journey had entailed.

Notes:

1. The full text of this address can be found in Nigel Hamilton's massive biography *Monty*, Volume I, 'The Making of a General 1887–1942'.
2. Towards the end of February 1943, Montgomery had assured Eisenhower's Chief of Staff, Major General Walter Bedell Smith, that his men would reach the port of Sfax by 15 April. Since this would necessitate their passing both the Mareth Line and the Gabes Gap, Bedell Smith was understandably incredulous and rashly promised that if this could really be done, then, as Montgomery explains in his *Memoirs*, 'General Eisenhower would give me anything I liked to ask for.' He immediately requested the use of a Flying Fortress and its crew – who would remain on the US payroll – for the rest of the war; duly carried out his promise and insisted the Americans honour theirs. Much to their credit, they did, but few would disagree with Bedell Smith's later comment that to serve under Montgomery would be a privilege but to serve over him was hell!
3. Montgomery's stepson, Major Richard Carver, who had been captured at the same time as Mainwaring, also succeeded in getting back to the Allied lines.
4. De Guingand's recollections are confirmed by Nigel Hamilton's *Monty*, Volume II, 'Master of the Battlefield 1942–1944', quoting from Montgomery's diary where he had recorded the notes used for his Presentation.

Chapter 5

'Enthusiasm, Enthusiasm'

Although de Guingand was the subordinate closest to Montgomery, the one who served under Montgomery for the highest proportion of his active career in the Second World War was Horrocks. He first did so during the retreat to Dunkirk, where the 2nd (Machine-Gun) Battalion of the Middlesex Regiment, of which he was Commanding Officer, performed a variety of difficult and dangerous tasks as part of Montgomery's 3rd (British) Division. Usually it was to be found guarding the division's flank or rear, and on one occasion Horrocks was the very last British soldier to retreat over a canal bridge before it was blown up by the sappers. On the night of 27/28 May, however, it was given a different mission – one crucial to the eventual salvation of the BEF.

By this time, the Belgian Army was rapidly disintegrating – it capitulated next day – as a result of which a gap was opening in the Allied front line on the left flank of the British II Corps. Its commander, Lieutenant General Alan Brooke, could only block this by withdrawing 3rd Division from an exposed position and directing it behind a sector where fierce fighting was taking place to the area of greatest danger. Moreover, the move had to be carried out during the hours of darkness, and for once the icily self-controlled Brooke was unable to conceal his anxiety from his staff.

Fortunately, as Brooke had observed, the perils of the retreat 'thrilled' Montgomery 'and put the sharpest of edges on his military ability'. In addition, he had conducted numerous exercises to make his troops proficient in moving at night. He sent his machine-gunners in advance to block the gap and Horrocks confesses that: 'I have never felt more naked in my life.' But by morning, 13,600 men and 600 vehicles had been brought safely to their new positions. Montgomery, in the words of an intensely relieved Brooke, 'had as usual accomplished almost the impossible.'[1] 'He was convinced that he was the best divisional commander in the British Army,' recalls Horrocks, 'and that we were the best division. By the time we had reached Dunkirk, I had come to the same conclusion!'

On 30 May, Horrocks received a promotion, if only a temporary one. Brooke departed for England; Montgomery, inevitably, succeeded him at the head of II Corps; Brigadier Kenneth Anderson, who would later command the British First Army in North Africa, was entrusted with 3rd Division; and Horrocks took over Anderson's 11th Brigade. It was ordered to retire to the beaches next day and on 1 June, Horrocks embarked on a destroyer. This was promptly sunk by German bombers (as were two other British destroyers and a French one) and Horrocks was taken aboard a small cargo boat where he manned an anti-aircraft gun. His efforts had no visible effect on the Luftwaffe but provided 'the only part of the withdrawal which I enjoyed'.

Horrocks quickly became a brigadier again, assuming command of 9th Brigade on 17 June. This was one of the formations in 3rd Division and Horrocks considered it 'wonderful news' that he would be 'back in the fold with Monty' – who had resumed his former command. In January 1941, however, Horrocks left 9th Brigade to become chief staff officer in Eastern Command; before being promoted to major general and placed in charge of 44th Division on 25 June. This was a formation in XII Corps, which in turn formed part of South-Eastern Command under Montgomery, now a lieutenant general, and Horrocks remained 'in the Monty sphere of influence' until 20 March 1942, when he moved to the Midlands to take over 9th Armoured Division. He had been particularly impressed by Montgomery's training methods with their insistence on realism and physical fitness and he now did his best to follow his teacher's example.

On 12 August, Horrocks was told that he had received a further promotion to lieutenant general and would be going to the Middle East to command a corps – XIII Corps as he would learn in due course – for which he had been personally selected. 'He's *very* good,' Montgomery had assured his staff, 'enthusiasm, enthusiasm.' Horrocks arrived in a Liberator bomber on the 15th, was warmly greeted by Alexander, then drove to Eighth Army HQ where he was treated by Montgomery to 'one of the most remarkable military appreciations I ever heard'. Horrocks was amazed alike at the way Montgomery 'had acquired a complete grip of the situation' in just a few days and the way in which he had thought ahead, outlining his intentions not only for dealing with Rommel's coming offensive but for mounting his own offensive thereafter.

At the moment, though, the first essential was preparing for the defensive battle, which would later be called Alam Halfa. It was a tense situation for time was desperately short and Rommel was predicting 'the final destruction of the enemy', which, Captain Liddell Hart confirms, he might well have achieved 'if his opponents had faltered or fumbled as they had done on several previous occasions when their advantage had seemed more sure.'

Throughout the Auchinleck regime, the Allies had always enjoyed a numerical superiority, most especially during the fighting in July 1942. They continued to do so after Alexander and Montgomery took charge, but at Alam Halfa, Liddell Hart points out, 'the strength of the two sides was nearer to an even balance than it was either before or later'. During August 1942, Rommel's original mobile infantry division, the famous 90th Light, had been joined by 164th Light and 288th Parachute Brigade, now used in an infantry role; his Italians had been strengthened by their finest division, the Folgore, another 'dismounted' airborne formation; his 15th and 21st Panzer Divisions had more than doubled the number of their Mark III Specials and received their first Mark IV Specials; his anti-tank guns had also doubled in number; and his supporting air forces had greatly increased in both size and quality.

Only in the matter of supplies could Rommel have had anxieties. Yet the arrival of nearly 800 lorries during August had rectified one former shortage, and although Malta's indefatigable striking forces had sunk three tankers in August, four others did reach Tobruk safely in the last ten days of the month.[2] Finally, on the 30th, Kesselring transferred 1,500 tons of fuel from Luftwaffe stocks, followed by a further 500 tons daily – though much of this was used up on the long journey to the front. This gave Rommel sufficient for the seven days that he believed would be enough to gain his crowning victory and his later claims of a petrol shortage would be rejected by his senior subordinates; Major General Gustav von Vaerst, Commander of 15th Panzer Division, for example, would bluntly label it a 'fallacy'.

Rommel's plan of attack was typically daring and employed all his forces except the Italian Bologna Division, which remained in reserve.

164th Light and Trento Divisions would make diversionary raids in the north; the bulk of the Parachute Brigade would assault the Ruweisat Ridge; the rest of the parachutists and the Brescia Division would attack the Alam Nayil Ridge on the left flank of 2nd New Zealand Division; the Folgore Division would take the 700-feet-high Qarat el Himeimat (Mount Himeimat) just north of the Qattara Depression; and General Walther Nehring's Afrika Korps – 15th and 21st Panzer and 90th Light Divisions – and the Italian XX Corps under Major General Giuseppe de Stephanis – Ariete (Armoured), Littorio (Armoured) and Trieste (Motorized) Divisions – would storm over the low ground between Alam Nayil and Himeimat.

This striking force was to race 30 miles to the east on the first night of the battle, then turn north-east, the Italian armour attacking Alam Halfa and Ruweisat Ridges from the rear while the Afrika Korps made for the coast some 35 miles east of El Alamein, where it would savage Eighth Army's supply units. The British tanks would doubtless move back to their assistance but Rommel was justly confident that his 88mms would deal with them. Then, leaving the bulk of his infantry to complete the destruction of Eighth Army's trapped formations, Rommel would send 21st Panzer to Alexandria and 15th Panzer, 90th Light and the Italian XX Corps to Cairo, from which the Germans would continue to Suez while the Italians followed the Nile southwards.

Rommel urged his soldiers to 'move fast'; the fighting was 'on no account to become static'. Ironically, this was also the wish of Auchinleck and Dorman-Smith. 'The essence of the defensive plan,' declares the former in his Official Despatch, was to be 'fluidity and mobility.' 'We have to be prepared,' announces Dorman-Smith in his Appreciation, 'to fight a modern defensive battle in the area El Alamein-Hammam' – and El Hammam lay some 40 miles by road east of El Alamein.

The form that this 'modern defensive battle' would take was suggested in Dorman-Smith's Appreciation and confirmed by subsequent Operation Orders issued by XIII and XXX Corps. When Rommel attacked, Eighth Army's infantry divisions – 9th Australian, 1st South African, 5th Indian and 2nd New Zealand – would retreat to strongpoints or 'boxes' known as 'Observation Posts', ten in number, established on prominent features some way to the east of the existing front line. Here they would split into battle groups, some to man the 'boxes', others containing the bulk of the artillery, to manoeuvre between them – which de Guingand among others feared would merely present 'a great danger of the guns being driven hither and thither and confusion setting in'.

Luckily, Montgomery's arrival completely altered the situation. He had no interest in fighting a fluid and mobile battle, at which he rightly believed Rommel's men excelled. He therefore cancelled the withdrawals to the Observation Posts, ordered his infantry to defend the existing front line 'at all costs' and stationed 23rd Armoured Brigade – previously kept back behind the 'boxes' – well forward in close support. These moves rectified the position for XXX Corps but that of XIII Corps, which was of course the special responsibility of Horrocks, was more complicated, since it was known that on it would fall the main enemy onslaught.

Montgomery instructed Horrocks that he must repel the assault but was 'not to get mauled' in the process because this would unduly delay the build-up of strength for Eighth Army's own coming offensive. If he could not prevent Rommel's striking force from penetrating the front line, then he must 'impose maximum delay' there and finally halt it at Point 102 and Alam Halfa. The arrival of 44th Division at Alam Halfa and the transfer of one of its brigades to give Freyberg sufficient manpower to hold both his front and his flank on Alam Nayil solved part of the problem, but the most crucial decisions to be made concerned the use of the British armour.

When Horrocks arrived in the Middle East, Eighth Army contained just one armoured division, the 7th; 1st Armoured Division had been withdrawn from the combat zone after the casualties it had suffered in July, though it had first transferred to the 'Desert Rats' its 22nd Armoured Brigade, commanded by Roberts. Auchinleck and Dorman-Smith had intended that 7th Armoured should also remain fluid and mobile, covering the infantry retirement to the Observation Posts and delivering counter-attacks on the enemy's armour. Montgomery would have none of this, warning Horrocks, who in turn reminded his corps about the Germans' 'known ways of fighting', particularly the use of their 88mms. 22nd Armoured Brigade was sent to Point 102 and when Gatehouse's 10th Armoured Division arrived to replace 1st Armoured, its 8th Armoured Brigade, which in practice was its only subordinate formation, was stationed south-east of Alam Halfa to block any wide sweep around the ridge. Both 8th and 22nd Armoured Brigades received additional anti-tank guns and were ordered to stand strictly on the defensive.

Even before Horrocks arrived, Montgomery had issued instructions that the British tanks should if possible ignore the enemy armour and 'shoot up' the 'soft-skinned' vehicles on which Rommel's supplies depended. Horrocks agreed wholeheartedly and would describe this tactic as 'really a case of "dog eat rabbit"', an expression that he may have got from Montgomery. He repeated it to Churchill when the Prime Minister paid a return visit to the Middle East on 19 August on his way home from Moscow, but it did not impress the old warrior; who found it too 'defensively minded'. He muttered it disgustedly at intervals and later told Montgomery that Horrocks was 'no good; get rid of him'. Montgomery naturally took no notice; instead, says Horrocks, realizing that 'I had been through a gruelling experience', he 'rang me up that evening and was most encouraging'.

Churchill was not the only one who disliked the new regime's policy for the armour. Major General Renton, commanding 7th Armoured Division, showed his disapproval so clearly that Horrocks became seriously concerned that 7th Armoured would not fight defensively and might well be mauled as a result. He therefore placed 22nd Armoured Brigade under direct corps control, with the entire approval of Montgomery and also of Roberts who, Horrocks was relieved to find, had little respect for Renton, less for Dorman-Smith's previous plans, and 'backed me up completely'.

The removal of 22nd Armoured Brigade left 7th Armoured Division holding the front line with only the weak 4th Light Armoured Brigade and the mobile infantry of 7th Motor Brigade, but Montgomery and Horrocks did their best to increase its strength in other ways. The previous regime had shown little interest in mines – it is difficult after all to think of anything less fluid and mobile – but as early as 14 August, Montgomery had ordered the 'enlarging and strengthening of minefields in 7th Armoured Div. front'. By the end of the month, two wide belts containing both anti-tank and anti-personnel mines were protecting the defenders and also restricting the enemy's movements to any gaps that could be made through them; this would greatly assist attacks by the Desert Air Force, the co-operation of which Montgomery regarded as one of the keys to success.

Horrocks set up his Headquarters on the Alam Halfa Ridge, where he went through some gruelling experiences of a different kind. The HQ was subjected to a number of Stuka attacks, one of them on the occasion of a visit by Montgomery. 'I couldn't help feeling this time,' recalls Horrocks as both officers went flat on the sand, 'that an unlucky strike which knocked out the commander of the Eighth Army before he had got into his stride might alter the whole war in the Middle East.' Happily the bombs fell some distance away.

Shortly after midnight on 30/31 August, says Horrocks, 'the whole of the southern flank seemed to go up in flames; everything opened up. This was obviously it.' The Battle of Alam Halfa had begun. Though tempted to spend the night at his HQ to watch its progress, Horrocks wisely retired to rest, and when he awoke next morning it was to learn that the changes that had been made were already having an effect. Folgore Division had captured Himeimat early on the morning of the 31st, but the subsidiary attacks on the Ruweisat Ridge and Alam Nayil, which might have caused chaos had they fallen on units preparing to retire to the Observation Posts, were repulsed comparatively easily. The majority of the Italian XX Corps and 90th Light were still trapped in the minefields; and though the German armour had finally managed to break through these by 0700 on the 31st, it had suffered heavy casualties, which included Nehring, severely injured by a bomb exploding just in front of his command vehicle, and the brilliant young leader of 21st Panzer Division, Major General Georg von Bismarck, killed possibly by mortar fire, probably by a mine.

On the coming of daylight, the Desert Air Force, which had previously attacked with the aid of flares, redoubled its efforts. The Baltimore and Boston light bombers, the Hurricane and Kittyhawk fighter-bombers created such pressure that the Afrika Korps, now led by von Vaerst, was only ready to move eastward at 1000, and soon had to halt while its battered supply units caught up with it. Unhappily, a dust storm, which reached a peak of intensity in the early afternoon, grounded the Allied airmen and enabled von Vaerst to resume his advance. Horrocks was bitterly disappointed but as the storm died away at about 1730, he saw to his delight that the German tanks were heading for Point 102, exactly as had been hoped and predicted. 22nd Armoured Brigade, fighting on the defensive as ordered, repulsed them, and as Horrocks declares, 'the crisis was over'.

On 1 September, the German armour attempted to attack Alam Halfa, apparently in the belief that if the front line, Alam Nayil and Point 102 were all defended, Eighth Army could not possibly have enough manpower to hold Alam Halfa securely as well. This had been true before 44th Division came forward but it was not true now and the move was easily thwarted; after which, Rommel's only hope was that Eighth Army, particularly its tanks, would revert to the fluid and mobile warfare that had proved so costly in the past.

Accordingly, relates Horrocks, 'the Germans tried over and over again to lure us out of our defences' – but without success. Horrocks refused to allow his tanks to attack the German positions, leaving it to the Allied artillery and the Allied airmen to harass and harm his opponents. Later critics have sneered at what they call Eighth Army's lack of enterprise and imagination, but they might like to reflect that Rommel would subsequently admit that:

> There is no doubt that the British commander's handling of this action had been absolutely right and well suited to the occasion, for it had enabled him to inflict very heavy damage on us in relation to his own losses, and to retain the striking power of his own force.

At the time, he expressed the same opinion much less politely: 'The swine isn't attacking!' he complained angrily to Kesselring, who was visiting the battle area. The 'swine', of course, was Montgomery.

By midday on 3 September, Rommel had accepted that Eighth Army would not become fluid and mobile and had begun a retreat to his start-line. Despite his claims of petrol shortages, German sources confirm that very few vehicles were abandoned for this reason, even though his supply units, on Montgomery's instructions, were made 'the principal target of both the Air Force and the Army'. Montgomery had also hoped that New Zealand infantry, pushing south from Alam Nayil, would put further pressure on the enemy, but Freyberg remembered only too well the suffering of his men during Auchinleck's July offensives. After much argument, he finally attacked at 2230 on 3 September, but only after insisting that 132nd (British) Brigade should join his two New Zealand brigades in the assault.

Both Montgomery and Horrocks disliked this idea, because they rightly believed that 132nd Brigade, like 44th Division as a whole, was

Harding (right) with two of the officers who commanded brigades in his 7th Armoured Division: Roberts (left) and 'Bolo' Whistler (centre). All three received the rare honour of two bars to their DSO.

Harding (right) in Italy with Alexander, whose Chief of Staff he was.

Leese with three of his divisional commanders at Alamein. Left to right: Morshead (9th Australian); Wimberley (51st Highland); Leese; Pienaar (1st South African). They made up a difficult team which Leese handled magnificently.

Another team – in Italy. Left to right, Leese; Alexander; Mark Clark.

The main commanders at the time of the reconquest of Burma. The photograph splendidly summarizes their different characters: Leese (right) grins broadly; Slim (centre) vainly attempts a smile; Mountbatten (left) eyes them both.

De Guingand (left) with Auchinleck of whom he was 'very fond' but whose handling of Eighth Army he considered deplorable.

De Guingand (right) at Tripoli with his new leader. He maintained that Montgomery gave the men of Eighth Army 'a new hope in our hearts'.

De Guingand as Chief of Staff, Twenty-First Army Group.

Horrocks (right) in eager discussion with Montgomery prior to the Battle of Alam Halfa. The changes of plan which they implemented would bring about a decisive victory.

Horrocks (right) confers with Freyberg prior to their delivering the 'Left Hook' that won the Battle of the Mareth Line.

Montgomery visits Horrocks and the commanders of his armoured division after their spectacular dash into and through Belgium. Left to right: Major General Allan Adair; Montgomery; Horrocks; Roberts.

Richardson as Eighth Army's Director of Operations.

Richardson (right) has a picnic lunch with Alexander on the beach at Salerno – both admirably cool at a time of crisis.

Roberts in the staff car which acted as his 'command post' during much of the campaign in North-West Europe.

Moment of Relaxation: An 'Alamein Reunion' dinner held at Brussels in October 1944. On the top table, (left to right): Roberts; de Guingand; Horrocks; Montgomery; Air Marshal Coningham; 'Bobby' Erskine.

The Master and one of his star pupils: Montgomery congratulates Roberts on his achievements after the conclusion of the war in Europe.

too inexperienced for offensive operations – indeed, Harding had particularly warned of this when he had arranged for the division to be sent to the front line. Freyberg persisted in his demands, however, so the Army Commander and XIII Corps Commander at last consented reluctantly – and unwisely, for the attackers suffered substantial casualties, 697 in 132nd Brigade alone, over two-fifths of the Allied total for the entire battle.

It was a grim confirmation of how wise it had been to refuse to indulge in all-out assaults. Thereafter the Axis soldiers suffered little interference save from the air and early on 7 September, Montgomery called off the battle. Despite Freyberg's failure, Montgomery had every reason to be proud of his men and he, for his part, had earned their trust and confidence; he had gained his victory in exactly the way he had said he would and as a result of the changes he had made to his predecessors' plans. 'Everyone,' recalls Horrocks, 'felt that a new dynamic force had entered into the tired, rather stale old body of the Eighth Army.'

Horrocks in particular had good reason to celebrate. He had fought his first battle as a corps commander; he had won it; and he had not 'got mauled'. It was also his forty-seventh birthday.

* * *

For Horrocks, triumph was followed not by tragedy, not by disaster, but by frustration. It will be recalled that in the Battle of El Alamein, as he rather sadly relates, Horrocks had 'only a subsidiary role' keeping part of the enemy armour in the southern sector of the front while the main assault was delivered in the north. For this, XIII Corps controlled 44th and 50th (British) Divisions, both under-strength, a brigade of the Fighting French and 7th Armoured Division, now under Harding. It also contained a number of 'Scorpions': tanks fitted with heavy chains that revolved so as to strike the ground and explode any mine that was encountered. These would demonstrate their worth later after improvements had been made, particularly on the beaches of Normandy; at Alamein, though, they proved unreliable and quickly broke down as a result of over-heating.

This was a great disappointment to Horrocks, who had hoped they might prove decisive, and despite the efforts of XIII Corps' Minefield Task Force led by Lieutenant Colonel Corbett-Winder, to whom

Horrocks sent his personal thanks, he was unable to make any substantial progress. On 26 October Montgomery, who wished to keep 7th Armoured Division 'in being' for future use, called off the offensive in the south, leaving Horrocks with only the consolation of knowing that he had at least retained sizable Axis forces well away from the main combat zone.

Horrocks must have felt still more frustrated over the next few weeks. When the enemy finally broke and X and XXX Corps set off in pursuit he was left to 'clean up' the Alamein battlefield with a command reduced to one salvage unit. In late November, he replaced Lumsden as head of X Corps but this was then stationed in reserve in the area between Benghazi and Tobruk to guard against any possible Axis counter-offensive. He was again disappointed when the final advance on Tripoli began, since X Corps took no part in the fighting but had to concentrate on bringing up supplies to the front. It should be said, though, that whatever his feelings about this task, Horrocks, in Montgomery's words, 'entered into it with the greatest enthusiasm and organized a first-class transportation service'.

Oddly enough, Horrocks would return to more satisfying duties as a result of a misfortune suffered by Eighth Army as a whole: the failure of Leese's coastal attack on the Mareth Line. News of this, first received in the early hours of 23 March 1943, came as a profound shock to an Army with grim memories of earlier days when the fighting had swayed backwards and forwards seemingly without end. Even Montgomery's cool self-confidence deserted him – for the first of only two occasions, according to his staff officers, when this happened during the entire war.[3] Happily, he quickly recovered his nerve and, with superb flexibility, set out to rectify the situation.

It was possible for troops to bypass the Mareth Line by crossing the Matmata Hills through a 'gap' bearing the name of its discoverer, Lieutenant Nicholas Wilder of the Long Range Desert Group, and then heading northwards. Any force doing so, however, would have to travel some 150 miles through extremely difficult waterless country and near the northern end of the hills its way would be blocked by marshes and it would have to swing back towards the coast through the Tebaga Gap which, at only 4 miles in width, was the narrowest 'bottleneck' of them all.

Montgomery had already dispatched a considerable force through

Wilder's Gap centred on Freyberg's 2nd New Zealand Division, which now contained 8th Armoured Brigade as well as its two infantry brigades. But Freyberg's task, at first anyway, was only to 'distract attention from the coastal sector'. In this he succeeded, for by 22 March, it was discovered that 'Plum Pass', as Eighth Army called the Tebaga Gap, was not only protected by strongpoints, minefields and an anti-tank ditch, but was guarded by 21st Panzer, 164th Light and seven battalions of Italian infantry. Freyberg can hardly be blamed then for concluding that he could only take it by a series of 'set piece' attacks over a period of from five to seven days, for which he would need massive reinforcements.

Montgomery, however, had determined that he would break through at Tebaga – and without delay before Messe could divert more troops to the area. De Guingand and Richardson – now Eighth Army's Director of Operations – therefore began at once to take the steps necessary to give this offensive its required air support and to send Briggs and his 1st Armoured Division through Wilder's Gap in order to take part in it. For reasons of morale, the operation was given the official code-name of SUPERCHARGE, but in practice it would always be known to the men of Eighth Army as 'The Left Hook'.

To command it, a delighted Horrocks and the Headquarters Staff of his X Corps were also sent to Tebaga, theoretically because the number of troops employed would need a Corps HQ to control them, but really because Montgomery rightly suspected that Freyberg would be reluctant to embark on this obviously risky operation, whereas Horrocks, for whom it was one 'after my own heart', could be relied on to provide the necessary drive. Horrocks arranged that all orders and messages should be sent to himself and Freyberg jointly but the latter was understandably aggrieved at being in effect superseded. Tuker was also critical of the appointment, declaring later that both Leese and Horrocks, but particularly Horrocks, lacked the strength of character to proceed on their own initiative outside Montgomery's control. Leese, however, had already proved him wrong during the final advance on Tripoli and Horrocks was about to prove him wrong again.

Horrocks planned that 2nd New Zealand Division, with 8th Armoured Brigade in the van, should make an initial advance of 4,500 yards, capturing the high ground on either side of the pass in the process. Then 1st Armoured Division, headed by 2nd Armoured

Brigade, should move through the positions gained and make for El Hamma, which was situated just south of the Gabes Gap. This caused considerable anxiety in the Allied ranks and Horrocks reports that the officers of 8th Armoured Brigade 'thought they were being launched on a second Balaclava', but his own confidence and resolution did much to reassure them. 'If we punch the hole,' asked a doubtful Freyberg, 'will the tanks really go through?' 'Yes, they will,' retorted the eager X Corps Commander, 'and I am going with them.'

At 1530 on 26 March, the new Operation SUPERCHARGE began with the first of a constant series of attacks by the Desert Air Force. Half an hour later, Eighth Army's artillery opened up and at 1623, the soldiers moved forward. 2nd New Zealand Division captured most of its objectives, though some pockets of resistance in the surrounding hills held out stubbornly until the following evening. 1st Armoured Division, accompanied by three tanks that contained Horrocks and the staff of his Tactical HQ, followed up as promised and though 15th Panzer Division arrived to swell the ranks of the defenders, nothing could stop Eighth Army. Both 15th and 21st Panzer were badly mauled, 164th Light lost almost all its vehicles and its heavy weapons, and early on 27 March, the enemy fell back, leaving behind 2,500 prisoners, all of them German. On the Mareth Line, the remainder of Messe's First Italian Army hastily withdrew to avoid being cut off, and by the 29th, having suffered some 14,000 casualties in the battle as a whole, all the Axis forces were retiring behind the defences in the Gabes Gap.

These, as even the forceful Horrocks quickly realized, were 'too strongly held to be bounced'. They could not be outflanked either since they ran between the sea and the impassable Chott el Fedjadj salt marshes, and they were based on natural features that seemed to have been designed to ensure a successful defence. In the centre of the position was the 1,000-foot-high Djebel Fatnassa, from which ridges 500 feet in height ran south-westward to the edge of the marshes and north-eastward to a final outcrop named El Meida. Beyond this came the Djebel Roumana, also 500 feet high, and guarded on both sides by wide anti-tank ditches and minefields. Finally the coastal sector was protected by the Wadi Akarit which, like the Wadi Zigzaou at Mareth, had been deepened, widened and mined and was filled with water after recent rains.

Montgomery's first intention had been that 51st Highland Division should cross the eastern anti-tank ditch while 4th Indian Division secured its flank by taking the Djebel Roumana. Horrocks with 1st Armoured and 2nd New Zealand Divisions would follow up, while 7th Armoured remained in reserve. Remembering the misfortunes of 50th Division at the Mareth Line, however, both Wimberley and Tuker wished the initial assault to be strengthened, and Tuker also professed to fear a counter-attack from the Djebel Fatnassa – though it is not clear why, because his reconnaissance patrols had confirmed that this feature was only weakly held.

4th Indian's reconnaissance had also revealed that the enemy had not sited any heavy weapons to cover the Djebel Fatnassa's forward slopes, the difficulties of which had been overestimated. Tuker therefore believed that his division, which was specially trained for mountain warfare, could attack these with every chance of success. For some reason, though, he did not put forward this proposal at the conference on 2 April at which the original programme was laid down; instead he raised it privately with his Corps Commander, Leese, later on. Leese was convinced and in turn persuaded Montgomery, but whatever the merits of Tuker's plan, it showed scant consideration for any formation in Eighth Army other than his own.

For a start, the departure of 4th Indian Division to Fatnassa left the Highlanders with the responsibility not only of crossing the anti-tank ditch east of Roumana but of taking Roumana itself as well. Then, in order to provide the link between Wimberley and Tuker, 50th Division – which in practice meant 69th Brigade as the division's other brigade, the 151st, had suffered very heavily at the Mareth Line – was ordered to strike over the anti-tank ditch west of Roumana, and had to be hurried forward, at such short notice that there was no time to bring up the divisional artillery. It is perhaps not surprising therefore that when the battle began on the night of 5/6 April, 69th Brigade proved unable to make much progress.

Elsewhere, both Wimberley and Tuker had achieved their initial objectives by early morning and 4th Indian Division was beginning to move round the flank of the western anti-tank ditch. When Horrocks visited its Headquarters at 0845, Tuker triumphantly announced that the way was clear for X Corps to break through the enemy lines, there was nothing to stop it and the end of the war in Tunisia was in sight.

Horrocks notified Montgomery, who gave permission for X Corps to advance at once. It did not do so and Tuker would heap much blame on Horrocks for this disappointment – understandably but unfairly, because Tuker had simply got his facts wrong.

In the first place, the way forward was not clear. There was another line of hills, the Oudane el Hachana, which still had to be taken and this was not even attacked until 0935. Not until it was captured could 1st Armoured Division move forward and when it did so in the late morning, Briggs discovered that there was a good deal to stop it: part of 15th Panzer Division, a line of 88mms, and field guns in protected positions which could only be attacked head-on and which, incidentally, were still killing some of Tuker's men as late as 1600. Tuker would claim that 1st Armoured should have rushed the anti-tank guns but this was not a practice recommended by the lessons of the past, and in any case the armoured commanders were by now reluctant to commit their forces until they knew where these were most needed.

Because the Axis reserves, in particular 90th Light and the rest of 15th Panzer, had begun a series of ferocious counter-attacks on 51st Division. The Djebel Roumana changed hands several times and the Highlanders both inflicted and suffered far more casualties than did 4th Indian Division. Yet they remained firm, and as darkness fell, Messe gave up his attempts and retired, cleverly covering his retreat with minor local thrusts.

Thereafter for a time, Eighth Army was handicapped mainly by the almost embarrassing number of prisoners it was taking; they were coming in at the rate of 1,000 every day. Sfax fell on 10 April; Sousse two days later; and by the evening of the 13th, Eighth Army had advanced 150 miles from the Gabes Gap and completed its conquest of the central Tunisian plain. It had also linked up with the forces that had taken part in the TORCH landings and subsequently been built up into the First British Army. Alexander, who as Commander of Eighteenth Army Group controlled both armies, decided that First Army, reinforced by 1st Armoured Division, would make the main assault on the last hostile enclave around Tunisia from the west where the country was well suited to the use of tanks, while Eighth Army provided a diversion by putting 'maximum pressure' against the Axis positions in the south around the village of Enfidaville.

The defences at Enfidaville, like those of the Gabes Gap, were based on a line of hills blocking a 'bottleneck'; the difference being that behind them was no wide plain but a series of other high points stretching almost all the way back to Tunis. Montgomery's hope that he would be able not just to distract his opponents but to break right through to Tunis, was therefore singularly optimistic. When his offensive began on the night of 19/20 April, 4th Indian Division captured most (though not all) of the 1,000-foot-high Djebel Garci and 2nd New Zealand Division took the steep-sided crag of Takrouna in what Horrocks, who was watching it, called 'the most gallant feat of arms I witnessed in the course of the war'. After that, progress slowed to a crawl with mounting casualties, yet Montgomery – who in fairness was far from well and also occupied with plans for the invasion of Sicily – showed none of his usual flexibility. He ordered Horrocks, who greatly disliked what was happening, to persist with his attacks; they culminated on 29 April with the savage repulse of 56th (British) Division, an inexperienced formation that had come forward all the way from Iraq. To make matters worse, First Army's offensive had also petered out on the previous day.

Horrocks had earlier warned Montgomery: 'Of course we can break through, but there won't be much left of your fine Eighth Army when we have done it.' Montgomery had 'merely grunted' but luckily Horrocks had made the point most likely to influence him, and his vision now cleared again. He cancelled all further attacks, and as he was too ill to travel, asked Alexander to visit him. When his superior arrived, Montgomery urged him to deliver a single concentrated thrust on the First Army front, promised him 'you'll be through in 48 hours', and offered to transfer 7th Armoured Division, 4th Indian Division and 201st Guards Brigade from Eighth Army to assist him.[4]

It is pleasant to record that Montgomery bore no resentment towards Horrocks over his forthright comments. It was decided to add the Eighth Army units to First Army's IX Corps, which already contained 6th (British) Armoured and 4th (British) Infantry Divisions. Since the Corps Commander, Lieutenant General Crocker – who would later command I Corps at the D-Day landings – had been injured during a weapons demonstration, Montgomery recommended that Horrocks should direct the assault, telling him to 'smash through to Tunis and finish the war in North Africa'. 'My heart leapt,' recalls Horrocks. 'This was the real art of generalship – a quick switch, then a knock-out blow.' He was off that afternoon, visiting forward units and inspecting the Medjerda Valley where his attack would take place, and his obvious eagerness, aided by tact and charm, quickly won over the officers of IX Corps who had not at first welcomed an Eighth Army Corps Commander being placed over them.

Operation STRIKE, as the offensive was appropriately named, began at 0300 on 6 May and followed the pattern that had served Horrocks so well at Tebaga: first air raids and a tremendous artillery bombardment; then the assault of the infantry; finally the breakthrough by the two armoured divisions. By noon, the tanks of both were, says Horrocks, 'grinding their way forward down the valley towards Tunis' with their armoured cars racing ahead of them. By the afternoon of 7 May, these had entered the city; Horrocks tactfully declares that they did so 'by different routes at exactly the same moment'.

After that the end came quickly. 7th Armoured swung north to engage the remnants of Fifth Panzer Army, which was already desperately short of fuel and ammunition; it surrendered on 9 May. 6th Armoured raced south, trapping First Italian Army between itself and Montgomery's men. At midday on the 13th, Messe, who had just been made a field marshal – a promotion well deserved for his earlier stubborn resistance, if scarcely appropriate in its timing – ordered his men to lay down their arms; then insisted on making his personal surrender to the renowned Eighth Army rather than to the forces closing in from the rear. General Fraser estimates that in these final days, 'over 100,000 German soldiers passed into Allied captivity – a greater number than taken at Stalingrad a few months before – and nearly 90,000 Italians'.

Horrocks accepted his triumph with a delightful modesty, assuring us that: 'I do not claim this as a great feat of generalship; it was nothing of the sort. I was merely fortunate to be in command of a battle in which victory was a foregone conclusion.'

* * *

Once again, triumph was followed by frustration, but this time for Horrocks personal disaster would not be far behind. X Corps did not take part in the Sicily campaign, being kept in reserve at Tripoli. This did not meet with the approval of the Corps Commander who, as

Montgomery recorded in a letter to Harding, was 'of course champing at the bit'. He was delighted to learn that he would lead his Corps into Italy, specifically Salerno, as part of Fifth US Army – but as he was watching a rehearsal for the landing, at Bizerta, a low-flying German fighter suddenly shot out of a smokescreen that had been laid on, with all guns blazing. Horrocks can best describe what happened next:

> A sledgehammer hit me in the stomach. I lost control of my legs and collapsed onto the ground, but even then I don't think I realized that I had been hit. I discovered afterwards that the bullet entered the top of my chest – I must have been leaning forward at the time – and then starting with my lungs it pierced almost every organ in my stomach and intestines, emerging at the bottom of my spine. It was pure bad luck; no one else was even scratched.

An immediate operation saved his life, but Horrocks remained desperately ill for some time. He was flown back to England, where he was subjected to several more operations. The last of these was performed at his own insistence, because he was determined to be back in action as soon as possible and not prepared to wait another six months for this as his doctors recommended. Even then it was only at the end of July 1944 that a medical board declared him fit for active service. Thereupon, however, Montgomery, who had been kept informed of his progress, at once appointed him to command XXX Corps, which he took over in Normandy on 2 August.

Shortly before this, on 30 July, Bradley had captured Avranches and Dempsey's Second British Army had commenced Operation BLUECOAT, a supporting attack on the Americans' left flank. The main objective of XXX Corps was Mont Pinçon, a steep-sided hill, 1,200 feet high, some 18 miles south-west of Caen, which dominated the surrounding country. Progress towards this had been very slow and costly and when Horrocks took up his post, he found that two of his three divisions, 7th Armoured and 50th Infantry, had become jaded, hating the fighting in the restricted terrain of Normandy, so different from the open spaces of the Desert, and beginning to adopt the dangerous attitude that they had already 'done their bit' and it was time for others to bear the brunt of the fighting. Horrocks therefore set out to restore morale by Montgomery's methods of visiting as many units as possible and explaining to them the present situation and his plans for the future.

'It was hard work,' Horrocks would later comment, 'but I am certain that it paid a good dividend.' Yet it was his third division, 43rd (Wessex), a formation that had not seen action prior to Normandy but, under the determined leadership of Major General Ivor Thomas, had already gained a deserved reputation, which most responded to his demonstration of trust and confidence. On the night of 6/7 August, despite heavy opposition, it triumphantly gained the summit of Mont Pinçon, which would provide an excellent observation post and artillery site for XXX Corps' subsequent advances.

Horrocks played a minor part in the fighting in the Falaise 'Pocket' since Montgomery, again thinking well ahead, intended to use XXX Corps in the pursuit once Normandy had been secured. Furthermore, Horrocks was still suffering from bouts of sickness and high temperatures and a particularly severe one struck him down just before XXX Corps crossed the Seine. Montgomery, having learned of this, had Horrocks brought to Twenty-First Army Group's Tac HQ, ensured that he received the best possible medical treatment, but forbade him to return to his Corps without permission; Horrocks remained in 'my pleasant bondage' until 26 August. In the meantime, Montgomery visited him daily, and their discussions, says Horrocks, 'proved more than usually interesting because this was the time when the big argument about the future conduct of the war was going on between Monty and Eisenhower'.

Montgomery's desire, first suggested to Bradley on 17 August and repeated to Eisenhower on the 23rd, was that once the Seine had been passed, all possible resources should be allocated to 'one powerful full-blooded thrust across the Rhine into the heart of Germany'. This would be made by Twelfth and Twenty-First Army Groups; the first making for Brussels, then for Aachen and Cologne, and finally swinging round the Ruhr from the south; the latter clearing the Channel coast and capturing Antwerp, after which it would head either through the Aachen 'gap' in concert with the Americans or into Holland prior to attacking the Ruhr from the north.

It can hardly be denied that this course of action contained a distinct element of risk. Yet it was scarcely the 'pencil-like thrust' that it was later dubbed by Eisenhower. If both Army Groups took part in it, they could provide 'a solid mass of some 40 divisions which would be so strong that it need fear nothing'; and at the very least Montgomery asked that twelve American divisions – in effect First US Army – should be put under his command. And if the risks were considerable, the prize to be won was far greater: the possible end of the war in Europe before the New Year.

After the war, an impressive number of senior German officers responsible for defending their country's western front would state without hesitation that Montgomery's scheme would have had an excellent chance of achieving just such a result. Von Rundstedt, for instance, declares that 'a concentrated thrust from Belgium in September must have succeeded'. General Günther Blumentritt argues that 'the best course of the Allies would have been to concentrate a really strong striking force with which to break through past Aachen to the Ruhr area. Such a breakthrough, coupled with air domination, would have torn to pieces the weak German front and ended the war.'[5] But the trouble was that this offensive would have to receive overriding logistical priority, which in turn would necessitate halting the advance of Patton's Third US Army towards Lorraine and the Saar – and that Eisenhower was not prepared to do.

Long after the event, it would be argued that Eisenhower was right, because had Third US Army gone onto the defensive, then the German forces tied down by its advance could have been sent to oppose Montgomery instead. Had this been done, however, the German infantry units in question would have lost the protection of those prepared positions at Metz and on the Siegfried Line that made their resistance so effective, and they would also have been vulnerable to attack from the air during the course of their move; while the panzer formations concerned had been formed in great haste, had had little training, and were equipped with tanks straight from the factories that broke down with distressing regularity. It is difficult therefore to believe that these troops could have posed much of a threat to Montgomery's 'full-blooded thrust', and their leader, General Hasso von Manteuffel, clearly did not believe it, declaring that:

> I am in full agreement with Montgomery. I believe General Eisenhower's insistence on spreading the Allied forces out for a broader advance was wrong. The acceptance of Montgomery's plan would have shortened the war considerably. Above all, tens

of thousands of lives – on both sides – would have been saved.

In any case, these later arguments appear somewhat irrelevant, for the reason why Eisenhower politely but firmly rejected Montgomery's proposals was not because of concerns over the risks involved but because he felt compelled to satisfy American popular demands. Nor, to his credit, did Eisenhower deny this, telling Montgomery to his face that he had no choice but to 'send the two Army Groups in such different directions that there could be no question of the American Army Group being under the operational control of a British general'. Bradley was equally honest. 'I get along with Monty fine enough,' he protested on 25 August, 'but we've got to make it clear to the American public that we are no longer under control of Monty's.'

Of course the Supreme Commander had to be a diplomatist and Horrocks for one considered that Eisenhower could not have acted otherwise – despite his own belief that Montgomery 'was right from the point of view of the actual fighting'. Unhappily, Montgomery could never understand or accept this, though in fairness to him it should be emphasized that he did tell Eisenhower that the matter was 'so important that if public opinion in America was involved, he should let Bradley control the battle and put me under Bradley'. The Supreme Commander refused, again for political reasons, but the offer confirms Montgomery's complete sincerity and explains, if it cannot wholly excuse, his subsequent actions.

During the next few weeks, tormented by the knowledge that if the Germans were given time to recover their balance a wonderful opportunity would be lost for ever, Montgomery strove by argument and demonstration to persuade his superior of the value of the northern advance. With this aim in view, he flung Second British Army forward through northern France and Belgium, although it had only its own resources on which to rely and was greatly handicapped by the inopportune discovery of a design fault in the engines of British-built lorries, which deprived it of the use of 1,400 of these and necessitated its VIII Corps being grounded. XII Corps protected the left flank of the advance and had reached Ghent by 6 September, but the main role was that of XXX Corps, with Horrocks back to lead it.

Montgomery ordered Horrocks to ensure his progress was 'swift and relentless'; he was 'to bypass enemy centres of resistance and to push boldly ahead creating alarm and despondency in enemy rear areas'. The instructions were hardly needed; Alan Moorehead in his *Eclipse* says that Horrocks had 'more volatility and fire and dash than one could have thought possible in a single man, an ideal breakthrough general'. Horrocks himself tells us that during the advance his command post was a tank with its gun removed and replaced by a map-table and cheerfully relates that: 'This was the type of warfare I thoroughly enjoyed.'

In performing his task, Horrocks, as he would be the first to admit, was brilliantly served by 11th Armoured Division under Roberts and Guards Armoured Division led by Major General Allan Adair, both of which were now part of XXX Corps. On 30 August for instance, he ordered Roberts to advance to Amiens, a distance of 30 miles, and seize the bridges over the River Somme during the hours of darkness. 'This,' he agrees, 'was asking a lot', but when he arrived at Divisional Headquarters early next morning, he learned that Roberts had captured the town, three intact bridges, a great deal of valuable Intelligence documentation, and General Heinz Eberbach, who had commanded the panzer formations in Normandy and had just been appointed head of Germany's battered Seventh Army. On 3 September, Guards Armoured Division entered Brussels, having covered 250 miles in six days, and on the 4th, 11th Armoured captured Antwerp and, with the help of Belgian Resistance fighters, secured its docks intact.

These dramatic events made Montgomery more than ever convinced that an assault in the north could capture the Ruhr – but it was already apparent that his opinion was not shared. Eisenhower was happy to agree to attacking through the Low Countries but only as one part of a general movement that would lead to the Allies 'crossing the Rhine on a wide front'. Bradley was a firm and sincere believer in the advance towards the Saar. And the luckless Hodges, forced to protect an impossibly wide frontage between the two offensives, was unable, through no fault of his own, to attack Aachen successfully, divert forces away from Dempsey, or even cover Dempsey's right flank.

Despite the absence of any material or moral support, though, Montgomery was still determined that Second British Army should make one last effort to secure a bridgehead of its own across the Rhine. This would at worst provide a good base for a subsequent attempt on the Ruhr and might just possibly persuade Eisenhower to 'invest in success' and give him the priority in manpower and supplies that he needed. He had already abandoned the thought of joining with Hodges in an attack through the Aachen 'gap': that was almost certain to cause delay while the arguments over who should control it were resumed. Instead he determined to sweep north-eastward and get into Germany over the Maas (as the Meuse was called in Holland) at Venlo, and then over the Rhine at Wesel.

The trouble with this route was that it was blocked by the two massive rivers, plus a number of smaller water obstacles, the bridges over which were likely to be blown up. On 4 September therefore, Montgomery met Lieutenant General Frederick Browning, Commander of I (British) Airborne Corps, and they discussed the possibility of Browning's 1st Airborne Division and 1st Polish Parachute Brigade landing behind the enemy lines ahead of Second British Army so as to seize the bridges before the Germans could destroy them.

When these proposals were put to the Allied Air Forces, however, the objection was raised that Wesel was only some 15 miles from Essen and Browning's valuable, vulnerable transport aircraft could fall easy victims to the anti-aircraft batteries in the vicinity. So Browning then urged that Dempsey should strike not north-east but north, with his own airborne troops as before securing the bridges over the Maas and the Rhine – or rather both Rhines, because on entering Holland that mighty river divides into a main branch, the River Waal, and a more northerly channel, the Neder Rijn.

Operation COMET, as this new plan was christened, thus presented Second British Army with a line of advance that included a third major river-crossing, a very restricted frontage and a considerably longer route to the Ruhr. On the other hand, it avoided the Peel Marshes, an area of reclaimed land stretching along the Maas for about 20 miles on either side of Venlo, where the going was exceptionally difficult; bypassed the Siegfried Line defences; and escaped the attention of the Ruhr's AA guns. It could also receive better aerial support as it would come within range of fighter and fighter-bomber bases in England; and once the rivers were crossed, Second British Army should find it easy to push on to the Zuider Zee, cutting off all German troops in southern and western Holland. Montgomery had hoped that this operation could commence on 7 September, but by that time, as Horrocks gloomily records, 'the situation had worsened dramatically'.

On 4 September, a growing shortage of supplies and an increasing exhaustion among the soldiers, particularly perhaps in 11th Armoured Division, had resulted in XXX Corps having to pause to 'refit, refuel and rest'. Horrocks would later wish that 'we had taken the chance and carried straight on with our advance', but he accepts that this would have been 'a considerable risk' and 11th Armoured at least could not have done so since the bridges leading north out of Antwerp over the Albert Canal had been blown up by the enemy. Furthermore, just as Dempsey's momentum started to fail, so the Germans, as Montgomery had feared, began to regain their balance and take the necessary steps to counter his threat.

On that same 4 September, the first German reinforcements arrived: the remnants of three infantry divisions that had been amalgamated under Lieutenant General Kurt Chill and sent to hold the Albert Canal. Next day, Chill was joined by forces previously guarding the Dutch coast, and he was also able to 'round up' literally thousands of stragglers from units swept aside in Second Army's great drive through Belgium. On the 6th, he was further strengthened by the advance guard of First Parachute Army whose leader, General Kurt Student, now took command of all ground forces on the Dutch mainland. First Parachute Army contained some 20,000 paratroopers and 10,000 Luftwaffe personnel and though many of the former and all the latter were untrained, they were fanatically loyal to their Führer and ready to fight to the death on his behalf.

This quickly became apparent when XXX Corps attempted to resume its advance on 6 September. 11th Armoured Division could not cross the Albert Canal at Antwerp. Guards Armoured Division did succeed in doing so at Beeringen further to the east but took until 10 September to cover the 10 miles to the next obstacle, the Meuse-Escaut Canal. The bridge at Neerpelt was then seized before it could be destroyed, but by then Montgomery had first postponed Operation COMET, then cancelled it altogether. Realizing that he must increase the scale of his offensive if his men were to reach the Zuider Zee, he won Eisenhower's approval to strengthen Browning's forces and, after initial hesitations, his promise to give Second Army priority in supplies. At 0900 on 10 September, Montgomery conferred with Dempsey, who in turn met Browning at Second Army's Tac HQ two hours later and informed him that 82nd and 101st US Airborne Divisions would be placed under his command. On the 17th, the revised offensive, Operation MARKET GARDEN, duly began.

The code-name chosen reflects the dual nature of the mission. Operation GARDEN was the advance by Second British Army, spearheaded by XXX Corps, intended to gain a foothold over the Rhine, threaten the Ruhr and cut off large numbers of German troops; Operation MARKET was the attempt to speed up its progress by securing bridges over the water obstacles in its path: 101st US Airborne Division would capture those across the Wilhelmina Canal at Son and the Zuid Willemsvaat Canal at Veghel; 82nd US Airborne those over the Maas at Grave and the Waal at Nijmegen; 1st (British) Airborne that over the Neder Rijn at Arnhem. The airborne assaults that are the usual focus of later attention were therefore only a means to a desired end: the success of Horrocks and his XXX Corps.

'I was under no illusion that this was going to be an easy battle,' recalls Horrocks. His only supply line would be a single road through low-lying marshy country which would make any deviations from the direct route very difficult. Attacks on that road would be likely to cause a monumental 'traffic jam' and these seemed certain to come from forces in Germany and western Holland once they had recovered from the initial shock of the assault. It had been hoped that Horrocks would be supported by XII Corps on his left and VIII Corps on his right but, despite the promises that had been made, Dempsey received hardly any priority for supplies during the period before MARKET GARDEN and most of those available were naturally allotted to XXX Corps. The other two corps could thus not be expected to make rapid progress and Horrocks appreciated that 'we should be operating on our own for a considerable period'.

In consequence, XXX Corps would indeed be subjected to attacks from the flanks. The attention paid to the airborne operations has led to much emphasis being placed on the unlucky presence of 9th and 10th SS Panzer Divisions north of Arnhem, whither they had been ordered on 5 September to recover from their heavy losses in Normandy, but their performance against the much more lightly equipped 1st (British) Airborne Division was not really very impressive. As Chester Wilmot points out, it took them three days to defeat Lieutenant Colonel John Frost's 2nd Parachute Battalion, the only one to reach the Arnhem bridge, and the bulk of 1st Airborne defied three times its own numbers until the night of 25/26 September. German accounts, by contrast, make little mention of the SS formations but stress the importance of the counter-attacks from east and west – a view supported by Horrocks, who states that it was these 'which finally turned the tide against us as more and more pressure was exerted along XXX Corps' line of communications'.

Bearing in mind XXX Corps' difficulties, it could well be suggested that a safer strategy might have been to direct Second British Army against a different important objective closer to hand. Although the Antwerp docks had been taken intact, they could not be used until the approaches to the port through the 50-mile-long estuary of the River Scheldt had been cleared of mines and the coastal batteries on either bank had been overrun. On 14 September, Montgomery gave this task to Crerar's First Canadian Army, which included I (British) Corps, but Crerar had also to secure the Channel ports, not only for their own value but because otherwise troops from them could have attacked the Canadians from flank and rear; it was too much to hope that he could do this and at the same time clear the approaches to Antwerp, for these presented a formidable problem.

The south bank of the estuary consisted of low-lying, marshy ground, the western part of which, known as the 'Breskens Pocket', provided an almost perfect defensive site, being protected by two parallel canals with only a dyke between them for about half its length and by heavy flooding for the rest of it. North of the river was the confusingly-named South Beveland Peninsula, joined to the mainland only by a narrow, easily defended isthmus, and into which as from 6 September, a stream of reinforcements had been pouring from the south bank; in addition, any Allied formations approaching it would themselves be liable to attack from enemy units stationed in northern Holland. Finally there was the island of Walcheren, connected to South Beveland by a single heavily fortified causeway and, apart from the port of Flushing on its south coast, surrounded by a steep and massive dyke designed to protect it against the sea. Walcheren in fact could only be captured by amphibious landings and these could only take place after attacks by heavy bombers had made breaches in the dyke and flooded most of the island.

Nonetheless, Montgomery did not direct Second Army to assist the Canadians in spite of these difficulties – or rather because of them. The time it was bound to take to secure the Scheldt estuary would entail a loss of momentum, which he was not prepared to accept. Horrocks entirely agreed; in fact on reflection, he wished that he had ordered 11th Armoured Division to concentrate on blocking the South Beveland isthmus, thereby reducing the attacks on MARKET GARDEN's supply line, even though this would have meant bypassing Antwerp and enabling the Germans to have destroyed its docks. 'In my opinion,' he declares bluntly, 'Monty was right. . . his eyes were focused on the big prize – to bounce a crossing over the Rhine and cut off the industrial heart of Germany, thus finishing the war in 1944. While there was still any chance of this succeeding he would have been wrong to deflect his resources to a subsidiary task.'

It may be added that on 9 October, Montgomery would direct that all priority in supplies must be given to First Canadian Army – to which he had already sent reinforcements of manpower two days earlier – and would also order XII Corps to assist by capturing the area between the Maas and the Canadians' existing front line, which, by this time, they had pushed north of Antwerp almost to the South Beveland isthmus. They had also, incidentally, occupied the eastern part of the Scheldt's southern bank and gained two footholds within the Breskens 'Pocket'. Nonetheless, South Beveland was not secured until 31 October; the Breskens 'Pocket' not until 3 November; and both the XII Corps' objectives and Walcheren not until the 8th. Even then the Scheldt had to be cleared of mines, 267 of which are said to have been removed, and it was only on 28 November that the first supply vessel, appropriately the Canadian *Fort Cataraqui*, arrived in Antwerp.

If Twenty-First Army Group had directed all its efforts to clearing the Scheldt estuary when Antwerp was first captured, it would probably have taken a similar time to achieve its task – in fact it would probably have taken longer, for on 9 October most of the plans had already been prepared and, as we have seen, many preliminary objectives had already been gained. In which case, MARKET GARDEN could hardly have commenced before the end of October at the very earliest and by then, as Horrocks points out, the Germans, who in any case made a remarkable recovery, would have been given another six weeks in which to organize their defences. In addition, the bad weather would have set in with a vengeance, the rainfall in November proving exceptionally heavy. There was thus no question of postponing MARKET

GARDEN until Antwerp had been made usable, as some critics have suggested, as 'it would have been impossible later on to carry out the swift advance up to the Lower Rhine at Arnhem'.

Montgomery's only choice therefore was whether to launch MARKET GARDEN or cancel it. A cautious, unimaginative leader would no doubt have preferred the latter course but it may be noted that this would not have met with the approval of those most directly concerned. Frost, for instance, greatly favoured the operation, which he considered 'the genuine airborne thrust that we had been awaiting'; while Horrocks, despite his knowledge of the dangers he was likely to face, was still 'confident that we should win through'.

For some time it seemed that his confidence was justified. On 17 September, Guards Armoured Division, leading XXX Corps, overcame a stubborn German defence with the aid of a powerful bombardment by artillery and rocket-firing Typhoons. Next day, the advance reached Eindhoven to join forces with 101st US Airborne Division, which had captured four bridges intact at Veghel. The bridge at Son had been blown up just before the Americans could reach it, but the sappers repaired it within twelve hours. On the 19th, Guards Armoured made contact with 82nd US Airborne, which had captured the bridge at Grave and secured a defensive perimeter through which XXX Corps could pass towards the widest obstacle in its path, the River Waal at Nijmegen.

Then XXX Corps' progress began to slow. The Germans defended the great road and rail bridges over the Waal so tenaciously that it was not until 1900 on the 20th that Guards Armoured and 82nd US Airborne Divisions captured both in a combined attack, which Horrocks calls 'one of the finest' of the war. Horrocks still 'went to bed a happy man', but, although poor communications prevented him from learning it, on the afternoon of the 20th, Frost's noble stand at Arnhem had ended and, as Wilmot relates, by the cruellest of ironies, 'three hours before the first British tank crossed the Nijmegen bridge heading north, the first German tank crossed the Arnhem bridge heading south'.

Therefore on 22 September, Horrocks found the direct route to Arnhem blocked by strong enemy forces, and to make matters worse, attacks from the flank cut his supply line north of Veghel, forcing him to send 32nd Guards Brigade back to help clear the road, which unfortunately could not be done for over twenty-four hours. Horrocks also learned at last of the desperate situation of the survivors of 1st Airborne Division, now trapped in a narrow salient in the outlying suburb of Oosterbeek, and he reluctantly concluded that he could no longer break through to the Zuider Zee or present an immediate threat to the Ruhr. On the previous day, however, 1st Polish Parachute Brigade, after lengthy delays caused by bad weather, had been dropped near the village of Driel on the south bank of the Neder Rijn opposite Oosterbeek. Horrocks accordingly sent 43rd Division to join the Poles in the hope that it would still be possible to cross the river and come to 1st Airborne's assistance.

It was not to be. Only a gallant handful of men were able to get over the Neder Rijn under heavy fire on the night of the 23rd/24th and next day the Germans again broke through to XXX Corps' supply route, this time south of Veghel, blocked the road for forty-eight hours and all but trapped Horrocks, who had returned from the front to discuss the situation with Dempsey. On the night of the 25th/26th, some 2,200 airborne troops withdrew across the river and several hundred more, hidden and protected by the Dutch, followed them later. They were the only members of 1st (British) Airborne Division to regain the Allied lines.

Horrocks has rarely received any praise for his part in what would be called 'the epic of Arnhem'. The heroes of this are the valiant parachutists and for many the villain is Horrocks, who did not come to their rescue in time. Yet his inability to do so was caused in the main not by the problems of his XXX Corps in Operation GARDEN but by those of the Airborne Corps in Operation MARKET.

Some of these arose from factors outside Browning's control. The troops had to be carried in three separate airlifts since there were not enough transport aircraft to take them all at once. Bad weather – which had not been forecast – ultimately resulted in the lifts being spread out over five days; this inevitably reduced the attackers' strength and, General Student acknowledges, was a major cause of their failure. On top of that, within two hours of the start of the offensive, a glider crashed near Student's Headquarters at Vught to the west of Veghel. In it was found a briefcase containing 'the orders for the complete airborne operation'. No wonder the German reaction was swift and effective.

The greatest problem, however, was of 1st Airborne Division's own making and it is regrettable that its importance has been concealed by a myth. We are told repeatedly that at the conference preceding MARKET GARDEN on 10 September, Browning warned Montgomery that 'we might be going a bridge too far'. This would scarcely seem likely since Browning had previously proposed for Operation COMET that the bridges at Son, Veghel, Grave, Nijmegen *and* Arnhem should all be seized by just 1st Airborne Division and the Poles and had assured his own subordinates that these alone would be sufficient. And it would also have been unlikely for Browning to have said this to Montgomery on 10 September, as he made his plans not with Montgomery, but with Dempsey – who at no time ever mentioned such a conversation. But in any event, it was not the case that 1st Airborne Division went too far; the problem was that it did not go far enough.

According to Chester Wilmot who, by the way, accompanied XXX Corps in its advance, 'the basic reason for the failure at Arnhem was that the 1st Airborne Division landed too far from the bridge' – up to 8 miles away to be precise – and then used much of its strength in securing a 'firm base', while sending only small and widely dispersed forces to gain its objective. Had it remained concentrated, Wilmot believes, the Germans in the Arnhem area, even though 'much stronger than had been expected', would still 'not have been strong enough' to overwhelm it.

Enemy accounts tell the same story. Student, for example, also says that 'the landing zones west of Arnhem were too far away from the objective' and the troops therefore 'arrived at the bridges too late'. Von Rundstedt in his official report to Hitler not only agrees but specifically states that the British had *not* 'selected a target too far in advance of the main defensive line'. On the contrary, if they learned their lesson they would probably land next time 'even further ahead' of their ground forces, but in strength and close to the objective. Had 1st Airborne done this at Arnhem, then German reinforcements would have been unable to move south of the Neder Rijn; in which case, XXX Corps would surely have reached Arnhem in time and Horrocks would have been acclaimed the hero of the hour.

Even accepting that he did not in fact achieve MARKET GARDEN's main objectives, Horrocks has still received less than justice from some later commentators who sneer that he had gained only 'a 50-mile salient – leading nowhere'. That was not how it appeared to de Guingand who, although he had not favoured the operation after Eisenhower had refused it full priority, still maintains that: 'The brilliant advance of XXX Corps led the way to the liberation of a large part of Holland, not to speak of providing a stepping stone to the successful battles of the Rhineland.' Even more to the point, Student calls MARKET GARDEN 'a great success. At one stroke it brought the British Second Army into the possession of vital bridges and valuable territory. The conquest of the Nijmegen area meant the creation of a good jumping-board for the offensive which contributed to the end of the war.'

That offensive would be delivered between the Maas and the Rhine and it brought about the battles of the Rhineland to which de Guingand refers. It was postponed, first while Montgomery attended to the clearance of the approaches to Antwerp, which he admits, he should have commenced immediately he had accepted that he would not get his bridgehead over the Rhine; then in December, it was postponed again by Hitler's desperate counter-offensive in the Ardennes. Horrocks took part in neither of these campaigns, though during the latter, his XXX Corps was stationed in reserve south of Brussels and he hoped, and even suggested, that the Germans might be allowed to continue their advance so that he could defeat them on the battlefield of Waterloo, which was a short distance away. Montgomery, who had already felt that Horrocks was becoming 'nervy and difficult' with his staff, was not pleased. He declared that Horrocks had 'gone mad' and ordered him back to England for a rest. He did, however, take care to advise Brooke that his Corps Commander was 'a valuable officer and I want him back'; and to assure Horrocks himself that he would be needed for 'a big battle I've got in store for you as soon as we've cleared up this mess here'.

So when Montgomery's offensive against the Rhineland, codenamed Operation VERITABLE, finally began on 8 February 1945, it was Horrocks who watched from a very temporary command post – a small platform halfway up a tree – as his XXX Corps, once more chosen as the spearhead, moved slowly forward behind a massive artillery bombardment. The corps had been placed under First Canadian Army for this occasion and expanded to contain Guards Armoured and six infantry divisions, two of them Canadian which, Horrocks states, 'more and more impressed' him as he got to know them. In all, he commanded 200,000 men – 'the biggest operation I ever handled in war'.

It was also, says Horrocks, a 'horrible battle', 'the grimmest battle in which I took part'. VERITABLE had originally been intended as one half of a pincer movement, of which the other was Operation GRENADE, an assault northward over the River Roer, a tributary of the Maas, by Lieutenant General William Simpson's Ninth US Army, which had come into the line on Twenty-First Army Group's right and been placed under Montgomery's control. Unfortunately, as the Allies had feared and anticipated, the Germans had wrecked the dams on the Roer and flooded this so effectively that it would be many days before Simpson could join in the Battle of the Rhineland.

The Maas and the Rhine had also been flooded, particularly the low-lying ground to the south of the latter between Nijmegen and Cleve. XXX Corps' advance was thus again restricted to a narrow frontage, and across this ran the northern extension of the Siegfried Line. It lacked the strong permanent fortifications to be found further south but did have a trench system protected by anti-tank ditches and barbed wire. In addition, complains Horrocks, 'the whole area was lousy with mines'. Small towns such as Cleve and Goch some 10 miles further south had become virtual fortresses, prepared for all-round defence; while alongside the main road between Cleve and Goch ran the dark, sinister Reichswald Forest, 4 miles deep, from which enemy forces could strike at XXX Corps' flank.

At first all went well, and XXX Corps had broken through the Siegfried Line by the morning of 9 February. Then continuous heavy rain caused further flooding and turned the ground into a sea of mud, which bogged down every vehicle attempting to move off the roads, crippled XXX Corps' supply line, and caused a 'traffic jam' of enormous proportions. Cleve was captured on the 12th, but thereafter, reports Horrocks, 'the battle developed into a slogging match as we inched our way forward through the mud and rain'. Fortunately, some of the pressure on XXX Corps was eased by II Canadian Corps being brought up on its left flank; the Reichswald was at last cleared on 16 February; and Goch, the key to the German defences, was entered on the 18th and finally secured on the 21st.

Horrocks rightly pays tribute to his soldiers, fighting 'under the most ghastly conditions imaginable . . . in which only two things mattered, training and guts, with the key men as always the battalion commanders'. Yet his own contribution should not be forgotten. Major

General Hubert Essame, who was then the commander of 43rd Division's 214th Brigade, declares in *The Battle for Germany*, that the head of XXX Corps' 'own enthusiasm and lively sense of humour infected his whole command. He never forgot a face or a friend nor missed a chance to praise work well done or crack a joke.' And furthermore, 'every day found him somewhere in the forward area'.

It should also not be forgotten that Horrocks had won more than his own battle. As early as 10 February, von Rundstedt recognized that VERITABLE threatened the integrity of the entire German front and rushed all the reserves he could find to meet it. Two armoured divisions, four parachute divisions and three infantry divisions were already battling the northern pincer when, on 23 February, Simpson launched GRENADE against much reduced opposition. By 1 March, Montgomery was rejoicing that 'the most sensational results have been achieved'; on 3 March, XXX Corps made contact with the GRENADE forces; and on the 10th, the enemy, abandoning great masses of equipment, retired over the two bridges at Wesel – which the Allied airmen had been requested in vain to bomb – and blew these up behind them.

It had been the last great 'stand-up' fight in North-West Europe. The Allies had had nearly 23,000 casualties but the German loss of some 90,000 of their best men, many hastily transferred from other sectors, was decisive. Resistance west of the Rhine began to collapse, allowing all Eisenhower's armies to close up to the river over its entire length from Switzerland to the sea. Late on 23 March, Second British and Ninth US Armies crossed the Rhine north and south of Wesel respectively. Horrocks and XXX Corps, now back under Dempsey's command, were unlucky enough to meet the strongest resistance and were unable to move forward as rapidly as XII Corps making for Hamburg or VIII Corps heading for the Baltic. It was XXX Corps, though, that captured the great port of Bremen. Horrocks had called on the city to surrender but his demand was ignored and Bremen was pounded by heavy bombers before finally being taken by assault on 27 April.

Horrocks had tried to prevent the resultant devastation in order to save lives, but it is fair to say that he was chiefly concerned with the lives of his own men. In the past, he had 'hated the thought' of having to request air raids on towns or cities – Cleve for instance – but now his attitude was different. South-east of Bremen was Belsen concentration camp. When Horrocks saw it he was physically sick and was so angry that he probably never realized that he had been provided with a justification, albeit a ghastly one, for all the horrible experiences of the past few years: the strain and tension, the agonizing responsibility; the pain of his near-fatal wound. He had now seen why he and so many others had endured them, and what might have been the fate of Europe if he and they had not.

Notes:

1. The only mishap befell Montgomery personally: the driver of his staff car took a wrong turning into a cul-de-sac, from which he was able to extract it only after a worrying delay and 'a great deal of fearful language'. A similar but still more alarming incident occurred during Montgomery's first day in the Desert on 13 August 1942: he was driven into a minefield. 'I wasn't too pleased,' he assures us in his *Memoirs*.
2. While Alam Halfa was being fought, aircraft or submarines from Malta sank four more tankers but by the time the first pair went down on the night of 1/2 September, Rommel's attack had already broken down irreparably.
3. The other was in December 1944, when Eisenhower warned that he was no longer prepared to tolerate Montgomery's insubordinate demands.
4. Alexander had in fact intended to order some such transfer in any event, but Air Vice Marshal Broadhurst, head of the Desert Air Force, who was present at the meeting, confirms that Montgomery's gesture was entirely voluntary; it shows the mutual understanding that existed between these two very different but very fine soldiers.
5. As described earlier, von Rundstedt was the C-in-C, West at the time of the D-Day landings. He had been dismissed on 2 July but was reinstated on 4 September. Blumentritt was Chief of Staff to von Rundstedt and his successors from D-Day to early September. Among the other officers who echoed their (and Montgomery's) views, were Blumentritt's own successor, General Siegfried Westphal, Lieutenant General Hans Speidel, Chief of Staff in Army Group 'B' from D-Day to early September, and General Kurt Student, head of First Parachute Army and later of Army Group 'H' in the Low Countries.

Chapter 6

Plans and Operations

It was mentioned earlier that during the retreat to Dunkirk, Horrocks had been the last man to retire over a canal bridge before this was blown up. It is possible that it had been prepared for demolition by sappers under the direction of Richardson, who also served in Brooke's II Corps on the Headquarters Staff of 4th Division commanded by Major General Dudley Johnson VC. Throughout his wartime career Richardson would perform a wide variety of tasks and his duties at this time included arranging bivouac areas for his division, ensuring that food, petrol and ammunition were available as required – no easy task in a period of rapid retreats – and overseeing the divisional sappers who covered the withdrawal by destroying bridges, laying minefields and strengthening whatever natural or man-made obstacles could be found. In ten days of continuous action, Richardson estimates that he had 'perhaps twenty hours' sleep'.

When the orders for the evacuation were given, Richardson took on the further role of Beachmaster, supervising the departure of large numbers of troops before receiving his own instructions to leave and wading out to a naval sloop at the head of a party of twenty soldiers. On board this, they were stripped and put into a warm boiler room while their clothes were dried. But at least Richardson, unlike Leese, had a uniform to wear by the time he arrived at Dover.

In late August 1940, Richardson, like de Guingand before him, travelled through the Mediterranean to take up the post of Instructor at the Staff College, Haifa, though Richardson's journey was much more exciting. Italy had declared war on Britain and France at midnight on 10 June, so Richardson went out in HMS *Valiant*, a battleship no less, being bombed ineffectually by Italian aircraft on the way. At Haifa he and de Guingand became and remained firm friends, but they ceased to be fellow instructors in December when de Guingand was transferred to Cairo.

Six months later, Richardson, now a lieutenant colonel, was also sent to Cairo with the task of trying to control the 'cloak and dagger' activities of the Special Operations Executive in the Balkans and Middle East. It was not a happy assignment, because Richardson, like everyone else who had experience of SOE at this time and place, was disgusted by its lack of organization and its corroding atmosphere of jealousy, suspicion and intrigue, redeemed only by the personal courage of the 'agents'. 'I am surrounded by mountebanks,' he reports in a letter home. 'The place is a madhouse, but there are no dull moments.' He was delighted when, on 25 June 1942, he was summoned to join the staff of Eighth Army – even though this was then falling back in a calamitous retreat.

Richardson's delight was quickly quenched by the events of July 1942. Like so many others, he was distressed by the failure of five offensives in succession despite Eighth Army's many and considerable advantages; he strongly condemned the preference for fighting in battle groups; and he lamented that co-operation with the Desert Air Force had ceased to be 'close and cordial'. As Director of Plans, however, he particularly deplored the way in which intentions were constantly changed and firm decisions a rarity; in consequence of which no proper preparations were ever made and the offensives deteriorated into a series of 'piecemeal unco-ordinated attacks' which were 'the negation of that careful "stage management of the battle" that was to be the hallmark of our next manager: Montgomery'.

Thus, for example, all the arrangements for Auchinleck's first offensive had to be altered at very short notice because of a last-minute change of plans. In a later one, the 'stage management' was so poor that attacks intended merely as diversions began only after the main assault had already broken down. In another, later still, a brigade that had just been transferred from another part of the front and was quite unfamiliar with the area where the attack was to take place, was forbidden to carry out any reconnaissance on the grounds that this might jeopardize surprise; when the offensive began several units got lost and it failed like all the others. No wonder that Richardson was depressed, and his depression deepened when the only long-term project entrusted to him was to prepare for a possible withdrawal to Khartoum.

'Auchinleck's frustrated planner', as Richardson styles himself, had no doubt where responsibility lay. He had previously known and liked Dorman-Smith but he was horrified by the way in which 'this dangerous supernumerary adviser' had gained an 'intellectual dominance' over Auchinleck and was influencing him to a quite unacceptable extent. Richardson describes 'an atmosphere of constant crisis' in which Dorman-Smith's 'vigorous, restless and inventive mind was continually looking for clever, unconventional and daring solutions to the dire battlefield problems with which Rommel confronted us. Few if any of these solutions were attuned to the capabilities of Eighth Army, which had recently been disastrously defeated. Moreover, 'Chink'' was seldom content with pursuing only one solution.' As a result, 'nothing constructive by way of seizing the initiative' was ever suggested.

Richardson's dejection was not lifted during the early days of August. Auchinleck gave still less direction to his staff and his Army, and Richardson 'observed him, day after day, sitting in the sand, spending long hours staring through binoculars at the distant void horizon'. Richardson acknowledges Auchinleck's 'striking personality, which dominated almost without speech, his courage and his manifest integrity', but he also states flatly that he 'was unconvinced that General Auchinleck could turn the tide, no matter what new resources might come our way', and in his opinion – and that of Belchem and Williams – 'the removal of Auchinleck was essential'.

In contrast, Richardson found Dorman-Smith 'still in ebullient form', but considered his activity as dangerous as Auchinleck's lack of leadership. When Dorman-Smith revealed his intention of meeting Rommel's forthcoming offensive by withdrawing Eighth Army's infantry divisions to the Observation Posts and then splitting them up into battle groups, some to defend, others to manoeuvre between them, Richardson, who had not been consulted, was simply appalled. He would later declare that:

> It would be difficult to conceive a tactical plan more unsuited to the units of the Eighth Army at that time. Depressed by defeat, dismayed by heavy casualties, and disillusioned by the collapse of all their hopes, they were in no mood to leave the comparative security of fixed positions, then marry up with units with whom they had never trained, and engage without pre-tested radio

communications in mobile manoeuvres against an enemy who had proved himself master of this form of fighting.

Happily, they would never have to do so. 'I'm for the Star Chamber tomorrow, Charles,' Dorman-Smith told Richardson on 4 August. 'I'm going to be sacked.' Richardson 'made a friendly reply, but in my heart thought "thank God!"'

The arrival of Montgomery did much to reduce Richardson's anxieties, but could not dispel them completely. He was 'much relieved' to learn that the withdrawal to Khartoum would never be put into practice; he was gratified that at long last he was given 'clear and definite' instructions; and like everyone else, he was impressed by Montgomery's 'clear thinking and his amazing confidence'. Nonetheless, he admits with commendable honesty that 'in many minds, certainly in mine, there lingered doubts: "Is this just a technique, and will it fall apart when we face the crunch with Rommel, still the bogeyman?"'

But then came Alam Halfa and all doubts were removed. Richardson was particularly pleased that Montgomery had restored and strengthened Eighth Army's former happy relationship with the Desert Air Force. Like his new chief, he regarded this as of prime importance – a belief that would become known and have a considerable effect on his subsequent career. He was also very impressed by the way Montgomery had continued to consider the needs of Eighth Army's future offensive even while Alam Halfa was being fought. Montgomery had, for instance, mounted a raid by the Australians against enemy positions in the north, partly as a diversion but mainly as an armed reconnaissance of an area where he intended to make his own attack when the time came. The clearest example of his foresight, however, was shown at the very end of the battle when he declined to make any attempt to recapture the peak of Himeimat despite the opinions of Horrocks that this could have been 'done quite easily' and of Roberts that it would at least 'have been worthwhile having a try'.

The concerns of these officers were understandable since Himeimat provided a superb vantage point from which everything that happened in the southern sector of the front could be observed. This, though, was why Montgomery preferred it to remain in Rommel's hands. As we have seen, he proposed to mount only a diversionary assault in the south where the Axis defences were weaker, and make his main effort in the north where he would have more chance of achieving surprise, particularly if he could deceive the watchers on Himeimat into believing that the major offensive would come in its vicinity. 'Leave them in possession of Himeimat,' he told Horrocks. 'That is where I want them to be.'

For Operation BERTRAM, as Montgomery's deception plan was called – that it had its own separate code-name is a measure of its importance – the 'co-ordinating brain', in Montgomery's own phrase, was Lieutenant Colonel Richardson. Armed with a letter of authority signed by Montgomery, and ably assisted by the camouflage staff at GHQ, Cairo, he set about his task with a will, personally visiting every corps and divisional commander to discuss security and to explain how each formation's activities fitted into the overall scheme. Everywhere he found 'loyal, intelligent support to the plan', though when he wrote home on 17 October, he remarks, naturally without giving any details, that he had 'seldom been so busy'.[1]

Richardson's aims were simple: to convince the enemy that Eighth Army's principal attack would be launched in the south and later than the real target date of 23 October. His means were far more elaborate. In the north, every attempt was made to conceal both the strength and the imminence of the offensive. Supply dumps were masked by their contents being stacked in such a way that from the air they resembled vehicles. Tanks and guns were hidden by having the shapes of lorries, called 'sunshades' fitted over them. Slit trenches for the infantry were dug well forward but disguised. So were any vehicles that were brought up close to the front line, while their places well back from it were taken by dummies; all such movements being made at night and the traces of them carefully obliterated. Since to the Axis commanders the existing situation appeared to remain unchanged, they can be excused for having concluded that preparations for the offensive had not yet been completed.

In sharp contrast, in the south, vehicles and supply dumps, many of which were false, were deliberately poorly camouflaged for the benefit of the Himeimat observers. 10th Armoured Division advanced into the area openly; then slipped away after dark, leaving dummies in its place. The Headquarters of 8th Armoured Division, which had no operational troops under its command, was also sent to the southern sector, from which it broadcast a heavy volume of wireless signals. A bogus water pipeline made from petrol tins, with accompanying fake pumping stations and water towers, was laid, moving steadily towards the southern part of the front. In an attempt to deceive the enemy as to the time as well as the place of the main assault, this progressed at a rate that indicated a completion date in early November.

Yet the real date of the attack was almost betrayed by an unfortunate signal for which Richardson had no responsibility or, indeed, knowledge. This was sent on 15 October, asking for reserves of stretcher-bearers to be sent forward from the Nile Valley. It was intercepted by the Intelligence staff of Panzerarmee Afrika, who recalled that such a message had preceded an earlier Allied offensive. Assuming that history was about to repeat itself and that a similar length of time would elapse between the signal and the offensive, they issued a warning that an attack might be expected on any day from 21 to 25 October.

In the circumstances, it is a testament to the thoroughness of Richardson's deception measures that this warning was simply ignored. On the 21st, Colonel Ulrich Liss, head of the Intelligence Department at the German Army High Command – Oberkommando des Heeres or OKH – visited Panzerarmee Afrika with the assurance that Montgomery's offensive would not commence until early November. Rommel would later admit that the attack came as a complete surprise to him; when it began he was enjoying a well-deserved rest in Germany, having handed over temporary command to General Georg Stumme. On the evening of 23 October, that officer sent a routine signal to Hitler: 'Enemy situation unchanged.'

His own Intelligence staff had already assured Montgomery that the Axis commanders showed no sign of expecting an imminent assault, and 'Ultra' would subsequently confirm that they believed Eighth Army would attack at several different points and try to develop the most promising, but that its greatest effort would come 'in the south'. One of Rommel's two panzer divisions, the 21st and Ariete, the better and more experienced of his two Italian armoured divisions, were therefore stationed in that sector, while two of his mobile infantry divisions, 90th Light and Trieste, remained in the north only because they could be supplied more conveniently there, and were kept well back in reserve, ready to engage Eighth Army wherever this should prove necessary.

Moreover the deception continued even after the Battle of El Alamein began. The fact that an attack was indeed made in the south added to the enemy's uncertainty. Tuker would later argue that it would have been better to concentrate on just the one assault in the north, with perhaps a supporting push along the coast road by the Australians. It is unlikely that they would have welcomed this as it would have taken them up against the strongest of the enemy's fixed defences, manned by 164th Light. Yet in any case had the diversion in the south not taken place, the Axis armour in that area and the mobile infantry in reserve would surely have been moved to deal with the northern attack in very short order.

Similar considerations provide the answer to another criticism of Eighth Army's initial assault by Tuker among others: that Montgomery should have employed all his artillery in the north, instead of holding some back in reserve and, worse still, using some to assist XIII Corps' diversion. It seems a somewhat carping complaint bearing in mind that the bombardment in the north, apart from impressing and heartening the attackers, as even the critics condescendingly allow, was powerful enough to inflict considerable damage on the Axis batteries, cause heavy losses to the Axis infantry, especially the Trento Division, completely shatter Panzerarmee Afrika's communications system, and thereby bring about the death of the wretched General Stumme who had gone too close to the front line in an attempt to clarify the situation. And as far as using his guns in the south was concerned, it would surely have been unwise in the extreme for Montgomery to provide the XIII Corps' attack with only token support, thereby 'giving the game away' that this was not a major effort.

As it was, his deception was not exposed and not until late on 26 October did 21st Panzer and Ariete begin to move northward and 90th Light and Trieste come forward from their reserve positions. Richardson, as later enemy accounts and intercepted enemy messages at the time all confirm, had succeeded brilliantly in his immediate task and had set a precedent for similar deception plans in the future. He was rewarded with an OBE (Military), an award made sparingly during the Second World War, and it may fairly be said that he had earned it.

* * *

During the actual fighting at Alamein, Richardson relates, 'there was little planning that could be done until the probable outcome of the battle could be more clearly seen'. So he became the 'odd-job man', dealing with the accounts of casualties, reporting the results of reconnaissance missions and acting as assistant to the hard-worked de Guingand. One task, which as Richardson remarks, was 'not catalogued in normal staff procedures', came as part of the preparation for SUPERCHARGE. Because of the congestion in the Allied salient, Richardson and Freyberg's chief staff officer, Lieutenant Colonel Ray Queree, spent nearly a day sending units not required for the operation back from the combat-zone in order to make enough room for the fresh troops who were – thus casting an interesting reflection on another of Tuker's complaints, namely that Eighth Army's main assault was put in on too broad a front.

Richardson did have a complaint of his own to make, however. On de Guingand's instructions he had drawn up a plan, code-named Operation GRAPESHOT, whereby a separate self-contained force of ninety-six tanks with supporting infantry, artillery and AA guns would be created to conduct the pursuit once victory had been achieved. Richardson would later admit to some doubts as to whether his scheme would have succeeded, and certainly there would have been delays while this formation was brought up through the minefields and past those units already in the front line. In any case, though, it was never attempted; as Richardson reports: 'Little by little, troops were removed from the force for more immediate tasks until only a remnant was left.' For this, it is difficult to blame Montgomery when the importance of the battle and the stubbornness of the defenders is considered. The ability to pursue a defeated foe would, after all, be of little use had he proved unable to bring about that defeat in the first place.

If Richardson's GRAPESHOT troops took no part in the pursuit, he personally, together with the rest of Eighth Army's staff, was dangerously close behind the retreating enemy, and it fell to him to report to Montgomery the capture of Mainwaring's party. Since one of those missing was Major Richard Carver, Montgomery's stepson of whom he was very fond, Richardson did not welcome his task, but 'my commander presented his usual demeanour of controlled professionalism', calmly telling Richardson to take over as Director of Operations and find a replacement for Carver.

In his new role, Richardson found that his most important duty was to 'co-ordinate with the RAF the minute by minute use of airpower in support of the forward units'. This support had always been Montgomery's greatest desire and during Alam Halfa and Alamein, for the first time in the North African campaigns, a joint Operations Room had been established at which Mainwaring and his staff had worked side by side with a similar team from the Desert Air Force. Having succeeded Mainwaring, Richardson enthusiastically set out to improve co-operation between the services still further, being greatly assisted in this task by Lieutenant Colonel Jock McNeill, the officer directly responsible for Army/Air liaison, and by the arrival at the Desert Air Force of a new Senior Air Staff Officer who would become almost an honorary member of Eighth Army.

When the future Air Chief Marshal Sir Harry Broadhurst took up his post in November 1942, he was a fighter 'ace' with a dozen enemy aircraft to his credit and held the rank of air commodore. Montgomery, de Guingand, Richardson and McNeill all found him a delight to work with and by the time that Tripoli fell, Montgomery was as proud of what he rather arrogantly called 'his' 'magnificent air striking force' as he was of 'his' Eighth Army. Indeed he claimed that these formed 'one fighting machine, and therein lies our great strength'. This unity would become still more pronounced after 1 February 1943, when Broadhurst became the Desert Air Force's Commander and the youngest air vice marshal in the RAF, and it would shortly be demonstrated in spectacular fashion.

Meanwhile, Montgomery was preparing for his coming assault on the Mareth Line and his advanced units were already moving against Axis strongholds in southern Tunisia. Ben Gardane was captured on 16 February, Medenine with its four landing-grounds on the 17th and Foum Tatahouine on the 18th. These gains, according to Rommel, were made 'rather earlier than we had bargained for' – another indication that Eighth Army's progress was hardly the ponderous affair beloved by certain critics.

Rommel was then conducting an offensive of his own against the British First Army in western Tunisia, but his uneasiness about Eighth Army's continuing successes was causing him to glance nervously over his shoulder. His anxiety was to be increased on 22 February, when General Alexander in his capacity of Commander of Eighteenth Army

Group appealed to Montgomery to exert as much pressure as was possible in order to discourage his old antagonist from any further aggression.

If he did this, Montgomery would be taking an undoubted risk. Only 51st Highland and 7th Armoured Divisions were well forward; 2nd New Zealand Division was still in Tripoli and X Corps as far away as Benghazi. Richardson, who knew his chief's insistence on remaining 'balanced' at all times, states that he 'would not have been surprised' had Montgomery 'answered that there was nothing he could do'. Instead, he declared: 'Alex is in trouble; we must do everything we can to help him.' Eighth Army's advanced units were ordered up to the Mareth Line at once, the Desert Air Force's Kittyhawk fighter-bombers were requested to increase their attacks, and Montgomery sent a cheerful signal to Alexander – which did not reflect his true feelings – that they might be able to get Rommel 'running about' between them 'like a wet hen'. 'It was Monty in his most generous mood,' Richardson comments.

Montgomery's action had immediate effect. Late on that same 22 February, Rommel met Kesselring and showed an 'ill-concealed impatience to get back as quickly and with as much unimpaired strength as possible to the southern defence line'. Rommel then reported to Hitler that he was abandoning his attacks in western Tunisia because the situation in the south 'made it necessary to collect my mobile forces for a swift blow against Eighth Army before it had completed its preparations'.

Since Eighth Army had not completed its preparations and Rommel could bring against it 10th, 15th and 21st Panzer Divisions with a total of 141 tanks, 90th Light, 164th Light and two Italian Infantry Divisions, it was not unreasonable for Montgomery to have 'sweated a bit at times!' Aerial reconnaissance, confirmed belatedly by 'Ultra' on 25 February, showed that Rommel's target was Medenine, but revealed neither the date nor the direction of his attack. Happily, brilliant work by Eighth Army's staff enabled reinforcements of infantry, armour and artillery to be rushed to the front line in time, and an all-round defence prepared that depended chiefly on some 460 anti-tank guns, including a few brand-new and formidable 17-pounders, which went by the innocuous name of 'Pheasants'.

Rommel's assault began at 0900 on 6 March. At about 2030, the last

Axis attacks were broken and the enemy retired with the loss of fifty-two tanks and 635 men dead, wounded or prisoners. Eighth Army had lost not a single tank, hardly any guns and 130 killed or wounded, 'all ranks'. Three days later, Rommel left North Africa forever; a sick, disillusioned man.

As at Alam Halfa, Montgomery has been criticized for not launching an immediate counter-attack against a beaten foe, but that would have brought his soldiers up against the fixed Mareth Line defences. Montgomery did not want to assault these until he had assembled his full strength, particularly since, as explained earlier, he had planned for a whole series of continuous encounters that would carry Eighth Army to Enfidaville, perhaps even to Tunis. And as it turned out, the interval between the Battles of Medenine and Mareth Line proved beneficial because during it another action was fought, small in scale but momentous in its consequences.

On 1 February, Eighth Army had been joined by General Philippe Leclerc and over 3,200 French and colonial troops, volunteers all, who had marched 1,000 miles over the desert from Chad in French Equatorial Africa. Richardson, the fluent French-speaker, now added to his varied roles that of liaison officer to Leclerc, with whom he got on well and who quickly became 'one of us'. 'Force L', as the Free Frenchmen were collectively known, was sent first to secure 'Wilder's Gap'; then on receipt of Alexander's call for help, it was ordered to advance along the west side of the Matmata Hills to the craggy massif of Ksar Rhilane, about a third of the way to Tebaga. Here, on 10 March, it was attacked by a strong German reconnaissance unit that included tanks.

Leclerc's men were too far away for the rest of Eighth Army to assist them and Richardson describes how 'we listened appalled' as news came in of the enemy assault and of mounting casualties. Mercifully, Eighth Army's partner, the Desert Air Force, could intervene. Raids by the Kittyhawk fighter-bombers of 250 and 260 Squadrons and particularly by the Hurricane IIDs of No. 6 Squadron, which were armed with two 40mm anti-tank cannons, drove the enemy away with ruinous losses. Messages of congratulation poured in for the successful pilots, but it is unlikely that they had any idea of just how important was the precedent that they had set.

When Montgomery's coastal thrust on the Mareth Line was

repulsed and he was forced to rely on his 'Left Hook', it was clearly impossible to provide at short notice the additional weight of artillery that Freyberg rightly thought necessary. Richardson and McNeill therefore urged de Guingand to request that the Desert Air Force give the support needed, much as it had done at Ksar Rhilane. Moreover they wanted the airmen to go in at very low level, in the belief that their cannons would be more disruptive than bombs dropped from a comparatively high altitude. This was quite a favour to ask, as only the anti-tank Hurricanes had made such strikes in the past and it seemed likely that the dual-purpose 88mms with which the sides of the Tebaga Gap were liberally supplied, would take a heavy toll of the attackers. Air Marshal Sir Arthur Coningham, the previous head of the Desert Air Force and now in Algiers commanding the North-West African Tactical Air Force of which the Desert Air Force formed part, was so concerned that he sent a staff officer to Broadhurst, warning him that in the event of failure his entire future career would be at risk.

Broadhurst, to his immense credit, took no notice: 'I will do it,' he promised de Guingand. 'You will have the whole boiling match – bombs and cannon. It will be a real low-flying blitz.' The Army and Air Force staffs set to work at once to determine the details of the assault, one of which was its direction by RAF officers sent to the front line in armoured cars – a technique later copied with great effect in North-West Europe, Italy and Burma. General Alexander was also brought into the scheme; he provided Spitfires from northern Tunisia to give Eighth Army fighter cover.

This was very necessary because, apart from one Hurricane squadron that specialized in night-fighting, all Broadhurst's units were committed to the close support role: two squadrons each of Boston, Baltimore and Mitchell light bombers; five squadrons of Spitfires; sixteen of fighter-bomber Kittyhawks or Warhawks; one of fighter-bomber Hurricanes; and the Hurricane 'tank-busters' of No.6. On 23 March, the Desert Air Force commenced strikes on enemy vehicles in the Tebaga area; these continued for three days and reached a culmination on the 26th, when the fighters and bombers, 'screaming in at zero feet' as Horrocks recalls, flew 412 sorties in support of the second Operation SUPERCHARGE. 'Brilliant and brave work by the pilots,' reports Montgomery in his *Memoirs*, 'completely stunned the enemy.' Furthermore, despite the fears expressed beforehand,

Broadhurst lost only one Baltimore and thirteen single-engined aircraft, and six of the pilots returned safely to their units.

As Director of Operations, Richardson had played a big part in arranging the rapid transfer of armour to Tebaga as well as the use of Broadhurst's 'flying artillery'. In his own account of the battle, he modestly omits almost all mention of his personal contribution, but his superiors clearly appreciated its value for they ensured that it was recognized by the award of a DSO. Richardson received a further mark of their favour not long afterwards. In mid-April, de Guingand was sent to Cairo as Montgomery's deputy to co-ordinate the planning of Operation HUSKY, the invasion of Sicily. As his own deputy, de Guingand selected Richardson who thus became acting Eighth Army Chief of Staff with the rank of brigadier.

Delighted and honoured, if somewhat startled by his promotion, Richardson was in just the right mood to appreciate the natural beauty of central Tunisia. He joyfully describes the olive groves and the 'masses of flowers: poppies, white and yellow daisies and many other kinds', and adds rather touchingly that for all his new rank, he was strongly tempted to pick some. Sadly, the pleasant interval was of brief duration. The flowers soon withered and Eighth Army's staff took little part in the 'triumphal rejoicings' after the final surrender of the Axis armies in North Africa. 'We had other preoccupations,' Richardson reports; he and his colleagues now joined those already involved in the problems and tensions that marked the preparations for HUSKY.

The conquest of Sicily had first been decided upon at the Casablanca Conference in January 1943. The occupation of the island would open the Mediterranean to Allied shipping and finally end the need to send convoys all the way round the Cape of Good Hope. It was also thought that it might provide the final blow to a tottering Italy – as would prove the case – and help reduce Axis pressure on Russia; an aim that became more urgent in February when the Germans, recovering with remarkable resilience from the disaster at Stalingrad, began a new offensive that would lead to the recapture of Kharkov on 15 March.

Responsibility for the planning and mounting of HUSKY was given to Alexander but in view of his many other concerns as ground force commander in Tunisia, he understandably delegated the planning part to a special unit under Major General Charles Gairdner known as 'Force 141'.[2] This recommended a series of widely dispersed landings.

Eighth Army was to make three such at first instance: on both sides of the Pachino Peninsula in the south-east of Sicily and on its south coast; to be followed by a fourth on its east coast three days later. Meanwhile Patton's Seventh US Army would deliver further separate assaults on western Sicily in the vicinity of Palermo. Alexander much preferred one concentrated attack against south-east Sicily but Gairdner assured him that the ports there could not handle the amount of shipping that would be required.

When Montgomery learned the details of the plan he disliked it intensely and on 24 April, set out his views in a forthright signal to Alexander. In this he warned that the Germans would certainly resist fiercely; the Italians, to judge from their conduct in Tunisia, might well do the same, and there was a good chance that the multiple separate bridgeheads would be overrun one after another. He therefore insisted that Eighth Army must land in the south-east of the island on a single front stretching from the Pachino Peninsula to just south of Syracuse.

Since this accorded with Alexander's personal views, he was naturally sympathetic to Montgomery's demands, but they aroused violent reactions from the Naval and Air Commanders, Admiral of the Fleet Sir Andrew Cunninghan and Air Chief Marshal Sir Arthur Tedder. Officially their main objection was that the cancellation of Eighth Army's landing in the Gulf of Gela in the south of Sicily would enable enemy warplanes to make unhampered attacks on the assault shipping from the Ponte Olivo airfields. It seems likely, however, that much of their hostility arose from an understandable resentment of Montgomery's attitude which, with regret, can only be described as typically dictatorial and dogmatic.

Whatever the reason, Cunningham and Tedder were adamant in their opposition. Montgomery, who was not well at this time, asked de Guingand to put forward his case at a conference at Algiers arranged for 29 April, but as we saw earlier, de Guingand's aircraft suffered a crash-landing and he was removed to hospital with concussion. Montgomery then sent Leese instead but such was the attitude of most of those at Algiers that he found no one to meet him at the aerodrome and had to get a lift to the city in a lorry. At the conference, Alexander, according to Leese, 'was splendid and stood up for me from the start,', but the other senior officers merely listened politely and refused to discuss the matter further unless Montgomery appeared in person.

So on 2 May, Montgomery flew to Algiers. On the way, he asked Richardson, who had accompanied him, to read a draft of the address he proposed to make at the coming conference and tell him whether this was clear enough. 'I knew this was no formality,' Richardson adds, because Montgomery 'never expected his staff, or indeed his ADCs, to agree to anything if they did not.' On this occasion, though, Richardson saw no reason not to agree: 'As usual he had summed up the strategic argument with great force and few words.'

Montgomery now made a final suggestion that the American landing at Palermo should be cancelled. Captain Liddell Hart regrets its loss, claiming that, had it proceeded, Patton 'would have been well on the way to the Straits of Messina, the enemy's line of reinforcement or retreat – whereby all the enemy forces in Sicily could have been trapped'. Yet it is difficult to accept this contention because, apart from the dispersal of ground and air strength that a landing at Palermo would have involved, any troops advancing from it towards Messina would have been attacked from flank and rear by 15th Panzer Grenadier Division and two mobile Italian divisions that were stationed in western Sicily.

Instead of landing at Palermo, Montgomery proposed that the Americans should come ashore in the Gulf of Gela. This would enable them to capture the Ponte Olivo airfields quickly and protect Eighth Army's left flank; it would also simplify the provision of fighter cover for the invasion. Richardson remarks, somewhat cynically, that 'knowing as I did something of the prejudices of Tedder and Cunningham', it seemed likely that they would be 'very disinclined to alter their arrangements to satisfy the "egotistical" Monty', and indeed both continued to raise objections. But Montgomery won over not only Alexander but Eisenhower as well and on their return flight Richardson found him 'contented and relaxed'.

It is worth emphasizing that Eisenhower would always maintain that Montgomery's determination that Seventh US Army should land in southern Sicily was absolutely correct, and it is clear that once the Naval and Air Commanders had been forced to swallow their natural indignation over Montgomery's disrespectful and hectoring manner, they reached the same conclusion. The Navy accepted that Montgomery's amendments to the HUSKY plan 'undoubtedly reduced the risks of failure'. Tedder went so far as to claim that he personally 'had always favoured it'.

Richardson now took up yet another new duty, as Montgomery's representative and liaison officer with Force 141 in Algiers. 'My role,' he confirms, 'was to ensure that the overall preparations, as they developed, were reconcilable at every stage with Monty's requirements.' He did not like his latest post very much, found Algiers an unhappy place and was always grateful when it was necessary for him to travel to the Middle East to attend planning conferences or rehearsals for the landings.

'Finally,' relates Richardson, whose relief can be sensed from the use of that word, 'at the beginning of July, I flew to Malta to make arrangements for the headquarters of Eighth Army to control the assault from that island.' Pleased as he was to resume his primary role as Director of Operations – or to be strictly accurate since his promotion, Brigadier General Staff (Operations) – he was disappointed with the Sicilian campaign, which he found confused by politics, compromises, and international and inter-service rivalries; though he accepts that the capture of the island achieved all the strategic aims that had been hoped for. The proposals for the follow-up campaign on the Italian mainland also concerned him. Like the rest of Eighth Army's staff, he considered that the BAYTOWN landing on the Italian 'toe' was pointless; the assault on Salerno, in his opinion, was 'much more promising'.

It was therefore with mixed feelings that Richardson learned of the next assignment in his remarkably versatile career. For Operation AVALANCHE, the Salerno landings, Mark Clark's Fifth US Army had been reinforced by the British X Corps which, after Horrocks had been wounded, was taken over by Lieutenant General Richard McCreery. It was decided to add a small British staff to Fifth Army's Headquarters with the duty of ensuring that it enjoyed close relations with McCreery's corps. Montgomery, who stated at this time that Richardson's 'good work and devotion to duty have contributed largely to the victories we have gained', recommended him to lead this contingent with the title of Deputy Chief of Staff (British). Richardson's pleasure was genuine but could not help being marred by regrets that he would be leaving Eighth Army. He was consoled by a charming letter from Montgomery, who assured him that he would be 'greatly missed. But when appealed to by the Americans we had to send our best.'

Rather ominously, Montgomery added that he did not 'altogether like the way' the Salerno operation was 'shaping up' and Richardson would soon learn that however attractive in theory, it had not been well planned. Clark's American troops were inexperienced; the 82nd US Airborne Division with which he had intended to seize the bridges over the Volturno River and so block the arrival of German reinforcements, was withdrawn in readiness for an airborne drop near Rome that was subsequently (and fortunately) cancelled; and he had unwisely decided against a preliminary naval bombardment in the hope of gaining surprise. Worst of all, on 8 September, Italy's surrender was officially announced and, despite the private warnings of Alexander and the public warnings of Montgomery, it was generally believed that the Italians would turn on the Germans and, among other benefits, would secure Naples.

Consequently, when the AVALANCHE landings began in the early hours of 9 September, little opposition was expected and it was confidently forecast that Fifth US Army would be in Naples within three days. Instead, Clark's men met violent resistance from 16th Panzer Division, which controlled four infantry battalions as well as some eighty Mark IV Specials and forty self-propelled guns, and which would soon be reinforced by every formation that Kesselring had to hand. The result was a near-disaster and Richardson, as he tactfully wrote home, was able to see 'quite a lot of the fighting, much more than in Eighth Army'.

That was very much an understatement. Richardson had sailed to Salerno on USS *Ancon*, a specially designed Combined Operations Ship that flew the flag of the American naval commander, Vice Admiral Kent Hewitt. Early on the 10th, he went ashore, to spend most of the day visiting the formations of X (British) Corps and the HQ of VI US Corps. At dusk, he attempted to return to the *Ancon*, only to find that she was moving out to the open sea and would not be back before morning. Richardson therefore took refuge for the night on USS *Biscayne*, a smaller Headquarters Ship that was the flagship of Rear Admiral Richard Conolly. He slept soundly on a narrow shelf in the wardroom, oblivious of repeated raids by the Luftwaffe; probably he was exhausted.

Next day, Richardson reported to a small and somewhat primitive Headquarters that Clark had set up ashore. This was dangerously near to the front line and, says Richardson, 'shells and mortar bombs fell alarmingly close'. German attacks were continuous and on 13 September, Clark personally drove forward in a jeep to rally a battalion that had started to give way. Nonetheless, despite his individual gallantry, for which he was deservedly awarded a Distinguished Service Cross, Clark was so concerned about the situation that early on the 14th, he ordered emergency plans to be prepared for the re-embarkation of his Headquarters and the transfer of VI US Corps to the X Corps sector or vice versa as might prove necessary.

This was the news that greeted Alexander when he arrived in a destroyer on the morning of the 15th. Remembering the damage done to Eighth Army's morale by Auchinleck's obsession about withdrawal plans, the Commander of Fifteenth Army Group, tactfully but very firmly indeed, quashed all suggestions of evacuation under any circumstances whatsoever. His calm, unruffled composure was wonderfully reassuring, not least to Richardson who was sent to meet him on the beach. Alexander, remarking that he had had no lunch, insisted on their sitting down together for a picnic. Only when they had started eating did Alexander ask about the present position. Richardson, who had also managed to remain cool throughout the crisis, replied – presumably much to Alexander's secret relief – that he thought the danger had passed.

So indeed, it had; on 17 September, the Germans reluctantly fell back, though it was not until 1 October that Fifth US Army finally captured Naples. Thereafter, Fifth Army to the west of the Apennines and Eighth Army on Italy's Adriatic side began their slow and painful advance northward against increasingly strong resistance in increasingly terrible weather, until in December, they came to a halt before Kesselring's Gustav Line.

During this period, Richardson, like Montgomery's other pupils, took pains to pass on the knowledge he had acquired. He liked the Americans and was impressed by the speed with which they learned from experience, but he felt that their staff procedures, particularly with regard to air co-operation, were slow, clumsy and cumbersome. In the Eighth Army, he reflects, 'things were done with the minimum of fuss or paper and in about half the time'.

Wisely, Richardson did not reveal this opinion to his new colleagues for, again like most of Montgomery's subordinates, he had learned to avoid his former leader's regrettable mannerisms which, usually quite unintentionally, gave so much offence. During the fighting at Salerno, for instance, Montgomery had sent a letter to Clark, meant to express sympathy and encouragement, but sounding merely condescending. Clark's brilliant Chief of Staff, Major General Alfred Gruenther, knowing that it would be resented, asked the Deputy Chief of Staff (British) for advice. Richardson sensibly suggested that he pass on only a summary to Clark without quoting Montgomery's unfortunate wording. Richardson adopted a similar tactful approach when trying to persuade the Americans to accept Eighth Army ideas and systems. He not only achieved his aim but retained the friendship and respect of his Allies, and when he left Fifth Army he was sporting the ribbon of the United States Legion of Merit.

Richardson was naturally pleased and flattered by the ready acceptance of his advice, but as the winter of 1943–44 dragged on, he became ever less happy about the Allied tactics. He did not like the plans for the early attempts on Cassino and he was one of those who deplored the destruction of the monastery, if only because it achieved 'nothing decisive'; he was also unimpressed by the accuracy of the US heavy bombers. He was still less enamoured of the proposed landing at Anzio, which he considered could only succeed if the threat it posed to the German supply lines and the pressure exerted by Clark on the Germans' southern front combined to break their will to resist. Since he never accepted the wildly optimistic Intelligence reports that this would be the case, he declares that Anzio 'was the only operation since Dunkirk which I was convinced from the start would never succeed'.

This belief, Richardson adds, 'started well before the assault and grew stronger and stronger as D-Day approached'. He was not remotely surprised when 'the bridgehead was duly bottled up', and his dislike for the whole enterprise was only increased by a number of lengthy visits that he and other members of Fifth Army's staff paid to Anzio to check the situation and encourage its defenders. The whole area was under constant shellfire, Richardson personally had some narrow escapes, and he describes his experiences with typical restraint as 'indeed most uncomfortable'.

Worst of all, though, Richardson had come to feel that Italy was now 'a secondary theatre'. He accepted that it was playing a vital part in preparing for the Normandy landings by tying down experienced

German formations that could otherwise have been employed in North-West Europe, but he was certain that Operation OVERLORD would be 'the key factor in achieving victory'. So he was overjoyed when in late March 1944, he was summoned to join the Headquarters Staff of Twenty-First Army Group and became, as he puts it, 'a "Monty man" once more'.

*   *   *

'Back among old friends', Richardson was appointed head of Plans; his task and that of his subordinates being to fill in the details of the basic strategy determined by Montgomery, examine all matters that might affect this, and anticipate the likely reactions of the enemy. On 7 April, Richardson attended Montgomery's Presentation, describing it as 'crystal clear and supremely confident', and on 8 May, he produced his own Appreciation of the probable future course of the struggle in Normandy.

Although Richardson would later record that 'we were all far too optimistic about the timings early in the battle', in fact his Appreciation did warn that the restricted terrain south of the initial bridgehead, combined with the respective rates at which the Allies and the Germans could build up their strength, would render a speedy breakthrough unlikely. He therefore supported Bradley and de Guingand in pointing out that the 'phase lines' were rough indications of proposed progress, not firm guarantees, and that whether operations would in fact develop in the way it was hoped, 'must of course depend on our own and the enemy situation, which cannot be predicted accurately at the present moment'.

It should be emphasized, however, that while Richardson doubted very much that everything would go exactly 'according to plan', he entirely understood and approved of the plan's basic intention. In his Appreciation, which was issued to both First US and Second British Armies, he confirmed that once through the difficult country, the Allied aim should be 'to contain the maximum enemy forces facing the eastern flank of the bridgehead' – that held by Dempsey – and 'to thrust rapidly towards Rennes' – which was situated some 40 miles south of Avranches.

In addition to his general role, Richardson's experiences in North

Africa resulted in his becoming closely concerned with plans for the involvement of the Allied Air Forces in OVERLORD, from their part in preliminary assaults on northern France to their more immediate support during the D-Day landings and subsequently. They also led, on 4 June, to Montgomery appointing him a personal liaison officer with the Allied Air Force Headquarters at Bentley Priory.

Having 'set up my caravan in the grounds', Richardson found himself in a 'very strange' environment. The Air Commander-in-Chief was Air Chief Marshal Sir Trafford Leigh-Mallory, a former head of RAF Fighter Command and, by the way, a brother of the Mallory of Everest fame. He was genuinely eager to give all possible assistance to the Allied ground forces, but he found it difficult to exercise control over his semi-independent British and American subordinates, particularly, in Richardson's opinion, over Coningham, now Commander of Second Tactical Air Force, the RAF units giving direct aid to the British Second Army. Moreover, he was subjected to considerable interference from Tedder, now also an air chief marshal and Deputy Supreme Commander to Eisenhower.

Luckily, Richardson established a happy relationship with Leigh-Mallory's Scientific Adviser, Professor Zuckerman, who was also on good terms with Tedder and remained unaffected by the disputes that frequently arose between the various subsidiary 'Air Barons', as Richardson calls them. Richardson adopted the practice of discussing Army needs with Zuckerman at first instance and relying, with justification, on the professor's influence to ensure that Montgomery's air support requirements were duly satisfied.

It was also Richardson's duty to 'brief' the airmen on the progress of the fighting in Normandy. This was a largely formal task at first and on 8 June, Richardson delivered a report on the current position to King George VI, Churchill and Field Marshal Smuts of South Africa. Very quickly, though, circumstances changed and Richardson found the atmosphere becoming increasingly tense and strained.

It will be recalled that Montgomery had originally hoped for an early capture of Caen and the airfield sites beyond it. By 8 June, the date on which Montgomery personally arrived in France, Caen had not been taken, a direct assault on the town would clearly be very costly, and the German armour was making vigorous, if ineffective counter-attacks. Nonetheless, Montgomery was far from dismayed; on the contrary, he

Plans and Operations 161

believed that he might soon be able not only to capture Caen but, as he wrote to de Guingand on 9 June, to 'checkmate the enemy completely' by cutting off and destroying the panzer divisions in its vicinity. On the previous day, Second British Army had begun to thrust south towards Villers-Bocage as a preliminary to out-flanking Caen from the west. Now in a conference with Dempsey, Montgomery decided that he would send 51st Highland Division across the River Orne to strike out of the bridgehead held by 6th (British) Airborne Division, and encircle Caen from the east as well. At Leigh-Mallory's Headquarters on 10 June, Richardson revealed these plans and also Montgomery's request that 1st (British) Airborne Division be dropped south of Caen between the two pincers to complete the encirclement of the German forces.

Though some critics have regarded Montgomery's intentions as out of character, it must by now have become clear that the picture painted of him as a commander who would never run a risk is wholly false, and indeed his action now was very similar to the one he had taken in Sicily on being presented with an unexpected opportunity to trap enemy formations opposing the bridgehead. Unfortunately, as in Sicily, he proved over-optimistic. By 11 June, he was already assessing the situation much less confidently, for he had learned that the provision of troops for his eastern pincer was proceeding more slowly than hoped; the direct advance on Villers-Bocage had been called off after making no real progress; and Leigh-Mallory had categorically refused to agree to the airborne operation, fearing it would suffer heavy casualties.

Montgomery was furious with Leigh-Mallory's 'gutless' decision, as he called it, but it would surely have become inevitable in any case following the further failures of Second British Army to encircle Caen. The attempt to advance from the 6th Airborne Division's bridgehead had been abandoned by 13 June. On the previous day, the move towards Villers-Bocage had been revived and Dempsey had sent 7th Armoured Division on a wide wheel that would close on the town from the west. 7th Armoured captured it on the 13th, but when it advanced along the road to Caen, it was taken by surprise by German armour, losing twenty-five tanks and eighteen other armoured vehicles, and that night it abandoned Villers-Bocage; ultimately falling back to its starting-point east of Caumont.

Despite these setbacks, Montgomery remained unperturbed. Later critics have assured us that his failure to capture Caen and hence the airfield sites beyond it had compelled him to adopt a 'new plan' and this is 'proved' by his having signalled to Brooke, Eisenhower and de Guingand on 11 June – and repeated to the CIGS on the 14th – that his 'general policy' was 'to pull the Germans on to Second Army so that the First Army can extend, and expand'. If this was really a new aim Montgomery would seem to be entitled to much credit for his adaptability, but in reality, this 'general policy', in essence if not in detail, was the same as he had laid down as long ago as 7 April in his Presentation of Plans.

In that Presentation, as already described, Second British Army had been ordered 'to protect the eastern flank of First US Army' by providing a 'strong front', a defensive shield beyond which the Americans could indeed 'extend and expand'. The capture of Caen and the airfield sites and the engagement of German forces by Second Army were not alternatives; they were both factors designed to enable Dempsey to give the Americans their required protection. They did, however, differ in their relative importance.

Montgomery never denied that the capture of Caen would have made Dempsey's task easier, by strengthening his protective shield and depriving the Germans of a valuable road and rail communications centre. As late as 7 July, he would tell Brooke that 'we cannot be 100 per cent happy on the eastern front until we have got Caen'. Yet in no way would or did the failure to capture Caen prevent Second Army from fulfilling its primary role of guarding First US Army's flank – provided that it was on the eastern front that the main German strength, especially armoured strength, was committed.

This was the vital factor and here Montgomery was successful. In the first days of the campaign, all three panzer divisions in Normandy were directed against Dempsey in defence of Caen, and 'Ultra' would quickly confirm that strong reinforcements, including a fourth panzer division, had been ordered to join them. It has been argued that this reflects no credit on Montgomery but surely he deserves praise for having correctly anticipated that the location of the German armour and the eagerness of his enemies, especially Rommel, to hurl it into action as soon as possible, would inevitably result in its initial assaults falling on Second Army.

Having got Rommel's tanks engaged on his eastern front, Montgomery had to make sure that they could not be transferred to oppose Bradley, should Rommel wish to do so. It was in this respect that Montgomery did show his adaptability. He was quick to see that even without the capture of Caen he could still protect the Americans as long as the German armour was tied down fighting to retain it.

This Montgomery achieved by his attempts to outflank and encircle Caen and by the actions of the Allied airmen in their support. On 10 June, the Headquarters of Panzer Group West under General Freiherr Leo Geyr von Schweppenburg, which had been detected by 'Ultra' interceptions 12 miles south of Caen, was subjected to a devastating attack by sixty-one Mitchell bombers and forty Typhoons armed with rockets; this knocked out all wireless communications and killed all the Group's senior staff officers except Geyr himself, who was only wounded. Next day, a raid on Caen wrecked more communications and caused further disruption. These setbacks, together with the casualties they had suffered in repelling Second Army's ground attacks – Panzer Lehr Division for instance had lost about 100 tanks – robbed the Germans of the initiative, and this they would never regain. On 11 June, von Rundstedt and on 12 June, Rommel both reported to Hitler that their armour was being compelled to fight on the defensive and, if the front line was to be held, could not be withdrawn from it to mount any organized full-scale counter-attack.

These admissions confirm that, in the words of de Guingand already quoted, Montgomery's 'original conception was followed and worked'. At Bentley Priory, another of Montgomery's staff officers had reached the same conclusion. In a report to the 'Air Barons' on 14 June, Richardson acknowledged that recent moves had not been as successful as hoped, but expressed his full confidence that the overall strategy was proceeding satisfactorily. His beliefs were not shared by Tedder or Coningham, both of whom talked of a 'crisis'. They so alarmed Leigh-Mallory that he flew out to Normandy that same day to confer with Montgomery. Happily, his visit reassured him and on 15 June he rejected the 'crisis' claims as inaccurate and declared that 'the appreciation of the military situation given at yesterday's conference by Brigadier Richardson was a truer picture'. Brigadier Richardson was suitably gratified and dismisses the whole affair as an 'unnecessary panic', which he felt may have been 'deliberately created, by those who had no faith in Monty'.

By which, of course, Richardson meant Tedder and Coningham. In their favour it must be said that they considered they had genuine cause for complaint. They had been warned, particularly by de Guingand, that Montgomery's intention of making a speedy capture of the airfield sites between Caen and Falaise must be regarded as an aim, not a guarantee, but it was perhaps only human that they should have felt that he had broken a promise to them. As a result, not only were there fewer aerodromes available than anticipated but the ones in the bridgehead were jammed so close together that there was a dangerous risk of collisions; they were potentially vulnerable to Luftwaffe attacks; and in the British sector at least, they were within range of German heavy artillery. The airmen's anger was in no way diminished by Montgomery's obvious and exasperatingly cheerful unconcern about his inability to gain the 'promised' airfields, which, as he declares in his *Memoirs*, 'were not all-important to me . . . I wasn't fighting to capture airfields; I was fighting to defeat Rommel in Normandy'.

Nevertheless, it was a fact that Tedder and Coningham did already cherish an active dislike for Montgomery. The former had clashed with him over planning in North Africa and Sicily, and had not been appeased by having been proved wrong. Coningham was frankly jealous. In sharp contrast to Broadhurst, he had always resented Montgomery's insistence that Army and Air Force in North Africa should form 'one fighting machine', and this for the not very commendable reason that it had resulted in most of the praise – and the newspaper headlines – being given to Montgomery and not to him.[3]

And regrettably, Tedder and Coningham now allowed their antipathy to cloud their judgement. They could not have known that the lengthy delay in securing the airfield sites would not prevent the Allies from gaining a colossal victory or, incidentally, from reaching the Seine earlier than Montgomery had originally predicted. They were, however, aware that it was clearly not preventing their Air Forces from gaining a total supremacy that protected their own troops and paralyzed the enemy's movements, because this was fully confirmed by all Allied sources and also by all the leading German commanders in Normandy, as was revealed by 'Ultra'. They chose to ignore this; their influence, says Richardson who could view it at close quarters, was 'controversial and unhelpful'; and their intrigues against Montgomery added greatly to his many burdens.

Shortly after the 'unnecessary panic' incident, Richardson, much to his relief, was recalled to the Headquarters of Twenty-First Army Group. Montgomery was planning another drive towards Caen and since he was most appreciative of the achievements of the Allied Air Forces – though they confirmed his belief that the shortage of airfields was not as crucial as some made out – he was anxious to ensure full Army-Air co-ordination. There was no one in Second British Army with the experience required, so Montgomery sent the knowledgeable Richardson to Dempsey as a temporary Brigadier General Staff (Air). Richardson was delighted to find an atmosphere completely different from that at Bentley Priory, with Second Army's staff willing to learn and the airmen below the very top commanders eager to oblige. Even so, success continued to elude Dempsey, for reasons largely outside the Allies' control.

On 19 June, the Channel coast was hit by the worst summer storm for forty years. The damage done was immense and by the time the gale abated on the 22nd, the Allies' inability to maintain their build-up of men and equipment had deprived them of 140,000 tons of stores and 20,000 vehicles, and Dempsey had three fewer divisions under him than had been anticipated. In addition, the Allied aircraft were grounded and this at last gave the Germans the chance to move during the daylight hours; they gladly seized the opportunity to bring up reinforcements and strengthen their defences. In consequence, the move towards Caen had first to be postponed and then when it was delivered did not gain nearly as much ground as had been hoped. This in turn resulted in Richardson going back to Bentley Priory in an attempt to initiate a new form of aerial support.

At the time of the artificial 'crisis' of 14 June, Leigh-Mallory had suggested that the Allied heavy and medium bombers might be allocated to give Second Army direct assistance. Tedder and Coningham, though their voices had been loudest in proclaiming the 'crisis', had promptly quashed the proposal, but Montgomery who in the opinion of Horrocks was 'the most air-minded general I ever met', was not likely to have forgotten it. A fresh attempt on Caen was planned for early July, and Richardson as Montgomery's trusted liaison officer, accompanied by the Canadian Brigadier Charles Mann – 3rd Canadian Division would form part of the attacking force – was sent to persuade the 'Air Barons' to allow Bomber Command, for the first time ever, to participate in an Army assault.

A conference on 6 July failed to reach any agreement on the subject, which was then dropped. Richardson was 'not greatly surprised', but he continued to urge that he must have a decision one way or the other. He was therefore sent to the Headquarters of Bomber Command at High Wycombe where he presented Second Army's case to the redoubtable Air Marshal Sir Arthur Harris. To his delight, that formidable figure proved very ready to help. Air Vice Marshal Donald Bennett, the Pathfinder chief, was called in for consultation, details were quickly worked out and a genial Harris even loaned his car and driver to Richardson and Mann so that they could have 'time for a decent dinner in London' before returning to Normandy.

In the evening of 7 July, 467 Lancasters and Halifaxes dropped over 2,500 tons of bombs on the northern fringes of Caen. Richardson, who watched them, remarks that 'the earth literally shook beneath our feet. The results, however, were disappointing.'[4] Yet Dempsey, according to Chester Wilmot, 'was less interested in the destruction of enemy material than he was in gaining the moral ascendency,' and this the raid had certainly given him by dramatically raising Allied morale and correspondingly disheartening and in some cases breaking the resolve of Caen's defenders. And, in part at least because of those effects, Second Army finally reached Caen late on 8 July and had secured it, apart from the suburbs on the south bank of the River Orne, by the 10th. Carpiquet airfield was also taken, though it could not be used for some time as it was too close to the front line.

After this diversion, Richardson returned to his duties as Chief Planner. Immediate operations were dealt with by de Guingand, Belchem and Williams, but it was the planning staff who decided what developments would be necessary, desirable or likely to occur some weeks into the future, thus enabling Montgomery to be ready for these and his logistics staff to anticipate his requirements. It was Richardson's planners who first suggested that it would be preferable not to direct the whole of Third US Army into Brittany once the Americans had broken through to Avranches, but to turn much of its strength eastward towards the Seine instead. It was Richardson's planners who recommended that when Second British Army made its great dash from the Seine into Belgium, First US Army should deliver a series of 'right hooks' towards it, so as to trap the German soldiers whom Dempsey had forced aside. Hodges accepted this advice and in the first five days of September, in the neighbourhood of Mons, his VII Corps took well over 25,000 prisoners.

Richardson modestly makes no mention of this achievement, preferring to describe a number of meetings that he had with Browning and his staff to consider possible airborne operations – all of which proved abortive. Nor did he take any part in the preparations for the one that was put into action. He accepts that 'MARKET GARDEN had a strategic objective which was crystal clear and of overwhelming importance', but this was 'Browning's plan'; Richardson had always urged that the advance towards the Ruhr should be made through the Aachen 'gap' and did not even know about the intended drive into Holland until after it had been agreed. Richardson's personal experiences during the operation were not pleasant either. Montgomery sent him to Nijmegen to report on the situation but his attempt to return was blocked when a German attack severed XXX Corps' line of communications and he was forced to spend 'a disturbed and frugal night in a Dutch cellar'.

Nor were Richardson's planning staff involved with the German counter-offensive in the Ardennes, which began on 16 December, for the simple reason that Allied Intelligence had utterly failed to predict the move, which achieved total surprise. Like the rest of Twenty-First Army Group's staff, however, Richardson watched in 'profound admiration' as Montgomery met the crisis with 'his accustomed, professional skill' – especially after 20 December, when Eisenhower gave him control of two additional armies: First and Ninth US under Hodges and Simpson respectively.

These formations were in action on the northern flank of the broad salient that the enemy had driven deep into Twelfth US Army Group's area, and Bradley, whose Tactical HQ was situated well to the south in Luxembourg, could not communicate effectively with their commanders. Eisenhower's action was thus a practical and logical one but it was bitterly resented by Bradley and his staff, who regarded it as a reflection on their ability, and by public opinion in the United States where it was believed, quite wrongly, to have been instigated by Churchill, if not by Montgomery himself.

An awkward and sensitive situation was made much worse by the deplorable attitude that Montgomery now chose to adopt. He bestowed well-deserved praise on the courage and skill of the ordinary American soldier, but his air of triumphant and rather pitying superiority and his shameful bullying belittlement of the unhappy Bradley, who had supported him so loyally in Normandy, did immense harm to the Allied cause. As also to Montgomery himself, for the ill-feeling that he aroused was deep and in many cases lasting and it found vent both at the time and later in vicious criticisms of his own conduct, which were entirely deserved when they related to his personal failings but were grossly unfair when directed at his handling of the battle.

Even before 20 December, Montgomery had taken care to see that British troops were deployed in reserve positions and to become thoroughly familiar with the situation in the American sector, thanks to liaison officers whom he had sent out to every part of the front over the previous two days. Consequently, when he was put in charge of First and Ninth US Armies, he was better informed of the progress of the fighting than either Hodges or Simpson and when he visited those officers, he displayed a cool appreciation of the position and a clear realization of what needed to be done, which they found most encouraging and to which they instinctively responded.

Montgomery's new subordinates also considered his management of the conflict was 'splendid' and though his tactical withdrawals, which enabled the defenders to 'roll with the punch', proved unpopular with some who called them 'un-American', they provided badly-needed reserves and, it might be remembered, saved the lives of many gallant Americans. Montgomery's greatest contribution to the Allied victory, however, was the control he was able to establish. In the words of one of his adversaries, General von Manteuffel, Commander of Fifth Panzer Army, 'he turned a series of isolated actions into a coherent battle fought according to a clear and definite plan.'

Montgomery's plans for the next battle, that of the Rhineland, had already been prepared; in fact they would have been put into force earlier had they not been postponed by the Ardennes action. Richardson meanwhile was planning for the next battle but one; the crossing of the Rhine, which was given the somewhat ominous code-name of Operation PLUNDER. It was a colossal task for in addition to the usual need to bring up supplies and arrange air and artillery support, there were the special problems of crossing a river 500 yards wide with a huge flood plain on either side still soaked from the winter rains. These included the use of DD tanks and other amphibious vehicles; analysis of the Rhine's gravel and mud to decide the details of the bridges the sappers would have to build across it; provision of the materials for these; and research on the likelihood and effects of flooding and the measures that could be taken to guard against this.

Finally, in addition to the main assault by Second British and Ninth US Armies, 14,000 men of 6th (British) and 17th US Airborne Divisions were to be landed by parachute or glider with orders to seize bridges, capture positions that might obstruct the ground forces, disrupt any German counter-attacks, and accelerate the enlargement of the bridgehead – a tremendous undertaking, with its own separate codename of Operation VARSITY, which had to be co-ordinated with the needs of PLUNDER. The amount of time and effort devoted to the tactical and administrative requirements of the Rhine crossing was therefore amazing but every detail was thoroughly and meticulously checked, so much so that even at the time sneers would be heard about cautious commanders who were not prepared to take risks – though not from those whose lives were saved as a result.

The foresight of the planners was deservedly repaid. To say that everything went 'according to plan' would no doubt inspire ridicule in certain quarters, so we must rest content with the judgement of Major General Essame, who took part in the operation, that the plan for it 'is impossible to fault', and its performance was 'Montgomery's final masterpiece, executed in a manner soon to be outmoded, but nonetheless, like a Constable, a work of art'. It began late on 23 March; by the morning of the 29th, the bridgehead was 35 miles wide and 35 miles deep, and although the war in Europe, with all its cost and misery, would continue for another month, it was clear to the staff of Twenty-First Army Group that they were taking part in their final advance. It would end on 4 May at Lüneburg Heath.

In Richardson's own case, the advance would continue a little longer, because a few days later, he was flown to Copenhagen to help supervise the surrender of the German forces there. Perhaps it was finding himself not in a conquered country but in one overjoyed by its liberation; perhaps as a younger man he was much less exhausted, mentally and physically, than such as de Guingand or Horrocks; in any case it is a pleasure to record that Richardson at least thoroughly enjoyed the celebrations that followed.

Notes:

1. In the same letter, Richardson mentions that on the previous night he had unwittingly shared his bed with a snake, which had apparently sought shelter there from a gale that was blowing. Since he expresses his sympathy for the 'poor creature', it was presumably a harmless variety.
2. So called from the number of the room in the Hotel St George, Algiers, in which its first meetings were held.
3. Chester Wilmot reports an outburst by Coningham to a group of war correspondents: 'It's always "Monty's Army", "Monty's Victory", "Monty Strikes Again". You never say "Coningham's Air Force".'
4. There were two main reasons for this. Anxious to avoid any risk to their own troops, the RAF had not bombed the German fortifications immediately in front of the British lines. Moreover, the raid had originally not been arranged for the evening of 7 July at all but for dawn on the 8th, shortly preceding the start of Second Army's offensive. It was brought forward at the last moment because of an unfavourable weather forecast and there was no time for Dempsey to change his own plans. As a result, the German front-line troops escaped unharmed and though they were at first disorganized, they had six hours in which to recover before the fighting started.

Chapter 7

The Armoured Commander

When Montgomery took premature control of Eighth Army on 13 August 1942, and began that series of victories that would lead to Lüneberg and subsidiary local surrenders, four of our six representative subordinates were already in the Middle East. Of these, the one who knew the area best was Roberts, who had been serving there since before the Second World War began. He probably needed all his experience, to say nothing of more than his fair share of luck, to survive the various perils that were lying in wait for him.

The first of these came soon after Italy entered the conflict in June 1940. Major Roberts was returning from a visit to the front line when his staff car was strafed by a CR 42 biplane fighter. Roberts and his driver sprang out and the former opened fire with a Bren gun; it jammed after a short burst but apparently this spirited reaction persuaded the Italian pilot to look for an easier target elsewhere. Roberts had taken his 'first offensive action of the war' – but there would be plenty of others.

After a temporary break attending the Haifa Staff College in August, Roberts became the Brigade Major of 4th Armoured Brigade; this was at his own request even though, despite his title, it meant his reversion to the rank of captain. He served with 4th Armoured during Operation COMPASS and the subsequent invasion of Cyrenaica and on 13 December, while the brigade was endeavouring to cut off the Italian retreat from Sidi Barrani, he again experienced an attack from the air, this time by enemy bombers whose raids, says Roberts, 'went on all day' and were 'quite horrifying'. As a change, he came under artillery fire just prior to the capture of Tobruk. On a happier note, he was awarded a Military Cross for his part in the campaign.

In March 1941, Roberts resumed his pre-war role as a staff officer of 7th Armoured Division, regaining his major's crown in the process, and in early October, he received further promotion to lieutenant colonel and a place on the staff of the newly-formed Eighth Army's XXX Corps. Much had happened in the interval between these events: at the end of March, Rommel had launched his first offensive, regaining the whole of Cyrenaica apart from the admittedly very important exception of Tobruk; in June, Auchinleck had replaced Wavell as Commander-in-Chief, Middle East; Eighth Army had come into existence in September; and massive reinforcements had arrived to support the British and Commonwealth forces as they prepared for a major new offensive of their own.

This was Operation CRUSADER, which began on 18 November. Even for those who took part, it was, according to Roberts – who on 24 November, added to his list of experiences that of being shelled by German tanks – 'the most difficult to follow in the whole of the war in any theatre'. Suffice then to say that on 7 December, Rommel was finally compelled to begin an orderly retreat, ultimately to El Agheila. The Allied success was brief, however, for on 21 January 1942, Rommel delivered a counter-offensive, which by 5 February had brought him to Gazala and deprived Eighth Army of most of the gains made in CRUSADER, particularly the crucial Martuba airfields.

Roberts took no part in meeting this counter-offensive, since he had just been appointed Commanding Officer of one of 4th Armoured Brigade's subsidiary units, the 3rd Battalion, Royal Tank Regiment, which together with the rest of 4th Armoured was then withdrawn from the Desert for rest and for re-equipment with the new American Grant tanks now beginning to reach the Middle East. The brigade returned to the front line in early May, to be stationed some 8 miles north-east of Bir Hacheim, the most southerly strongpoint in the 'Gazala Line' as the Allied defences were collectively called. Here, towards the end of the month, warning was received – from 'Ultra', though Roberts did not then know of its existence – that Rommel would attack some time between the 25th and the 28th. Roberts awaited the event with confidence because it would be the first time that the Germans would have encountered the Grant and he was certain that 'they were in for a very nasty shock'.

In his official Despatch, long after the close of hostilities in the Desert, General Auchinleck would state, not as an opinion but as a fact, that British tanks were inferior to those of the Germans. This would become an article of faith throughout Eighth Army but Roberts would never accept it for the period of the Gazala and later July battles, and even for the period of CRUSADER he admits that: 'careful tests carried out after the war have shown that we were unduly pessimistic regarding the performance of our own tanks.'

That indeed was the case.[1] The Allied tanks at the time of CRUSADER certainly had their faults. The aging Matildas and the Valentines, particularly the former, lacked speed; the Crusaders lacked mechanical reliability; the American Stuarts or 'Honeys', as they were called, lacked range. On the other hand, the 2-pounder gun in the British tanks and the 37mm in the Stuarts had greater penetrative power than the short-barrelled 50mm of the German Mark III and the short-barrelled 75mm of the Mark IV, the latter of which in any case at that time fired not armour-piercing but high explosive shells for use against 'soft-skinned' targets. Furthermore, all Eighth Army's tanks originally had thicker armour on the front of their hulls and on their turrets. The Germans attempted to rectify the situation by adding a further front plate; where this was done their tanks were better protected than the Crusaders and Stuarts though not the British heavy tanks. The Germans' turrets, however, remained as vulnerable as before, and in practice the majority of such conversions had not been completed before CRUSADER ended.

By the start of the Battle of Gazala, the quality of both sides' armour had improved. All the standard German tanks now carried the additional frontal protection and new Mark III and Mark IV Specials had made their appearance. There was, however, no ammunition then available for the latter, which would only become a threat at the time of Alam Halfa. The Mark III Special had increased strength of armour for its hull though not its turret, and a new long-barrelled high-velocity 50mm gun, superior to that of all Allied types previously in use. Yet only nineteen of these were on hand when the battle began on the night of 26/27 May, and they never numbered more than twenty-seven in June or sixteen in July.

Eighth Army by contrast contained 167 Grants at the start of Gazala and there was every reason for thinking that these would indeed give the Germans 'a nasty shock'. The Grant carried a 37mm gun in the turret and a 75mm in a sponson on the side of the hull – an unusual configuration that resulted in an unnecessarily high silhouette and gave the 75mm a limited arc of fire. This, though, as Roberts confirms, did not prevent it from being 'superior in anti-tank capability to any guns mounted in the German tanks', including the Mark III Specials. In addition, the Grant's armour was equal to that of the Specials on the hull and much stronger on the turret, and it had little to fear from the standard German tanks that made up the bulk of Rommel's armour, even at close range. Enemy accounts relate how their 50mm shells literally bounced off the Grant's armour, while Roberts reports that during the early exchanges at Gazala, his Grant was hit eight times without being penetrated and another Grant resisted twenty-five hits successfully.

No wonder then that Roberts believes that Eighth Army 'had a magnificent opportunity of inflicting a heavy defeat on the Germans'. It was to be only a brief opportunity, for by the end of August, Rommel had his Mark IV Specials and these mounted a long-barrelled 75mm weapon which, Roberts reflects sadly, 'was far superior to the gun in the Grants'.[2] And it was to be a missed opportunity, 'lost', says Roberts, 'by vacillation at the top and failure to understand tank warfare'.

The main problem at the start of the Battle of Gazala was that General Auchinleck was convinced that Rommel would never attempt to outflank his defences by a move south of Bir Hacheim except perhaps as a diversion, but would mount his assault in the centre of the Gazala Line, probably accompanied by a seaborne landing further east. Since Rommel had not considered either of these courses for one moment, the reasons for Auchinleck's conclusions must remain a mystery, but so steadfastly did he cling to them that even after the outflanking attack had taken place, he would issue warnings to be ready for a follow-up assault further north.

Although none of Auchinleck's senior subordinates shared his views, it was inevitable that these should influence the outlook of the lower formations and particularly, it seems, that of their Intelligence staffs. As a result, when 4th Armoured Brigade was called on to investigate an 'enemy movement' in the south reported in the early hours of 27 May, Roberts, whose 3rd Royal Tanks was the leading regiment, was assured that this was only 'a sort of SINBAD' – code-name for a reconnaissance in force. Confronted by 'a whole ruddy panzer division', Roberts and his men were compelled to retire after a fierce encounter; Roberts reversing away very slowly so as not to make the movement obvious to the enemy, with his Grant all but out of ammunition and the crews of two disabled tanks clinging on to its back.

This was only the first of a whole series of engagements during which 4th Armoured Brigade incurred mounting losses; most of these, as Roberts recognizes, were caused by the enemy's lethal 88mms. It was not to be expected that Roberts, who had previously suffered the attention of enemy fighters, bombers, artillery and armour, would escape that of anti-tank guns, and on 28 May, a shell from one of them went clean through his tank from front to rear, miraculously without causing any casualties.

It was a reprieve only. On 6 June, another 88mm struck home and, says Roberts, perhaps a shade unimaginatively, 'all hell seemed to have been let loose'. One of his crew was killed, two others were fatally wounded and Roberts himself had to be evacuated, ultimately to a hospital in Ismailia in the Nile Delta, with wounds in his face, right arm and right knee. Happily, he made a swift and complete recovery, being cheered by the news that he had been awarded an immediate DSO, and on 29 July, he returned to the Desert, promoted to command of 22nd Armoured Brigade, then part of 1st Armoured Division but soon to be transferred to his old division, the 'Desert Rats'.

His injuries had caused Roberts to miss Auchinleck's five failed offensives in July, but he had of course heard all about them and he deplores the way the British armour had attacked 'positions which were well defended by anti-tank guns' and the inability of his superiors to develop 'a greater co-operation between all arms, particularly between the tanks and the artillery'. He was therefore most concerned to learn that for Rommel's coming offensive his brigade was intended to engage in just that 'fluid and mobile' warfare at which Panzerarmee Afrika most excelled.

And as Roberts discovered how fluid and mobile the fighting was likely to be, so his concerns mounted. In typical Dorman-Smith style, a 'multiplicity of plans' was foisted onto him: 'On code-word "so and so" we would move to a specific area with a certain task; on another code-word we would move somewhere else etc, etc.' Since the chances were high that the wrong action might be taken in the confusion of combat or as a result of communications problems, Roberts felt strongly that the prospect 'did not inspire the greatest confidence'.

Then came the change of command which, says Roberts, would

'have a marked effect within a few days on our plans, on our life and on our outlook generally'. 22nd Armoured Brigade, as described earlier, was placed under direct XIII Corps control and ordered to 'select and prepare static defensive positions' at Point 102.

> 'Gone were all the other plans,' Roberts reports exultantly, 'and we gladly destroyed the mass of traces with different code-names which had been prepared with laborious staff work to indicate the alternative positions. There was one firm plan and one position to occupy and we all felt better.'

Roberts personally was not feeling well on 30 August, the day before the Battle of Alam Halfa, spending it resting in 'a spare ambulance truck which could be made fly-proof and was a little cooler than a bivouac tent'. His mind, however, was calm and relaxed. Of 22nd Armoured's four regiments, three, described rather unkindly by Roberts as 'a motley collection of combined units', were equipped with tanks that had seen so much service recently that their mechanical condition was 'precarious' and Roberts had therefore feared they would be 'unsuited to mobile operations'. Now they were no longer being asked to conduct any; instead, as Roberts delightedly informed his men on 19 August, 'for once the enemy may have to attack us in good positions of our own choosing'.

So during the long hours of 31 August, apart from a reconnaissance force which Roberts sent out in the early afternoon and which came under fire, losing four Crusaders, 22nd Armoured Brigade remained in its good positions, tensely awaiting the arrival of Rommel's panzer divisions. Roberts had stationed his three hard-worked regiments in the foothills south of Point 102 covering a front of about 3 miles. On the right or western flank were 1st and 6th Royal Tanks, now forming one combined unit containing twenty-three Grants and nineteen Stuarts, supported by the 6-pounder anti-tank guns of 1st Battalion, the Rifle Brigade, and with an anti-tank battery close behind. In the centre came 4th County of London Yeomanry, with a squadron of 3rd County of London Yeomanry under command: twenty-one Grants and fifteen Crusaders in all. The eastern flank nearest to Alam Halfa Ridge was held by the combined 5th Royal Tanks and 2nd Royal Gloucestershire Hussars with twenty Grants and fifteen Crusaders, backed by the 25-pounders of 1st Regiment, Royal Horse Artillery.

Roberts with the four Crusaders allocated as his Headquarters remained just south-east of Point 102, while his reserve regiment, the Royal Scots Greys under Lieutenant Colonel Sir Ranulph Fiennes, took station some 2 miles behind the front line on the north-eastern slopes of Point 102. It was equipped with twenty-four Grants and twenty-one Stuarts, which were comparatively new and so less likely to experience mechanical difficulties.

At about 1730, Roberts at last sighted the German armour heading across his front towards Alam Halfa. As soon as the panzer divisions realized there were British tanks at Point 102, however, they turned towards them and shortly after 1800 attacked, 21st Panzer moving directly against the centre of 22nd Armoured Brigade's position and 15th Panzer circling to come in on its left flank. Roberts found it 'fascinating to watch them, as one might watch a snake curl up ready to strike'. A deadly snake at that, for Rommel had increased the number of his Mark III Specials to seventy-three and for the first time the British were about to engage Mark IV Specials, of which the enemy now had twenty-seven. Roberts identified a number of these in the van of 21st Panzer and noted grimly that they had 'a very long gun on them, in fact it looks the devil of a gun. This must be the long-barrelled stepped-up 75mm the Intelligence people have been talking about.'

So it was and with it the Mark IV Specials opened fire at a range of over 1,000 yards on Major Alexander Cameron's 'A' Squadron of the County of London Yeomanry, destroying all its twelve Grants in short order before losses of their own forced the Germans to pause. Roberts, left with 'a complete hole in our defence', hastily called on the Royal Scots Greys to 'move at all speed from their defensive positions and plug the gap', but before they could arrive, 21st Panzer resumed its advance. This time it headed for 1st Rifle Brigade which, with splendid coolness, held its fire until the range had decreased to less than 300 yards, when its 6-pounders inflicted a heavy toll. At almost the same moment, artillery fire from every British gun that could be brought to bear crashed down on the German tanks and again they were halted temporarily.

There was still no sign of the Royal Scots Greys and Roberts urged them over the wireless to 'get out your whips'. 21st Panzer began edging forwards once more; was checked by artillery fire once more; and then the Greys poured over the crest of the ridge to the north in a great cloud of dust, losing four Grants but blocking the gap left by the destruction of Cameron's squadron. 'They have not really been long,' recalls Roberts feelingly, 'but it has seemed an age.'

At about 1900, 21st Panzer finally fell back, but looking over to the east, Roberts could see that 15th Panzer was still in action, though meeting sturdy resistance from the Grants of 5th Royal Tanks, supported by the guns of both 1st Royal Horse Artillery and 44th Division on Alam Halfa. He quickly transferred the County of London Yeomanry's remaining armour to the threatened flank and at about 1930, 15th Panzer also broke off its attack. In all, twenty-two German tanks had been destroyed and several others disabled. Despite its own tank losses, the human cost to 22nd Armoured Brigade was just three killed and some fifty wounded.

Though 1 September would see a further minor clash on 22nd Armoured's right flank between 1st/6th Royal Tanks and 21st Panzer Division, and some shelling of Point 102 – a particularly heavy concentration greeting a visit by Horrocks – for Roberts and his brigade, Alam Halfa was virtually over and won. And they had won far more than just Alam Halfa. 'In that hour's battle,' declares Field Marshal Lord Carver in his *El Alamein*, 'on a front of only a few miles, in which certainly not more and probably less than 100 tanks had actually fired their guns against each other, the tide of battle in the desert had turned.'

*   *   *

For the Battle of El Alamein, 22nd Armoured Brigade was back with 7th Armoured Division now led by Harding. The Royal Scots Greys had been transferred to 4th Light Armoured Brigade leaving Roberts with just his three battle-worn regiments, so he was not surprised these were given only a diversionary role in the south or that they were unable to break through the minefields confronting them. Once the battle had been won and the pursuit had started, however, 22nd Armoured would again be well to the fore. At about 1300 on 4 November, it fell on the remains of the Ariete Armoured Division. 'We out-gunned them,' says Roberts, 'so we stood back and picked them off; there was no object in closing in and getting casualties.' 22nd Armoured in fact had only three casualties, all wounded, and lost one Stuart tank. The Italians who, it should be said, fought bravely and well, lost thirty tanks and 450 prisoners. 'It was a very good little mobile battle,' Roberts reflects cheerfully.

On 6 November, 22nd Armoured had another clash with 21st Panzer Division, destroying sixteen of its tanks as well as a number of guns. Unfortunately, in the expressive words of 22nd Armoured's brigadier: 'At the same time as our gunners started firing, so did the skies – it started to rain and steadily got heavier and heavier.' The downpour lasted all day and all night and by turning the desert into a quagmire, it ended Eighth Army's last chance of cutting off Rommel's retreat.

It did not, however, end Eighth Army's relentless pressure, and particularly that of Harding's 7th Armoured Division. On 15 November, his 4th Light Armoured Brigade regained the Martuba airfields, then entered Benghazi on the 20th. Meanwhile on the 18th, 22nd Armoured Brigade was re-equipped with new Shermans and ordered to strike across the base of the Cyrenaican 'Bulge'. It pushed forward as fast as possible but on reaching Agedabia, it came up against the redoubtable 90th Light Division, which fought a skilful delaying action throughout the whole of 22 November before slipping away after dark to join the rest of Rommel's men behind the El Agheila 'bottleneck'.

Before setting out on this mission, Roberts had been warned by Montgomery: 'Now you are not to get a very bloody nose – you must keep your armoured regiment in good shape.' Roberts felt that such instructions were 'rather frustrating', but Montgomery was again thinking ahead: he wanted as few casualties as possible in 22nd Armoured since he intended it should be his Army Reserve for the final advance on Tripoli. It was therefore withdrawn for a well-deserved rest soon afterwards, though not before, on 25 November, it had suffered the unwelcome attentions of half a dozen Junkers Ju 87s:

> 'I kept my field-glasses on the leading Stuka,' recalls Roberts. 'He was aiming straight for my tank; he let his bombs go and the first one seemed to be coming straight at us; I put my head down into the tank and shut my eyes; there were loud explosions all round, but the bomb aimed at us didn't go off and landed about 10 yards away. A close thing.'

Montgomery had already ensured that Roberts was awarded a bar to his

DSO, and now recommended him to Brooke in glowing terms as 'easily the best commander of an armoured brigade' in Eighth Army. He proposed that Roberts should return to England and should be made a divisional commander 'very soon', adding that 'the division that gets him will be very lucky'.

As in the case of de Guingand, Brooke did not agree, but when on 19 January 1943, Harding was wounded during the fight for the Tarhuna Pass, Montgomery was able to give Roberts a division anyway, if only on a temporary basis. After a quick talk with Leese, his Corps Commander, Roberts set out for Tarhuna to take over 7th Armoured. On the 21st, he directed the 1/7th Queens Royal Regiment, one of the battalions of 7th Armoured's 131st Infantry Brigade, to capture the ridge forming the western edge of the Pass, and, accompanied by a staff officer, Major Robert Brooke, went forward himself in an armoured vehicle to check the situation from close quarters. Like Harding before him, Roberts came under fire from heavy artillery, and he describes how: 'We huddled down and mercifully had no direct hit, but when all was quiet we thought it prudent to move and did so unmolested.'

It would have been especially tragic if Roberts had come to harm during this reconnaissance, for that night the pressure exercised by Eighth Army along the coast road convinced Rommel that further resistance at Tarhuna would be futile. 7th Armoured was able to resume its advance on the 22nd. It was checked for a time south of the great Castel Benito airfield by an enemy force holding a double anti-tank ditch but this was stormed by Lieutenant Colonel Roy Kaulback's 1/6th Queens on the night of the 22nd/23rd. By early morning, Roberts had set up his Tac HQ near the best hotel in Tripoli, from which he greeted Wimberley and his Highlanders as they entered the city from the east.

Two days later, Roberts handed over 7th Armoured to Erskine, Montgomery's acting Chief of Staff, and while awaiting the decision as to whether he would return to England or not, he requested leave in South Africa, to which his wife and children had been evacuated from Egypt after Italy's entry into the war. Montgomery 'was most sympathetic' and Roberts embarked on the first stage of his journey on 17 February.

On his return to the Middle East on 5 March, Roberts was advised that he would be sent not to England but to French North Africa where, it was hoped, he could pass on the benefits of his experience and his knowledge of Eighth Army methods and beliefs to the Allied forces there.

As a true pupil of Montgomery, Roberts was eager to oblige. He was initially attached to 1st US Armoured Division and visited all its regiments in turn talking informally to their officers and suggesting ways in which he could help them. The Americans 'could not have been more welcoming' and Roberts, for his part, was able to give good advice, particularly on the need for 'co-operation between all arms, armour, infantry and artillery' that of course had been one of Montgomery's principal aims. He was careful, though, to avoid the lack of tact and impression of superiority that Montgomery too often displayed and was rewarded by finding his listeners 'most attentive to anything I had to say'.

In late March, Roberts had the chance to give good advice to a British formation, taking command of 26th Armoured Brigade that formed part of 6th (British) Armoured Division. It had just exchanged its Valentines for Shermans, thereby giving Roberts 'a wonderful opportunity of putting my ideas across' without causing any offence or resentment: 'I did not have to say "In the Eighth Army we did this"; it was possible to say "Now, with the Sherman tank you can do this".'

The officers and men of 26th Armoured Brigade responded with 'spirit and enthusiasm'. Roberts 'felt that here was terrific material and I was sure that if given the opportunity they would do really well'. Unfortunately, he was soon to discover that whatever the case with his own brigade, the Allied forces in western Tunisia had still to become an effective fighting force. On 25 March, Alexander directed Patton's II US Corps to make a series of full-scale assaults towards the Gabes Gap from the north, hoping that these would trap Messe's men between the Americans and Eighth Army. Yet to Patton's fury, despite overwhelming odds in its favour, all II US Corps' attempts were repulsed. Montgomery took first the Mareth Line, then the Gabes Gap defences, but Patton's failures meant that Messe was able to withdraw safely. He was pursued by Eighth Army and harried from the air but his lines of communication remained open.

It was still possible to block Messe's retreat to Enfidaville if the Allies could break through the Fondouk Pass in time. Alexander therefore provided Patton with reinforcements and instructed him to clear the Pass, through which he would then send his Army Reserve, Lieutenant General Crocker's IX (British) Corps. Once again, though, the American attacks failed and on 8 April, Alexander ordered 6th (British) Armoured Division, which was part of Crocker's Corps, to capture the Pass regardless of casualties.

Such was the background to the appearance at Fondouk of Roberts and his 26th Armoured Brigade. Before delivering his assault on the Pass Roberts wisely intended to discover the extent of the minefields that he was certain would have been laid and to clear the hills on his flanks which were liberally covered with anti-tank guns. But Crocker who now arrived unexpectedly, no doubt with Alexander's imperative commands ringing in his ears, was not prepared to countenance any delay. 'In a not very friendly tone', he demanded that Roberts take immediate action. Roberts pointed out that this would prove expensive, but: '"Attack now," said the Corps Commander, and went off.' Roberts naturally obeyed orders but suffered very heavy losses, and it was not until the mines had been lifted and the anti-tank guns eliminated that the British armour finally emerged from the Fondouk Pass – too late to do more than capture a few stragglers.

'It was a useless and unnecessary loss of life and equipment,' Roberts complains angrily. He was little more impressed by the major Allied offensive that began on 22 April and was intended to deliver the final blow to the hapless remnants of the Axis forces in Tunisia. This gained some important positions, and better still, almost exhausted the German armoured formations' fuel and ammunition, but it was badly co-ordinated and had ground to a halt by the 28th. Roberts, who had come under heavy attack from enemy aircraft and whose Sherman tank had been blown up by a mine, happily without any casualties, concluded that the operation was 'just like Fondouk over again' – an observation not intended as a compliment.

But then, Roberts reports with relief, 'Horrocks came over from Eighth Army to take over IX Corps temporarily.' His enthusiasm and ability and the reinforcements Montgomery had sent with him had their effect, and Roberts declares that when the Battle of Medjerda began on 6 May, 'there were no real problems'. Tunis fell next day and by midday on the 13th, Roberts was directing his armour's fire against anti-tank guns that in turn were engaging Eighth Army's 56th Division. 'Soon after that,' Roberts concludes, 'everything collapsed and the Germans were surrendering on all fronts.'

Roberts, as his old leader Harding had once done, received the rare honour of a second bar to his DSO. He was also told that he would be returning home where, it was hinted, there would be the probability of a promotion. On 1 July, he set foot in England for the first time since the start of the war, to find his wife and family, whose departure from South Africa he had previously arranged, awaiting him. On 1 August, Roberts took over 30th Armoured Brigade and on 1 December, he did receive his promised promotion, becoming at the age of 37 the youngest major general in the British Army. His new command was 11th Armoured Division, which controlled two brigades, 29th Armoured equipped with Shermans and 159th Infantry, plus an 'armoured reconnaissance regiment', which at various times had Cromwell tanks or armoured cars, two artillery regiments with 25-pounder guns, one anti-tank gun regiment and one light AA regiment; 'I could not have wished for anything better,' Roberts declares.

It was clear to all that the long-awaited 'Second Front' would take place in the summer of 1944 and Roberts set to work preparing his division for the great task ahead of it, concentrating particularly on improving the gunnery of his armoured brigade, practising the techniques of getting vehicles off landing craft onto beaches, and, as to be expected from one who had served under Montgomery, developing 'the co-operation between all arms which would be required', Roberts attended Montgomery's Presentation of Plans which he considered 'superb'. He felt that 'we could not possibly fail,' though 'I had a slight twinge of disappointment that we were not going to be one of the assault divisions.'

Indeed it was not until 11 June that Roberts personally came ashore in Normandy with a small Tac HQ. His division arrived over the next few days but its build-up, like that of the rest of VIII Corps of which it formed part, was interrupted by the great Channel storm. During this period, Roberts was summoned to see Montgomery, who wanted to know how 11th Armoured was shaping. Apart from Roberts himself and a few other experienced officers, the division had never seen combat before, but Roberts assured his chief that his men were ready to 'have a go' and were very eager to prove that they could fight just as well as any in the veteran formations that had seen action in North Africa.

They were soon to be given plenty of opportunities.

* * *

The first of these came at 0700 on 26 June, which marked the start of Operation EPSOM. For this Roberts and his 11th Armoured were joined by two infantry divisions, 15th Scottish and 43rd Wessex, the latter transferred to VIII Corps from XII Corps, each supported by an armoured brigade. Their orders were to cross first the River Odon, a tributary of the Orne, then the Orne itself, thereby threatening Caen from the south and, it was hoped, forcing the Germans to employ their armoured reserves in the city's defence.

This was a matter of urgency because the great storm, by disrupting the Allied build-up and grounding the Allied Air Forces, had given Rommel a priceless opportunity to receive reinforcements. Four panzer divisions, 2nd, 21st, 12th SS and Panzer Lehr, were already committed to opposing Second British Army, but 1st SS from Belgium and 2nd SS from the south of France had by now also reached Normandy, while 9th SS and 10th SS were just arriving. Their presence had been revealed to Montgomery by 'Ultra', as had the intention of both Hitler and Rommel to use them against First US Army, then still completing its conquest of the Cherbourg Peninsula, prior to making its long-envisaged thrust south through St Lô to Avranches.

Since such a development would have ruined his whole basic strategy, Montgomery dared not delay the date of EPSOM – already postponed by the storm – even though it would have to proceed under a number of disadvantages. VIII Corps was not yet at full strength and the supply of ammunition to it was five days behind schedule. A preliminary attack on the previous day by XXX Corps, designed to secure VIII Corps' right flank, had failed to gain its objectives and there was no time for a fresh attempt to be made. And Montgomery had his usual ill-luck with the weather that prevented the Allied airmen from making a planned strike on enemy strongholds and from giving close support throughout 26 June.

In addition to these particular difficulties, Roberts and his men had problems common to all the Allied armoured formations in Normandy. The chief of these was that their tanks were inferior to those of the enemy. The earlier Matildas and Valentines, slow but heavily-armoured, had been replaced by the Churchill, but this was now rarely used in combat with the German tanks, serving instead in a variety of specialized forms, of which the chief was the 'Crocodile' equipped with a hideously effective flame-thrower. Normandy did, however, see the first appearance of the Cromwell, which carried a 75mm gun and, despite having armour of much the same thickness as the old Matilda, was very manoeuvrable and, with a speed of 40 mph, faster than any of its German opponents. Also present was the familiar Sherman, by this time extremely reliable, easy to maintain and, since February 1944, armed with a much superior high-velocity 76mm gun.

Against these, the Germans could employ three different types. There was the Mark IV Special with that long-barrelled 75mm gun that had so alarmed Roberts long ago at Alam Halfa. There was the Mark V 'Panther' which with a 75mm gun, 80mm armour and a speed of 28 mph, possessed an ideal mixture of fire-power, protection and rapidity. There was the Mark VI, the notorious 'Tiger', with its lethal 88mm gun, 102mm armour-plate and a speed not far inferior to that of any Allied tank then in use except the Cromwell. All three were superior in strength of armour and in the range and penetration of their fire-power to any standard Allied tank that saw action in Normandy.

It was an unhappy situation and despite later criticism, Montgomery was surely right in attempting to 'play down' the issue, so as to avoid a repetition of the harm done to morale during the earlier Desert campaigns by constant talk of German tank superiority – which had then not even been true! Moreover, the critics fail to mention the positive steps that he took to mitigate his armoured divisions' difficulties. In *The Battle for Normandy* (written in collaboration with Eversley Belfield, who also served in Normandy but with the Canadian Army), Major General Essame points out that Montgomery tried to counter the superior German armour by skilful use of the superior Allied artillery and air arm – as indeed he would do in EPSOM. He also on his personal initiative 'pressed on as rapidly as he could with the conversion of the Shermans into "Fireflies"' – which mounted the British 17-pounder gun. Some 600 of these were ultimately produced but such adaptations took a considerable time and Montgomery, as Roberts relates, therefore spread what 'Fireflies' were available equally among the various Sherman-equipped units. Nonetheless, the fact remained that even the 'Fireflies' were only slightly superior to the Mark IV Specials and still undeniably inferior to the Panthers and Tigers.

When it is added that the Germans had more effective anti-tank guns and the advantage of fighting on the defensive from prepared positions, it can be seen how severe a test faced 11th Armoured Division. Even the country over which it would have to fight was not of a type that an armoured commander would wish to encounter. This was the 'bocage', an area of tiny fields separated by thick hedges and high banks of earth covered with a profusion of trees and bushes, the claustrophobic atmosphere of which inhibited many of those who had fought in the open spaces of the desert, including perhaps the VIII Corps' Commander.

Lieutenant General Sir Richard O'Connor was the officer who had inflicted the spectacular defeat on the Italians in Operation COMPASS and the subsequent conquest of Cyrenaica but had then been taken prisoner during Rommel's first offensive. When Italy collapsed, he was able to make his way to the Allied lines, which he reached in November 1943. He took over VIII Corps on 21 January 1944 amid general approval: Montgomery, for instance, had suggested him as a suitable leader of Eighth Army.

Sadly, however, as head of VIII Corps, O'Connor did not live up to his high reputation. Possibly this was because his dashing temperament was ill-suited to the savage close-quarter brawls in the 'bocage'. Or it may be that his long captivity had 'taken its toll': this at least was Montgomery's opinion. On the other hand, Roberts considers that O'Connor's best-handled operation was a strictly limited one on the west bank of the River Maas as late as mid-October 1944. This may indicate that O'Connor – whose great triumph had been won against an Italian army, greatly superior in numbers but neither prepared nor equipped for modern warfare – simply took time to appreciate how very different it was to fight well-led, well-trained and well-equipped Germans, not to mention fanatical SS troops.

Whatever the cause, Roberts, though he accepted that O'Connor was 'one of the straightest and most honourable men that I have ever met', considered that many of his Corps Commander's tactical decisions were most unfortunate. So for that matter did O'Connor's own immediate superior, General Dempsey. A number of disagreements between them ended in late October when O'Connor requested that he be relieved of his command. Dempsey did not try to dissuade him and Montgomery made no attempt to intervene: he had also concluded that O'Connor was 'often only a ghost of his former self and that a new leader of VIII Corps was needed'.[3]

Roberts first disagreed with O'Connor on the opening day of EPSOM. The Corps Commander had ordered 11th Armoured's 'Recce Regiment', 2nd Northants Yeomanry, to 'rush' the bridges over the Odon. 'I never had much hope of this succeeding,' declares Roberts, 'unless the enemy were highly disorganized and virtually in flight' – which he was sure was not likely to happen. His protests were ignored; the move was duly made and duly failed; and the only consolation that Roberts could find was that the Yeomanry lost 'a number of tank casualties but fortunately not many men'.

By the end of the day, VIII Corps had still not reached the Odon and on the 27th, while 43rd Wessex Division consolidated and strove to widen the salient so far captured, 11th Armoured and 15th Scottish Divisions attempted to resume the advance. Roberts was still not happy because O'Connor had taken no steps to ensure co-ordination of effort between the two attacking divisions. He generously accepts that 'no doubt this was to some extent my fault', but when after the battle O'Connor suggested that it might be difficult to use 11th Armoured effectively 'in the country we are likely to be operating in', Roberts would make the tart comment: 'I felt that with closer co-operation between the infantry and the armour, we might get along reasonably well.'

Despite this lack of co-operation, VIII Corps made steady, if slow, progress during 27 June, and that evening, captured a bridge over the Odon intact. By next morning, 11th Armoured Division was across the river and its 29th Armoured Brigade and some infantry units battled forward against increasing opposition to take Hill 112 – so called from its height in metres – where they were joined in the afternoon by 44th Royal Tanks from 4th Armoured Brigade, the formation supporting 15th Scottish Division. Rather oddly, the new arrivals were not put under 11th Armoured's command but Roberts tactfully decided that: 'I would only be an unnecessary cog in the wheel if I tried to control them.'

O'Connor now wanted to continue his advance to the River Orne but Dempsey refused. It has since been claimed that his caution lost a splendid chance of achieving EPSOM's objectives – by which is meant its territorial objectives. Yet the majority of those who took part in the operation strongly doubt whether VIII Corps could possibly have reached the Orne in any event. Resistance was increasing: 1st and 2nd

SS Panzer Divisions had already joined the ranks of the defenders and 9th and 10th SS Panzer Divisions were about to do so. The attackers had suffered very high casualties, particularly 15th Scottish Division, and were faced with ever more difficult terrain. Major General Essame reports that 'it became desperately hard to push on up the well-fortified slopes beyond the far bank of the Odon Valley', while Roberts who visited the top of Hill 112 on 28 June, recalls that 'there was no way' of getting beyond it as it 'was well covered from several directions'.

In short, to quote Roberts again, VIII Corps was 'out on a limb' and if it had somehow managed to reach the Orne regardless of losses, the long, narrow salient it would have created – even north of the Odon, this was no more than some 2 miles wide – could have been supplied only by a single road well within range of German artillery, and would have been very vulnerable to the counter-attacks by fresh German armoured divisions, which Intelligence reports had revealed were already being prepared. It was thus inevitable, Roberts felt, that: 'We would have to go over to the defensive.'

So also thought Montgomery, but he was far from being depressed by this, since he had never been very interested in gaining ground, as long as he could thwart any major German attack on Bradley. The knowledge that all the newly-arrived panzer divisions were committed to opposing Dempsey instead was not a 'consolation prize' as has been suggested, but evidence that EPSOM, in Essame's words, 'had achieved a notable success'.

This success was emphasized by the losses that the Germans suffered in their counter-attacks on 29 and 30 June. Many of their tanks were put out of action by Typhoons before they could even reach the battle area. Many more were immobilized by fighter-bomber strikes against their precious petrol-tankers. Still others were destroyed by the Allied artillery. And when they did come into action, their effectiveness was further reduced by the fighting taking place at very close quarters where the stronger German armour-plate was most vulnerable, the longer range of the German guns was irrelevant, and conditions generally favoured the defenders.

In consequence, VIII Corps was able to retain almost all its salient south of the Odon and the only loss was that of Hill 112, which was abandoned during the night of 29/30 June. This would later be considered a grievous error, but it did not seem so to the men of VIII

Corps at the time. Roberts certainly approved of the retirement from this 'exposed position'; he had again personally gone to Hill 112 on the 29th, been shelled, and decided to 'withdraw with what dignity I could'. Essame reports that the hill was subjected to 'murderous and sustained' fire that was beginning to cause 'intolerable losses'. It has been pointed out that subsequent attacks on the hill would prove long and costly but at least these were made as part of a new offensive. On 29 June, the present offensive had come to a halt, there was 'no way' of moving forward from Hill 112 as Roberts had already observed, and any troops remaining on or brought up to it would, therefore, have had to endure the shelling and the 'intolerable losses' without any real purpose.

Moreover, as it transpired, even this withdrawal added to the Germans' problems. Chester Wilmot sums up their situation at the end of EPSOM as follows: 'By his timely thrust Montgomery compelled them to commit their armoured reserves piecemeal and in haste; then by assuming the timely defensive he was able to inflict on the SS Panzer Divisions a costly defeat; and finally, by withdrawing his armour into reserve at the height of the battle, he re-created the threat of a major offensive in the Caen area.'

And there was one other result of EPSOM, though not of EPSOM alone but of the continuous British efforts 'to protect the eastern flank of First US Army'. While VIII (British) Corps was fighting its way to the Odon, VII US Corps finally took Cherbourg. Montgomery, on 18 June, had declared that 'Caen is really the key to Cherbourg', a remark that aroused some sarcasm at the time, which would later increase in direct proportion to the distance in time and space between the person uttering it and the battlefield. Yet the protection that the fighting at Caen gave to the Americans advancing on Cherbourg can be summarized very easily: in mid-June, there were seventy German tanks opposing First US Army and 520 opposing Second British Army; by the end of EPSOM, there were 140 German tanks on the American front and 725 holding the British back from Caen.

If such considerations seem to have been of little interest to Montgomery's critics, they were horribly apparent to his professional opponents. On 28 June, they drove General Friedrich Dollmann, the unfortunate head of Seventh Army, to his death, either from suicide or more probably from a heart attack induced by worry. He was replaced by SS General Hausser, later to be so badly wounded in the 'Falaise

Pocket', who was shortly to urge the abandonment of Caen and a retirement to the south – a recommendation seconded by Geyr von Schweppenburg, chief of Panzer Group West.

These proposals echoed the wishes of von Rundstedt and Rommel, who were already pleading, in the former's words, for 'a free hand to order extensive adjustments to the front', which was a tactful way of describing withdrawals. By 1 July, von Rundstedt could tolerate the situation no longer: he ordered plans for retreat to be prepared at once. They were promptly countermanded by Hitler and the next day von Rundstedt was relieved of his command. Geyr von Schweppenburg was also dismissed and succeeded by General Eberbach. Hitler retained Rommel for the time being but refused to promote him to C-in-C, West, giving that post to Field Marshal Günther von Kluge whom the Führer believed, quite wrongly, to be his loyal supporter.

In any case, Rommel's days even as Commander of Army Group 'B' were numbered. On 17 July, his staff car was strafed by a low-flying Allied aircraft, almost certainly a Spitfire of 412 Squadron, Royal Canadian Air Force flown by the appropriately named Flight Lieutenant Charles Fox. Rommel's driver was fatally wounded, the car crashed, and the 'Desert Fox', unconscious and with a fractured skull, was carried to a nearby village, which, by a further curious quirk of fate, was named Sainte Foy de Montgomery.[4]

That Montgomery's strategy was succeeding was also appreciated by General Omar Bradley – as well it might be, for when First US Army's long-planned offensive southward from the Cotentin Peninsula began on 3 July, the diversion of German strength to the eastern front had given it a superiority of three to one in infantry and eight to one in tanks. Even so, the Americans soon learned that German fixed positions in 'bocage' country presented a formidable obstacle, and their slow progress compelled Montgomery to distract the enemy with further assaults by Second British Army, one of which, as we saw earlier, finally captured Caen. It is worth adding that Montgomery uttered no word of impatience or reproach and refused to harry Bradley into premature action. Not everyone proved capable of similar restraint.

The problems on the American front had greatly concerned Eisenhower who, on 7 July, suggested that the decisive attack might perhaps be delivered on the Caen front instead. Montgomery replied that he wished to stick to the original plan but his knowledge that

Eisenhower's anxieties would increase the influence of critics such as Tedder served to cloud his normally clear vision. When on 10 July, Dempsey expressed a belief that a breakout in the east would indeed be possible, it seems that Montgomery wavered and decided on a potentially dangerous compromise.

By 12 July, the plans for Operation GOODWOOD were taking shape. Dempsey was to transfer 7th Armoured and Guards Armoured Divisions to join Roberts and his 11th Armoured Division in VIII Corps, which would strike out of the Allied bridgehead east of the Orne, sweep first east then south of Caen, and seize the important Bourguebus Ridge and the road to Falaise. I (British) Corps would protect O'Connor's left flank, II Canadian Corps would clear those suburbs of Caen that lay beyond the Orne, and the Allied Air Forces would give maximum assistance. The date of the offensive was fixed for 18 July.

Dempsey was confident that he could penetrate the enemy defences and though he never intended to advance towards Paris as Eisenhower apparently came to believe, he did mean to capture 'all the crossings of the Orne from Caen to Argentan'. This would have threatened the rear of the German forces facing Bradley, though despite Liddell Hart's contention to the contrary, they would not have been trapped since they could always have escaped south of Argentan, just as the Americans would wheel south of it when the Allied breakout was really achieved.[5]

Montgomery was more doubtful. He would claim in his *Memoirs* that he had 'never at any time' contemplated any breakout in the east but it seems, as General Fraser says, that he had at least 'envisaged' some 'exciting possibilities' there, especially at this early date when it was hoped that the American advance to Avranches – Operation COBRA – would begin on 19 July, and so follow closely on the heels of GOODWOOD. His refusal to admit this was doubly unwise because not only would it give ammunition to his critics but, as Fraser points out, such adaptability 'was surely good generalship to be declared, rather than disavowed . . . He was a better general than autobiographer.'

At the same time, Fraser accepts that Montgomery 'had no intention of letting Second Army overreach itself', and in particular, no intention of sacrificing his armour, which might prove very vulnerable if it attempted to reach Falaise, let alone Argentan. And, as Liddell Hart points out, while Montgomery was ready to exploit a German collapse should one occur, he 'was not banking on it'. It would be sufficient for his purposes if VIII Corps gained the Bourguebus Ridge, retained the German armour in the east, and mauled it as much as possible, and he sent written confirmation of this to both Dempsey and O'Connor on 15 July.

As for any subsequent exploitation to Falaise, Roberts, whose division would provide the spearhead of the offensive, dismisses this as 'just a nice idea if the miraculous happened'. With every day that passed it became more obvious that it would not. The Americans only reached St Lô on 18 July, the day when GOODWOOD began, and could not possibly embark on COBRA in time to influence Second Army's assault. Intelligence reports made it equally clear that the Germans, having detected the movements of O'Connor's tanks, had realized the offensive was going to be delivered from the Orne bridgehead; they were sending reinforcements to the threatened area and strengthening and deepening its defences. Even Dempsey had apparently accepted the situation by 17 July; his orders to O'Connor on that day mentioned only that VIII Corps must 'establish' its armour in the Bourguebus area.

Unfortunately in previous signals Dempsey had reflected his original optimistic beliefs and specifically mentioned Falaise as one of his objectives, much to the delight of the airmen, who thought that at last they were about to gain their missing aerodrome sites. Equally unfortunately, Montgomery's own comments at this time lacked their usual uncompromising clarity and could be misinterpreted. Thus in a letter to Brooke of 14 July, he declares that: 'The possibilities are immense: with 700 tanks loosed to the south-east of Caen and armoured cars operating far ahead, anything may happen.' Yet in fairness, he records flatly in the same letter that his offensive was 'designed to write off and eliminate the bulk of the enemy's holding troops. I doubt if he can collect more troops to rope us off again *in the west* and it is in the west that I want territory.'

These statements, moreover, were not really inconsistent. Montgomery's 'design' in GOODWOOD was to tie down and 'write off' the German forces on the Caen front so as to prepare the way for the American breakout in the west; more dramatic achievements were 'possibilities', not essentials. Montgomery would later be accused of neglecting to keep either Eisenhower or his own Twenty-First Army Group staff properly informed, but the suggestion would have astonished de Guingand and Montgomery's Military Assistant, Lieutenant Colonel Christopher Dawnay, who on 14 July, were sent to Eisenhower and Brooke respectively with orders to make these considerations clear beyond doubt.

That the Supreme Commander (but not Brooke) did misunderstand Montgomery's intentions was therefore mainly his own fault: possibly he heard only what he longed to hear. Nonetheless, in the tense, heated atmosphere of early July it was certainly unwise of Montgomery to have made dramatic comments about how 'decisive' GOODWOOD might prove. Furthermore, while Montgomery tried to give Eisenhower the full picture, Roberts for one considers that he did nothing to warn the airmen that Dempsey's hopes of reaching Falaise were highly optimistic, 'for fear of having the bombing programme' – which he considered of crucial importance – 'reduced'. This was no doubt very reprehensible of him – until one notes the comments of Leigh-Mallory that Tedder and Coningham had adopted a 'policy of double dealing, the effect of which has been to deny the Army what it wanted in the field', and of Dempsey that 'the air people' as he tactfully calls them, 'were almost guilty of disloyalty'.

The 'bombing programme' was not reduced and starting at 0530 on 18 July, 1,000 British 'heavies' attacked the German positions on the flanks of VIII Corps' line of advance. At 0700, some 400 American medium bombers joined in, dropping anti-personnel bombs along the line of advance itself, and at 0745, Roberts ordered his 11th Armoured Division forward. The aerial bombardment had appalled and confused the defenders as well as inflicting heavy casualties on men and tanks, so Roberts encountered little resistance at first, captured considerable numbers of stunned prisoners and saw his 29th Armoured Brigade cover some 6 miles to reach a 20-foot-high railway embankment just short of the Bourguebus Ridge – where problems started to accumulate.

Behind 29th Armoured's advance, matters were already going badly. Only 11th Armoured Division had been able to occupy the restricted Orne bridgehead prior to GOODWOOD; when the operation began, Guards Armoured and 7th Armoured had first to cross both the river and the Canal de Caen, which ran parallel to it. They then had to get through a minefield laid by the British to protect their salient, but O'Connor had decided not to have this cleared but only to make gaps through it in a vain attempt to achieve surprise. Roberts had felt that these gaps were in any case 'quite inadequate' and urged that they be increased in number and width. 'In the end,' he reports, 'it was just all right, but only just.' In reality, while the gaps may have been sufficient for 11th Armoured, they caused massive delays for the other two divisions, which were increased by poor traffic control.

O'Connor's tactics also proved far from impressive. In particular there was, says Major General Essame, 'a lamentable lack of co-operation between the infantry and the armour', one aspect of which had become clear to Roberts even before the operation began. He had originally been given orders that on reaching the Bourguebus Ridge, 29th Armoured Brigade would take up station on the right of VIII Corps but only after capturing the strongpoint of Cagny on the Corps' left flank. Roberts thought this 'a stupid arrangement', especially since it would require the help of infantry and he had been deprived of his 159th Infantry Brigade. This had been detailed to take Cuverville and Demouville, fortified villages to the west of 29th Armoured's line of advance. Roberts had argued, verbally and in writing, that they should be left to 51st Highland Division, which had been holding the Orne salient, but O'Connor had curtly refused, though he did agree that 29th Armoured might 'mask' Cagny rather than seizing it.

Roberts reluctantly felt that 'I really had no alternative but to accept' the situation, but it would cause him immense difficulties on 18 July. As 29th Armoured passed Cagny, anti-tank guns opened fire from the flank and it had suffered heavy losses among its Shermans before it even reached the railway embankment. Then south of this it was faced with other strongpoints, behind which on the Bourguebus Ridge were heavy guns, including seventy-eight 88mms, that earlier attacks by US Flying Fortresses had left almost entirely unscathed. Progress halted abruptly and Roberts, who had been shelled twice already on his way forward, again became a target and was forced to seek shelter in a slit trench.

The mistakes previously mentioned meant that Roberts received virtually no support from the rest of VIII Corps. Guards Armoured began to come up at about 1000, but when it approached Cagny it lost nine Shermans to anti-tank guns and, greatly overestimating the strength of the opposition, it did not succeed in capturing the village until 1600. The advance guard of 7th Armoured Division only reached the front line at 1800, too late to be of service. And even its own 159th Infantry Brigade could not come to 11th Armoured Division's aid. It had captured Cuverville by 1015, but O'Connor ordered it to make no further advance until it was relieved – ironically by a battalion from 51st Highland Division, which Roberts had requested take the position in the first place. In consequence, 159th Brigade could only set out for Demouville at midday, and having taken this, was again ordered to wait for relief by the Highlanders. It was 1800 before it was able to move on to join Roberts and it is little wonder that he recalls feeling 'so soured up by the Corps Commander's orders to be responsible for taking these two damned villages!'

During the night, German reserves strengthened their positions on and around the Bourguebus Ridge and VIII Corps was compelled to try to subdue these one by one. Roberts, whose day had begun with more shellfire that, he reports indignantly, had spilled his tea, captured the village of Bras on a spur of the Ridge and other small gains were made but the Ridge itself remained out of reach. On 20 July, a tremendous thunderstorm broke, the ground was reduced to a quagmire and Operation GOODWOOD came to a premature end.

O'Connor had lost over 400 tanks, but it should be remembered that only about a third of these were destroyed, the rest being recovered later, and that the tanks' crews had suffered reasonably lightly, making later talk of a 'death ride' somewhat ridiculous. Moreover, the German tank casualties, though much fewer in number, were at least equally serious, as their total armoured strength was considerably smaller and their losses much less easy to replace. Nonetheless, the scanty territorial gains made, even including the remaining suburbs of Caen that had fallen to the Canadians on 18 July, seemed a poor return for so much cost and effort. To make matters worse, on the evening of the 18th, Montgomery had received Intelligence reports that the Bourguebus Ridge was in Allied hands. Delighted that the armour had taken its main objective and perhaps thinking that he might now be able to get to Falaise after all and silence his critics in the air rorces, he gleefully passed on the news to Brooke and, as he admits in his *Memoirs*, was far 'too exultant' far too soon. Sadly, the reports were of course quite inaccurate and when this became apparent it resulted in widespread disillusionment.

It is perhaps not surprising that the 'Air Barons' should have redoubled their complaints, with Tedder raging that Montgomery had 'stopped his armour from going further' – though one might think that the Germans had had something to do with this – or that certain later critics should have eagerly echoed such comments. 'But the real achievements of the operation,' as Roberts rightly declares, 'are seldom mentioned.' GOODWOOD had forced both 2nd Panzer Division, ordered to take up station south of St Lô, and 116th Panzer Division, on its way to the same area from north of the Seine, to move to the Caen front instead – as during July did five of the six fresh German infantry divisions to reach the battle area. It had thereby left the way clear for Bradley and by convincing the Germans that the Allies intended to break out on the east, had distracted almost all their attention from him as well. On 25 July, COBRA struck, and its bite was soon to prove fatal.

Dempsey planned to support Bradley's advance with an attack south of Caumont by VIII Corps on 2 August, but Montgomery, in contrast to his doubts before GOODWOOD, strongly favoured this move and on 28 July, he gave orders that Operation BLUECOAT, as it was codenamed, should begin in two days' time and be made by both VIII and XXX Corps. 11th Armoured Division was stationed on the far right of the British advance, in touch with 5th US Infantry Division on the Americans' far left.

Roberts had by now achieved full co-ordination of the different arms within his division, its 29th Armoured Brigade containing infantry battalions and its 159th Infantry Brigade including tank regiments, and despite certain problems caused by the date of the operation being brought forward and some not very clear instructions from O'Connor, he was able to push 12 miles through the German defences. By the night of 1/2 August, his armoured cars were approaching the important road centre of Vire, which they reported to be only weakly held. 'However,' records Roberts, 'orders came through that Vire was within the American boundary and we were to keep clear of it.'

Though both Montgomery and Bradley were sensitive about interArmy boundaries, in fact the main reason for halting 11th Armoured Division was that it had outstripped the forces advancing on either side of it, and had it entered Vire it would have been left at the end of a long, narrow and isolated salient. Roberts was disappointed at the time, especially since Vire was not captured by the Americans until 4 August, but on reflection he admits to being 'rather thankful that we were not allowed to take it', and could instead fight off the inevitable counter-attacks from the nearby Perrier Ridge where he could be supported by the Allied artillery. In any case, BLUECOAT had fulfilled its purpose. The British advance had first diverted forces, including 9th and 10th SS Panzer Divisions, intended to oppose Bradley, and then tied them down, preventing them from being used in the Mortain counter-offensive. Nothing could now stop COBRA.

Roberts, whose division was placed under XXX Corps as from 12 August, took little part in the resulting destruction of the German armies in the Falaise 'Pocket' or the subsequent advance to the Seine, but it may be recalled that during the Allied dash into Belgium, 11th Armoured Division was responsible for the dramatic captures of Amiens and Antwerp. The former, described by Dempsey as 'a magnificent performance', also entailed the capture of General Eberbach, whom Roberts introduced to his new Corps Commander, Horrocks, looking, says the latter, 'exactly like a proud farmer leading forward his prize bull'. The seizure of Antwerp was a less complete success because although the docks were secured intact, the bridges over the Albert Canal were not: an omission that prevented the immediate continuation of the Allied advance.

Since 11th Armoured Division reached Antwerp in the evening of 4 September and the bridges were not blown up by the Germans until about 0900 next day, it is clear that they could have been seized easily enough. Some commentators have excused Roberts on the grounds that he received no specific instructions to do so, but perhaps most would agree with Wilmot that 'it is strange that so astute a divisional commander as Roberts did not secure the bridges immediately as part of his general brief to capture Antwerp'. Indeed, Roberts honestly admits that he was aware of his superiors' desire to continue the advance north of Antwerp and that regardless of whether he was ordered to or not, he should have taken the bridges as a matter of course, just as he had taken those over the Somme at Amiens. He declares:

'This was, I think, the worst mistake I made in the campaign.'

Yet Roberts was surely being unfair to himself. He had had every intention of securing those bridges but the vital information that would have ensured that he did so was not available. As he tells us:

There was a great shortage of maps which took us as far as Antwerp, and those that were available were very small scale;

Antwerp was a little red circle with a very thin blue line going through the middle of it, which was the Albert Canal . . . As it appeared on the map, if one captured the city one was automatically across the Canal.

In reality, the Canal was just north of the city and by the time Roberts found out, it was too late. Ironically then, the main cause of the disappointment was that the Allied advance had simply been too fast.

Had the advance continued, it seems unlikely that 11th Armoured Division would have taken part in it, since it was now exhausted and short of supplies. Similar considerations no doubt prompted Horrocks to choose Guards Armoured Division to spearhead MARKET GARDEN, though Roberts was 'a little disappointed' that his own division 'had not been selected for this great but hazardous operation'. Instead it returned to VIII Corps on 16 September, and began a series of actions to clear Holland of the enemy up to the west bank of the River Maas. Next, 29th Armoured Brigade retired to rest and re-equip, being replaced by 4th Armoured Brigade. This, together with 11th Armoured's existing 159th Infantry Brigade, then participated in the Battle of the Rhineland on 26 February 1945, as part of II Canadian Corps led by Lieutenant General Guy Simmonds. The Canadians pushed over the ridge between the fortified towns of Calcar and Udem in the face of fierce resistance; after which 11th Armoured and 4th Canadian Armoured Divisions raced on to the final German defensive position, called the Hochwald Layback. Here, though, they were checked until early on 4 March, when the enemy retired towards Wesel and subsequently over the Rhine.

Roberts confirms that this battle had been 'the most unpleasant' in which he ever fought, and the one which presented the greatest obstacles to his armour: 'impenetrable forests, impassable bogs, numerous craters, roadblocks, mines and every form of demolition'. Happily, after the crossing of the Rhine – in which Roberts was not involved, though he had a good view of it as a passenger in a light aircraft flown by Air Vice Marshal Broadhurst – his division would be operating in the open plains of North Germany. Moreover, 29th Armoured Brigade that now rejoined it, had replaced its Shermans with Comets – a development of the Cromwell with a new high-velocity 77mm gun, which provided a considerable improvement in armour-piercing capacity over that of the standard Sherman, if not of the 'Firefly'.

For this final campaign, 11th Armoured Division was once more back in VIII Corps, now commanded by Lieutenant General Evelyn Barker, with whom Roberts 'got on well'. Roberts again used his two brigades as mixed armour and infantry formations and on suitable terrain, in improving weather, these made steady progress. It was 159th Brigade that liberated Belsen, which Roberts describes as 'absolutely ghastly' and 'the worst and most horrible thing I have ever seen in my life'.

On 19 April, 11th Armoured was brought to a halt at the River Elbe, over which the last bridge had just been blown up, and when it was able to cross on the 30th, the objective given to it was not Berlin, as Roberts had hoped, but the city of Lübeck on the shores of the Baltic. By this time, says Roberts, 'the opposition was sporadic' and 11th Armoured covered the 60 miles to Lübeck in two days, taking large numbers of German prisoners and liberating large numbers of Allied ones in the process. Its capture, as Dempsey generously acknowledged, 'set a seal on the truly great achievements' of Roberts and his men.

Roberts personally, as he tells us, 'was given one final task'. He was sent to Flensburg, also on the Baltic but very close to the Danish frontier. Here Hitler's successor, Grand Admiral Karl Dönetz, and the staff of Oberkommando der Wehrmacht (OKW), the Supreme Command of all the German Armed forces, had taken refuge and Roberts had been told to make it clear to them that they must henceforth take their orders from Montgomery's Tac HQ, pending final instructions from Supreme Allied Headquarters. He was accompanied by Lieutenant Peter Heath, an Intelligence Officer who would act as his interpreter, and who later recounted with amusement that the Germans, all of them in splendid uniforms covered with medals, found it hard to believe that Roberts really was a major general: he was not remotely pompous, he was wearing ordinary battledress, and above all he was far too young. Roberts had indeed come a long way, figuratively as well as literally, since he had exchanged machine-gun fire with that Italian fighter five years earlier.

Notes:

1. All details of the Allied and Axis tanks which fought in the Desert, as set out hereafter, can be confirmed from the *Official History* (Volume III); from *The Tanks* (Volume II) by Captain B.H. Liddell Hart; and from *Tobruk* by Field Marshal Lord Carver.

2. It might be added that it was also superior to the gun in the original Shermans; this was a 75mm similar to that in the Grants but with the advantage of being installed in the turret.
3. Montgomery's views on O'Connor are set out in Nigel Hamilton's *Monty*, Volume III: 'The Field Marshal 1944–1976'.
4. Three days later, came the famous attempt to kill Hitler with 'the bomb in the briefcase'. Four staff officers died but the dictator miraculously escaped with comparatively minor injuries, to take a terrible revenge on the conspirators. Rommel, who had been in contact with some of them, though he had neither approved of Hitler's assassination nor translated talk into action of any kind, was given the choice of arrest or suicide. He was promised – truthfully – that if he chose the latter and so avoided a dangerous scandal, he would receive a state funeral and his family would not be harmed. On 14 October 1944, he swallowed a poison capsule. Von Kluge, who had been similarly implicated, had already done the same on 18 August.
5. Of course Hitler might have prevented his soldiers from escaping by forbidding any withdrawal, but that does not alter the fact that they would not have been *trapped*.

Chapter 8

Latter Days

Great as was the relief and satisfaction that came with the end of the conflict in Europe, most of those who had been through it felt like de Guingand, that 'the past makes the future look pretty drab'. There was sadness also that the 'Monty team' of officers, both on the staff and in the field, was breaking up. Some like Leese and Harding were long gone, but now the process accelerated. One departure was particularly tragic. Colonel Joe Ewart, who had been an Intelligence Officer on Eighth Army's staff, Intelligence Chief at Twenty-First Army Group's Tac HQ with responsibility for handling the 'Ultra' interceptions, and Montgomery's interpreter for the surrender at Lüneburg, was killed on 1 July 1945, when his jeep struck a land-mine.

De Guingand's departure was another, if very different kind of tragedy. In July 1945, Montgomery was informed that he would become Chief of the Imperial General Staff when Brooke retired, though the appointment was only officially announced on 26 January 1946 and Montgomery did not take up the post until 26 June. In July 1945, as mentioned earlier, de Guingand was on sick leave but Montgomery was already considering him for Vice Chief (VCIGS) in due course. He therefore arranged with Brooke that de Guingand should be given experience at the War Office as Director of Military Intelligence, which de Guingand duly became on 19 September.

It was not a happy appointment. De Guingand was still far from well; his arrival was resented by those who disliked Montgomery or feared that only Montgomery's chosen subordinates could expect high office; and Brooke had never shared Montgomery's high regard for him. On 3 January 1946, Brooke – Viscount Alanbrooke, as he had become two days earlier – explained these problems to Montgomery and declared bluntly that he could never agree to de Guingand becoming VCIGS: 'I don't trust him. He is an unbalanced chap.'

In fairness to Brooke, it should be mentioned that in a few years' time, Eisenhower, a much greater friend and admirer of de Guingand, would not want him in a high administrative office either. During 1950, '51 and '52, de Guingand put out numerous feelers indicating his readiness to serve in some capacity in the North Atlantic Treaty Organization (NATO), of which Eisenhower had been appointed Supreme Commander in November 1950, and all his offers were courteously but firmly declined. In 1946 then, Montgomery who had immense respect for Brooke and acknowledged that the doubts he had raised were valid ones, could scarcely have been expected to dispute his judgement.

Nonetheless Montgomery's handling of an admittedly difficult and delicate situation was appallingly bad. He could surely have explained the circumstances fully and sympathetically, softening the blow as much as possible. On the contrary, he curtly told de Guingand that he did not want him 'for my Vice' on the grounds that 'it would not do me any good'. 'He then,' says de Guingand bitterly, 'rushed off.'

While many explanations have been given for Montgomery's disgraceful behaviour, it seems most probable that he was simply embarrassed by having to disappoint an ever-loyal subordinate, especially after having persuaded him to cut short his sick leave and undertake a task for which he had proved unsuited. He therefore got the unpleasant duty out of the way as quickly as possible and tried to forget about it. Perhaps also he did not appreciate just how grievous was the hurt that he had so unthinkingly inflicted.

For de Guingand's reactions, while not excusing Montgomery, do give further point to Brooke's comment that he was, at least at this time, 'an unbalanced chap'; when he recounted the event to his wife, he broke down in tears and he recorded a long series of complaints about Montgomery which when later made public would be seized upon eagerly by Montgomery's critics. It must therefore be said that they were by no means entirely fair. We are told, for instance, that Montgomery had assured de Guingand that his appointment as VCIGS was guaranteed, but de Guingand's own correspondence shows that this was never more than a good possibility; that de Guingand had received no new British honours since his knighthood in June 1944, but not that he had gained five foreign decorations all initiated by Montgomery; that Montgomery had not asked de Guingand to join him in a Victory

Parade through London, but not that none of the other leading commanders had invited their Chiefs of Staff either.

It should also be remembered that on 7 January 1946, Montgomery did try to make some amends by a letter acknowledging the debt he owed to de Guingand and promising that if there was another war, 'I would pull you straight in as Chief of Staff'. By mid-February, the two men were again corresponding amicably, but de Guingand could never entirely escape the feeling that he had been cruelly rejected by his old chief and since he could no longer see any future in his job at the War Office, he resigned from it on 26 February, to resume his sick leave, typically perhaps in Cannes. Here he decided to quit both the Army and England and in November, he and his family departed first to Southern Rhodesia and later to South Africa.

In his adopted country, de Guingand began a new life as a successful and influential businessman that culminated in the award of 'The Great Star of the Order of Good Hope', South Africa's highest decoration. Yet it would appear that he always secretly regretted that he was no longer a serving officer, as his attempts to persuade Eisenhower to consider him for a NATO post indicate. Moreover, he continued to be dogged by illnesses, including, towards the end of his life, a brain tumour, and it is sad to report that his divorce in 1957 only formally terminated a marriage that had been unsatisfactory for quite some years.

For all these reasons de Guingand never seems to have attained real happiness and it was therefore the more tragic that in 1967 came another rupture with his old leader. Arrangements had been made for Montgomery to visit the Alamein battlefield in May and de Guingand had expected to be invited to accompany him. When he wrote to Montgomery on the subject, however, he was curtly informed that Montgomery was taking only 'a very small party and a very "closed shop"'. De Guingand was naturally disappointed and all the resentment he had felt over his 'rejection' in January 1946 was re-awakened.

Montgomery's attitude is usually ascribed to jealousy, but he was probably prudent to restrict the numbers of his party severely since he and they were guests of the Egyptian government and diplomatic relations between Britain and Egypt had been severed more than ten years previously and not yet resumed. Montgomery was accompanied only by Leese and Mainwaring. Leese, as the commander of the crucial XXX Corps in the battle and subsequently the organizer of the official

Alamein Reunion functions was the obvious first choice, and had de Guingand gone as well, it might have been the turn of Horrocks, Montgomery's other Corps Commander, and perhaps Robertson, his Senior Administrative Officer, to feel aggrieved. The inclusion of Mainwaring is less easy to justify and it has been suggested that Montgomery was offering him a belated apology for having brought about his captivity by taking Eighth Army's HQ dangerously close to a retreating enemy. Perhaps, though, Montgomery's main reason was that Mainwaring, as a brigadier, was of sufficiently high – but not too high – a rank to act as a superior ADC – a role that he played to perfection.

Once again, if Montgomery had only explained his reasoning, much trouble could have been averted. Not only did he not do so but when de Guingand protested, Montgomery, whose eightieth birthday was to be celebrated on 17 November with a dinner at the Royal Hospital, Chelsea, threatened to exclude him from attending this as well. Happily he was persuaded to change his mind and de Guingand rightly formed part of a distinguished gathering that included Leese, Harding, Richardson, Robertson, Graham, Mainwaring, Dawnay and Williams. Cordial relations were somewhat tentatively resumed and after the old Field Marshal's death on 24 March 1976, de Guingand, although gravely ill himself, acted as a pall-bearer at the funeral, which took place at St George's Chapel, Windsor on 1 April. Thereafter he returned to Cannes where he had taken a flat in 1972, and in which he remained until his own death on 29 June 1979.

Of our six soldiers, only Leese had predeceased de Guingand – on 22 January 1978 – and he had enjoyed a longer life, having been born over five years earlier than de Guingand. All the other four not only outlived de Guingand but survived him by many years; for the sake of completeness we should perhaps record here the dates of their passing: Horrocks on 4 January 1985; Harding, the longest-lived of them all, on 20 January 1989; Richardson on 7 February 1994; Roberts on 5 November 1997, his ninety-first birthday. All inevitably suffered illness; Leese for instance had circulation problems, which necessitated his use of a wheelchair and ultimately the amputation of his right leg below the knee. All knew sorrow; Horrocks for example lost his daughter in a tragic accident when she was swimming in the River Thames. Yet with none of them is there that aura of unhappiness that follows de Guingand and it may be symbolic that his marriage was ended by divorce while those of all his colleagues was ended only by the death of one or other of the parties to it.

That included Richardson, the sole remaining bachelor at the end of the war. He married in 1947 and his new responsibilities led him to reject a call from de Guingand to come to South Africa; the correctness of this decision would be shown by the increasingly important military appointments that he received. By 1955, he was a major general and Commandant of the Royal Military College of Science at Shrivenham. In 1958, he became a Companion of the Bath; two years later, he was summoned to the War Office to establish a new Directorate of Combat Development, 'the "think tank" of the future army' as he calls it; and a year after that, he was appointed Director General of Military Training.

In 1962, Richardson's varied services were recognized by his being made a Knight Commander of the Bath; a year later, he was head of Northern Command; and he joined the Army Board in 1965 as Quartermaster General to the Forces. In 1967, he became a Knight Grand Cross of the Bath, Master General of the Ordnance and, for three years, ADC General to Queen Elizabeth II. He retired from the Army as a full general in 1971, but from 1972 to 1977, he was Chief Royal Engineer – a highly suitable honour for an officer who had, after all, begun his career as a sapper, even if he had successfully performed many other duties thereafter.

Harding, who proved equally versatile, also remained in the Army, to his and its advantage. In 1947, he returned from Italy to England, where he took over Southern Command; only to set off again in 1949 to Malaya as Commander-in-Chief, Far East Land Forces; shortly afterwards becoming a full general. Unfortunately, the climate did not suit his health, which soon began to decline badly. He was therefore delighted to return to Europe in 1951, to assume the leadership of the British Army of the Rhine; this in turn was followed by his appointment as Chief of the Imperial General Staff on 1 November 1952 and his promotion to field marshal on 19 November the following year.

During his time as CIGS, which lasted until September 1955, Harding once again gave valuable assistance to his old leader. On 1 November 1948, Montgomery had become Chairman of the Western Union Commanders-in-Chief Committee – the Western Union being a military alliance between Britain, France and the Low Countries, in which he had an almost obsessive belief. He had therefore been most concerned that his successor as CIGS was going to be Slim. Montgomery had recommended Crocker, then C-in-C, Middle East, for the post, since he was certain that Crocker would reassure the other members of Western Union that Britain would fight alongside them in the event of another European war. By contrast, he feared that Slim, an Indian Army officer who had spent the last three years of the Second World War in the Far East, would at best be indifferent to a 'continental strategy'.

This indeed proved to be the case. Slim promptly disavowed previous undertakings that Britain would guarantee to help defend France's frontiers – with the inevitable result that the French concluded that 'perfidious Albion' could not be trusted. This in turn made Montgomery's position as military head of Western Union all but impossible. Accordingly he decided, despite objections and warnings from Slim and the other Chiefs of Staff, that he would visit the United States in late 1949. NATO had formally come into being on 4 April of that year and Montgomery hoped that the Americans might give the French the promises they longed for. His hopes were justified: he was able to persuade them to make at least verbal declarations of support, and these would lead, on 2 April 1951, to Eisenhower setting up the Headquarters of NATO near Paris, taking over Western Union and appointing Montgomery his Deputy Supreme Commander.

By the time that Harding became CIGS, NATO was already well established, but he still felt the need to keep 'a watchful eye' on the situation. Eisenhower had left on 30 May 1952, shortly to be elected President of the United States. Most of NATO's officers had wanted his Chief of Staff, General Alfred Gruenther, to take over as Supreme Commander but the British Chiefs of Staff had again intervened, objecting that Gruenther lacked experience as a battlefield commander. In consequence, Eisenhower had been succeeded by General Matthew Ridgeway, who unfortunately proved unable to maintain the level of international co-operation that Eisenhower had achieved and for this reason was not regarded with favour by Montgomery. Harding had known Gruenther in Italy and, unlike Slim, he agreed with Montgomery that Gruenther would make a much better leader of NATO. On becoming CIGS therefore, he gave Montgomery steadfast support, while tactfully making sure he did not offend the Americans.

Gruenther did become Supreme Commander on 11 July 1953; he and Montgomery got on excellently; and Harding earned the gratitude of both by leaving the conduct of NATO affairs to them, yet always being ready to provide help and encouragement if required.

Harding in fact always retained his respect and affection for his old chief and in due course would, like de Guingand, be one of the pallbearers at Montgomery's funeral. Later on 30 October 1977, he would give the address at a service of dedication when a memorial window to Montgomery was unveiled in Sandhurst Chapel. For his part, Montgomery had approved of Harding's appointment as CIGS and, not surprisingly, valued his actions in that office very highly. Perhaps, though, that part of Harding's post-war career that is most often remembered is his service as Governor and Commander-in-Chief in Cyprus from October 1955 to October 1957, after which he retired from the Army. Cyprus had then been in the grip of terrorist violence and Harding once more found himself in the front line; he spent the night of 20/21 March 1956 blissfully unaware that there was a bomb under the mattress of his bed. Mercifully, this failed to explode; it was discovered next morning and was removed to a place of safety where it went off four minutes later. Harding afterwards declared that he 'had never slept better' than on the night in question.

If the military careers of Field Marshal the Baron Harding of Petherton (as he became in the 1958 New Year Honours List) and General Sir Charles Richardson, Chief Royal Engineer had flourished exceedingly, many of their colleagues followed the example of de Guingand and sought careers elsewhere. Roberts appropriately became Director of the Royal Armoured Corps at the War Office in 1948, and was also made a Companion of the Bath but a year later, he chose to be nearer to his family and left to become a successful businessman. He was only 42 and much as one admires his unselfish action, it is difficult not to feel that whatever others had gained, the Army was very much the loser.

Leese also decided at the end of the war that he must spend more time at home. He therefore declined posts at the head of the British Army of the Rhine and the British Troops in Palestine in favour of Eastern Command in England, retiring from this and from the Army at the end of 1946. It has been suggested that the military life had been soured for him by the activities of Mountbatten and Slim, but this seems unlikely as he would later send both of them cheerful congratulations on their subsequent appointments. Indeed, Leese always seemed much more concerned with other people's misfortunes than with his own – he was one of the principal protestors against Montgomery's threat to ban de Guingand from his eightieth birthday celebrations for instance – and his generosity extended not only to friends but to a former enemy.

In 1947, a British military tribunal found Field Marshal Kesselring guilty of the deaths of Italian hostages who had been killed in retaliation for a partisan bomb attack, and sentenced him to be shot. The verdict horrified most independent observers who pointed out that the real responsibility had been that of SS officers who were, at most, only nominally under Kesselring's command. Field Marshal Alexander led the protests but he was strongly supported by Churchill and Leese, and Leese later received a message from Kesselring saying he was 'honoured and touched' by the trouble taken on his behalf. It proved worthwhile, for Kesselring was reprieved and though sentenced to twenty years' imprisonment was released, officially on the grounds of ill health, in 1952.

It seems more likely that Leese left the Army because there were so many other things that he wanted to do. His management of the Alamein Reunions has already been mentioned and it was he who, after Montgomery's death, was the principal figure at the last of these in 1976. He became an enthusiast for cacti and other desert plants, which he both exhibited and sold commercially with great success, on which he wrote and lectured extensively, and in search of which he made several journeys abroad. In 1954, Alanbrooke, who had been made Constable of the Tower of London, chose Leese to be his Lieutenant, a post which Leese held for three years and that perhaps indicates Alanbrooke's final opinion of Leese's actions and achievements in the Far East. From 1962 to 1969, Leese was President of the Royal British Legion, which he rightly considered of tremendous importance. He also received several cricketing appointments and it was typical of him that whether these were President of his local club, Worfield near Wolverhampton, President of Warwickshire County Cricket Club, an office he held from 1959 to 1975, or President of the MCC, which he became in 1965, they all received his equal attention and all gave him equal pleasure.

Horrocks had been very sorry to learn of Leese's retirement, reflecting that they had 'served together very happily in many places and I hate seeing the old ties broken'. His own retirement, however, was soon to follow. In 1946, he had taken over Western Command but 'I kept on getting attacks of fever accompanied by pain and sickness.' Another operation was considered necessary and on recovery he was presented by his surgeon with 'a piece of my shirt which had been lurking in my bile duct ever since I was wounded at Bizerta'. By this time, Horrocks records: 'my stomach was beginning to resemble an abstract painting, with scars running in every direction.'

Prior to this operation, Horrocks had been chosen to head the British Army of the Rhine and, in his eagerness to become an Army Commander, he took up his post 'before I had properly recovered' – only to find that his health made it impossible for him to carry out his responsibilities. In 1948, he reluctantly took up civilian duties, the best-remembered being Gentleman Usher of the Black Rod in the House of Lords. He will be remembered still more, however, for his television appearances when he presented an outstanding series of programmes on the art of warfare, in which, despite a confessed dread of the television camera, his clarity, objectivity and personality ensured he would be an unqualified success. It was perhaps the culmination of that desire held by all Montgomery's pupils to pass on the lessons they had learned from him to the widest possible audience.

Retrospect

'All of us who were there at the time and knew the mess we were in and saw what he did for us – I think all of us would be "Monty men" for life.'

So, quite independently, at different times, but in identical words, both General Sir Charles Richardson and Major General 'Pip' Roberts described to the author the effect of Montgomery's arrival in the Middle East in August 1942. All our six officers were 'there at the time' or shortly afterwards and the loyalty that Montgomery then inspired in them and in many thousands of others was deep and lasting. As we have seen, they made immense contributions to his successes and to the Allied cause in general but none of them ever denied that he was the leader and the inspiration: Horrocks spoke for them all when he said that Montgomery had 'more influence on my life than anyone before or since'.

Not that this loyalty was ever given unthinkingly. As we have also seen, all our six officers had their own ideas and if they had any doubts about their chief's proposed course of action, they did not hesitate to say so – though they all accepted that the final decision was his and once it had been reached, no further argument was permissible. Nor were any of them unaware of his personal faults and foibles, over which they sometimes smiled, sometimes shook their heads in disbelief, and which they tried to avoid in their own conduct; it was simply that they regarded these as a trivial price to pay for the benefits of his leadership.

Their loyalty in fact rested on two firm foundations: gratitude and respect. The gratitude was earned by the way Montgomery guided and trained his subordinates. Horrocks records that, following Alam Halfa, Montgomery wrote to him, sending congratulations but also advising him of minor errors that had marred his performance. Far from being upset or offended, Horrocks telephoned his leader to say 'Thank you very much'. 'Who else,' demands Horrocks, 'on the day after his first major victory, which had altered the whole complexion of the war in the Middle East, would have taken the trouble to write a letter like this to one of his subordinate commanders?'

Montgomery's staff officers were equally appreciative of his interest and concern. De Guingand wrote to him on 2 June 1945: 'It is no good my trying to say all I feel, or to thank you adequately for all you have done for me . . . It has been a most wonderful experience for me. I was a very raw and untried Chief of Staff when you arrived to command Eighth Army. But under you I have learnt a lot. I owe you a debt for this alone.'

And the reason why all Montgomery's subordinates, whether field commanders or staff officers, so valued his guidance and were so determined to practise the lessons he had taught, even, perhaps especially, when they were not under his direct control, was that they had total respect for his ability. They were all career soldiers and when they describe Montgomery's actions and attitude, the word that appears over and over again is 'professional'. Richardson, the Cambridge scholar, believes that: 'Four talents marked him out as an exceptional leader: professionalism, self-confidence, an intuitive grasp of the psychology of leadership, and the ability to simplify the issues of battle', and adds that the first of these, which encompassed and informed the other three, 'was based on twenty-five years of profound study of war'.

Montgomery, Richardson concludes, 'was without doubt a supreme master of the battlefield'. How supreme is echoed by Richardson's colleagues. 'Greatly as I admired Alexander and Slim,' reports Harding, 'if I had to go to war again, I would sooner go under a plan prepared and conducted by Monty than by anybody else who lived through either war.' Leese, who had had a close view of how both Alexander and Slim conducted their battles, considers that Montgomery was 'the greatest soldier of our age', often 'most difficult and even exasperating' to his equals and superiors, yet 'as a commander to serve under on the battlefield, it's Monty for my money any day'.

So greatly did Montgomery's professionalism impress his subordinates that even the most charming and tactful of them were contemptuous of critics who, they felt, could not or did not appreciate his worth. Horrocks, referring to those who decried Montgomery for not being 'a dashing, romantic figure' in the way that, say, Rommel was, remarks caustically that admittedly one would be unlikely to find Montgomery 'leading a forlorn hope in person', but that was 'for the simple reason that if he was in command forlorn hopes did not occur'.

De Guingand states that many of the attacks on Montgomery's strategy in Normandy in particular were 'rather overdoing it' and that much of the criticism of Montgomery generally was 'ill-informed and unfair'. 'There were some at the time,' recalls Harding, speaking in 1977, 'and there are more now who write books and so on, who think they could have done better. For my part I am thankful they weren't given the chance to try.'

By the time the war ended, gratitude and respect had merged in a realization of the magnitude of Montgomery's achievements.

> 'I should like to close my reminiscences,' says Roberts, 'with a tribute to Monty. I do not believe there was anyone else at the time who could have won Alamein; I do not say that if we had lost Alamein we would have lost the war but it would certainly have prolonged it. . . . And then it is my view that no-one else could have won the invasion in Normandy; there were some setbacks, but the Seine was reached on the day he said it would be, and that made certain that the war in Europe would be won.'

With all respect to Roberts, however, perhaps it would be even more convincing to close with a different tribute. Only a year after his hopes of becoming Vice Chief of the Imperial General Staff had been cruelly dashed, de Guingand could still testify that he was one of Montgomery's 'greatest admirers'. As for 'the job he has done', de Guingand declares simply that the campaigns fought by Montgomery – and by Montgomery's chosen subordinates – represent the 'golden pages of the history of British arms'.

Acknowledgements & Bibliography

My thanks as always to all those who helped and in particular to: Pamela Covey, my editor; Brigadier Henry Wilson and his team at my publishers, Pen & Sword Books Ltd.; Andrew Hewson and his team at my Agents, Johnson & Alcock Ltd.; Sylvia Menzies-Earl for her assistance with the manuscript; the staff of the Taylor Library for their assistance with the photographs.

My thanks also to some who helped in a different way. The six officers who represent 'Monty's Men' were selected partly because their careers and characters are so varied but partly because a great deal about their personalities, beliefs and feelings has been revealed in reminiscences or biographies or, in the case of perhaps the most important, de Guingand, in both.

The memoirs, all extremely frank and open, are:
DE GUINGAND, Major General Sir Francis: 'Operation Victory', Hodder & Stoughton 1947.
HORROCKS, Lieutenant General Sir Brian: 'A Full Life', Collins 1960.
RICHARDSON, General Sir Charles: 'Flashback: A Soldier's Story' Kimber 1985.
ROBERTS, Major General G.P.B.: 'From the Desert to the Baltic', Kimber 1987.

The Biographies:
CARVER, Field Marshal Lord: 'Harding of Petherton', Weidenfeld & Nicolson 1978. Field Marshal Carver served under Harding in North Africa – he dedicates his 'El Alamein' 'To John Harding My Commander in the Battle' – and wrote this biography 'with Lord Harding's full approval and cooperation'.
RICHARDSON, General Sir Charles: 'Send for Freddie', Kimber 1987. 'Freddie' was de Guingand, of whom Richardson was a close friend as well as colleague.
RYDER, Rowland: 'Oliver Leese', Hamish Hamilton 1987. The author, who served with Eighth Army, was given 'unrestricted access' to Leese's papers, including Leese's own unpublished memoirs and, even more valuable, his letters to his wife. From September 1942 to July 1945, Leese wrote over 600 of these and though obviously he could not be completely candid, if only for reasons of security, they do give a faithful portrait of his character and his opinions.

These works provided the main sources as well as the inspiration for this study of some of Montgomery's ablest followers. With them should be coupled the definitive and detailed biography of the man whose career bound all theirs together:

HAMILTON, Nigel: 'Monty', Hamish Hamilton.
Three Volumes:
'The Making of a General 1887-1942' 1981.
'Master of the Battlefield 1942-1944' 1983.
'The Field Marshal 1944-1976' 1986.

To all the above my gratitude and my appreciation.

Further details of the six soldiers, their relationships with Montgomery and the campaigns in which they fought can be found in:

ALEXANDER, Field Marshal the Earl: 'The African Campaign from El Alamein to Tunis', *London Gazette Supplement* 1948.
ALEXANDER, Field Marshal the Earl: 'The Allied Armies in Italy', *London Gazette Supplement* 1950.
ALEXANDER, Field Marshal the Earl: 'The Conquest of Sicily', *London Gazette Supplement* 1948.
ARNOLD-FORSTER, Mark: 'The World at War', Collins 1973.
AUCHINLECK, Field Marshal Sir Claude: 'Operations in Middle East 1/11/41 to 15/8/42', *London Gazette Supplement* 1948.
BEEVOR, Antony: 'D-Day: The Battle for Normandy', Viking 2009.
BEHRENDT, Hans-Otto: 'Rommel's Intelligence in the Desert Campaign', Kimber 1985.
BELFIELD, Eversley and ESSAME, Major General H.: 'The Battle for Normandy', Batsford 1965.
BRYANT, Sir Arthur: 'The Turn of the Tide 1939-1943', Collins 1959.
BRYANT, Sir Arthur: 'Triumph in the West 1943-1946', Collins 1959.
CARELL, Paul: 'The Foxes of the Desert: The Story of the Afrika Korps', Macdonald 1960.
CARVER, Field Marshal Lord: 'Dilemmas of the Desert War: A New Look at the Libyan Campaign 1940-1942', Batsford 1986.
CARVER, Field Marshal Lord: 'El Alamein', Batsford 1962.
CARVER, Field Marshal Lord: 'The Imperial War Museum Book of the War in Italy 1943-1945', Sidgwick & Jackson 2001.
CARVER, Field Marshal Lord: 'Tobruk', Batsford 1964.
CHURCHILL, Sir Winston: 'The Second World War', Volume IV: 'The Hinge of Fate', Cassell 1951.
CLARK, Lloyd: 'Arnhem: Jumping the Rhine 1944 and 1945', Headline Review 2008.
CLARK, General Mark: 'Calculated Risk', George G. Harrap & Co 1951.
CLARKE, Sir Rupert: 'With Alex at War: from the Irrawaddy to the Po 1941-1945', Leo Cooper 2000.
COLLIER, Richard: 'The Sands of Dunkirk', Collins 1961.
CONNELL, John: 'Auchinleck', Cassell 1959.
DE GUINGAND, Major General Sir Francis: 'Generals at War', Hodder & Stoughton 1964.

ELLIS, John: 'Cassino: The Hollow Victory', Andre Deutsch 1984.
ESSAME, Major General H.: 'The Battle for Germany' Batsford 1969.
FOLLAIN, John: 'Mussolini's Island', Hodder & Stoughton 2005.
FRASER, General Sir David: 'Alanbrooke', Collins 1982.
FRASER, General Sir David: 'And We Shall Shock Them: The British Army in the Second World War', Hodder & Stoughton 1983.
FRASER, General Sir David: 'Knight's Cross: A Life of Field Marshal Erwin Rommel', HarperCollins 1993.
FULLER, Major General J.F.C. : 'The Decisive Battles of the Western World', Volume III, Eyre & Spottiswoode 1957.
FULLER, Major General J.F.C.: 'The Second World War 1939-1945', Eyre & Spottiswoode 1948 (Revised Edition 1954).
HIBBERT, Christopher: 'Anzio: The Bid for Rome', Macdonald 1970.
HIBBERT, Christopher: 'The Battle of Arnhem', Batsford 1962.
HINSLEY, F.H. with THOMAS, E.E., RANSOM, C.F.G. and KNIGHT, R.C.: 'British Intelligence in the Second World War: Its Influence on Strategy and Operations', Volume II, HMSO 1981.
HOLLAND, James: 'Together We Stand', HarperCollins 2006.
HOWARTH, T.E.B. (Edited): 'Monty at Close Quarters: Recollections of the Man'. Articles by: DAWNAY, Lieutenant Colonel C.P.: 'Inside Monty's Headquarters'; HARDING, Field Marshal Lord: 'In Memoriam'; WILLIAMS, Brigadier Sir Edgar: 'Gee One Eye, Sir', Leo Cooper 1985.
JACKSON, Robert: 'Dunkirk', Arthur Barker 1976.
JACKSON, General Sir William: 'The Battle for Italy', Batsford 1967.
JACKSON, General Sir William: 'The Battle for Rome', Batsford 1969.
JACKSON, General Sir William: 'The North African Campaign 1940-43', Batsford 1975.
KESSELRING, Field Marshal Albert: 'Memoirs', Kimber 1963.
KIPPENBERGER, Major General Sir Howard: 'Infantry Brigadier', Oxford University Press, 1949.
LEWIN, Ronald: 'Montgomery as Military Commander', Batsford 1971.
LEWIN, Ronald: 'The Life and Death of the Afrika Korps', Batsford 1977.
LEWIN, Ronald: 'Ultra Goes to War: The Secret Story', Hutchinson 1978.
LIDDELL HART, Captain B.H.: 'History of the Second World War', Cassell 1970.
LIDDELL HART, Captain B.H.: 'The Tanks: The History of the Royal Tank Regiment and its Predecessors', Cassell 1959.
LUCAS, James and BARKER, James: 'The Killing Ground: The Battle of The Falaise Gap August 1944', Batsford 1978.
LUCAS PHILLIPS, Brigadier C.E.: 'Alamein', Heinemann 1962.
LUNT, Major General James: 'A Hell of a Licking: The Retreat from Burma 1941-2', Collins 1986.
MACINTYRE, Captain Donald: 'The Battle for the Mediterranean', Batsford 1964.

MACMILLAN, Harold: 'The Blast of War', Macmillan 1967.
MAJDALANY, Fred: 'Cassino: Portrait of a Battle', Longmans, Green & Co 1957.
MAJDALANY, Fred: 'The Battle of El Alamein', Weidenfeld & Nicolson 1965.
MASTERS, David: 'With Pennants Flying: The Immortal Deeds of the Royal Armoured Corps', Eyre & Spottiswoode 1943.
MELLENTHIN, Major General F.W.von: 'Panzer Battles', Cassell 1955.
MERRIAM, Robert E.: 'The Battle of the Ardennes', Souvenir Press 1958. (Reissued as 'Battle of the Bulge' 1965).
MOLONY, Brigadier C.J.C.: 'The Mediterranean and Middle East', Volume V: 'The Campaign in Sicily 1943 and the Campaign in Italy 3rd September 1943 to 31st March 1944', HMSO 1973.
MOLONY, Brigadier C.J.C. and JACKSON, General Sir William with GLEAVE, Group Captain T.P.: 'The Mediterranean and Middle East', Volume VI: 'Victory in the Mediterranean', HMSO 1973.
MONTGOMERY, Field Marshal the Viscount: 'El Alamein to the River Sangro', Hutchinson 1948.
MONTGOMERY, Field Marshal the Viscount: 'Memoirs', Collins 1958.
MONTGOMERY, Field Marshal the Viscount: 'Normandy to the Baltic', Hutchinson 1947.
MOOREHEAD, Alan: 'Eclipse', Hamish Hamilton 1967.
MOOREHEAD, Alan: 'The Desert War: The North African Campaign 1940-1943', Hamish Hamilton 1965.
NICOLSON, Nigel: 'Alex: The Life of Field Marshal Earl Alexander of Tunis', Weidenfeld & Nicolson 1973.
OWEN, Roderic: 'The Desert Air Force', Hutchinson 1948.
PACK, Captain S.W.C.: 'Operation Husky: The Allied Invasion of Sicily', David & Charles 1977.
PARKER, Matthew: 'Monte Cassino', Headline 2003.
PLAYFAIR, Major General I.S.O. with FLYNN, Captain F.C., MOLONY, Brigadier C.J.C. and GLEAVE, Group Captain T.P.: 'The Mediterranean and Middle East', Volume III: 'British Fortunes Reach their Lowest Ebb', HMSO 1960.
PLAYFAIR, Major General I.S.O. and MOLONY, Brigadier C.J.C. with FLYNN, Captain F.C. and GLEAVE, Group Captain T.P.: 'The Mediterranean and Middle East', Volume IV: 'The Destruction of the Axis Forces in Africa', HMSO 1966.
RICHARDS, Denis: 'Royal Air Force 1939-1945', Volume I: 'The Fight at Odds', HMSO 1953.
RICHARDS, Denis and SAUNDERS, Hilary St G.: 'Royal Air Force 1939-1945', Volume II: 'The Fight Avails', HMSO 1954.
RICHARDSON, General Sir Charles: 'From Churchill's Secret Service to the

BBC: The Biography of Lieutenant General Sir Ian Jacob', Brasseys (UK) 1991.
ROMMEL, Field Marshal Erwin (Edited by LIDDELL HART, Captain B.H.): 'The Rommel Papers', Collins 1953.
ROONEY, David: 'Wingate and the Chindits: Redressing the Balance', Arms & Armour 1994.
SAUNDERS, Hilary St G.: 'Royal Air Force 1939-1945', Volume III: 'The Fight is Won', HMSO 1954.
SEATON, Albert: 'The Fall of Fortress Europe 1943-1945', Batsford 1981.
SLIM, Field Marshal the Viscount: 'Defeat into Victory', Cassell 1956.
SMITH, Brigadier E.D.: 'Battle for Burma', Batsford 1979.
SMITH, Michael: 'The Emperor's Codes', Bantam Press 2000.
SMITH, Peter C.: 'Pedestal: The Malta Convoy of August 1942', Kimber 1970.
STEWART, Adrian: 'Eighth Army's Greatest Victories', Leo Cooper 1999.
STEWART, Adrian: 'The Campaigns of Alexander of Tunis 1940-1945', Pen & Sword 2008.
STEWART, Adrian: 'The Early Battles of Eighth Army', Leo Cooper 2002.
STRAWSON, Major General Sir John: 'The Battle for Berlin', Batsford 1974.
STRAWSON, Major General Sir John: 'The Battle for North Africa', Batsford 1969.
STRAWSON, Major General Sir John: 'The Battle for the Ardennes', Batsford 1972.
THOMPSON, R.W.: 'The Battle for the Rhineland', Hutchinson 1958.
TREVELYAN, Raleigh: 'Rome '44', Secker & Warburg 1981.
TUKER, Major General Sir Francis: 'Approach to Battle', Cassell 1963.
TURNBULL, Patrick: 'Dunkirk: Anatomy of Disaster', Batsford 1978.
VERNEY, Peter: 'Anzio 1944: An Unexpected Fury', Batsford 1978.
WHITING, Charles: 'The Last Battle: Montgomery's Campaign April-May 1945', Crowood Press 1989.
WILMOT, Chester: 'The Struggle for Europe', Collins 1952.

War Diaries of the various Theatre Headquarters, armies, corps, divisions and brigades: Public Records Office, Kew.

General Index

Aachen, 124-5, 127-8, 167
Abbeville, 45
Adair, Major General A., 127
Adige River, 43
Adrano, 58-9
Agedabia, 179
Agheila El, 18, 30-1, 50, 85-6, 172, 179
Aircraft Types – Allied:
　Baltimore (Martin), 113, 151-2
　　Boston (Douglas), 113, 151
　　Dakota (Douglas), 66-68, 100
　　Flying Fortress (Boeing), 88, 106, 194
　　Halifax (Handley Page), 166
　　Hudson (Lockheed), 88
　　Hurricane (Hawker), 16, 68, 113, 150-1
　　Kittyhawk (Curtiss), 90, 113, 149-51
　　Lancaster (Avro), 166
　　Liberator (Consolidated), 46, 108
　　Mitchell (North American), 151, 163
　　Spitfire (Supermarine) : 151, 190
　　Typhoon (Hawker), 99, 101, 133, 163, 188
　　Warhawk (Curtiss), 151
Aircraft Types - Axis:
　　Fiat CR 42, 21, 171, 199
　　Junkers Ju 87, 31, 45, 113, 179
　　Mitsubishi Zero, 72
Air Forces - Allied, 43, 66, 128, 138, 148, 151, 160, 163-5, 193
See also: Desert Air Force
　Squadrons:
　　No. 6 RAF, 150-1
　　No. 20 RAF, 68
　　No. 250 RAF, 150
　　No. 260 RAF, 150
　　No. 412 RCAF, 190
Air Forces – Axis, 19, 78, 156
Akyab, 68
Alamein El, 1, 20-5, 28, 30, 60, 70, 81, 83, 110
Alamein El, Battle of, 15, 26-31, 43, 46-52, 54, 56, 76, 83-5, 108-109, 115-6, 123, 146-8, 178, 203-204, 208, 212
Alam Halfa Ridge, 14, 24-5, 110-14, 176-8
Alam Halfa, Batlle of, 25, 47-9, 82-3, 109, 113, 139, 143, 148, 150, 173, 176-8, 185, 210
Alam Nayil Ridge, 24, 110-11, 113-4
Albert Canal, 129, 197-8
Alencon, 101-102
Alexander, General, later Field Marshal Sir H., 15, 23-4, 26, 33-43, 46, 49, 52, 54-5, 57-8, 60, 63, 72, 80, 84, 90, 92-3, 108-109, 120-1, 139, 148-54, 156-7, 181-2
Alexandria, 19, 22, 80, 83, 110
Algiers, 55, 88, 151-55, 170
Allfrey, Lieutenant General C., 90, 92
Amiens, 127, 197
Anders, General W., 60-1

Anderson, Brigadier K., 108
Antwerp, 124, 127, 129, 131-3, 136, 197-8
Anzio, 35-6, 38-40, 60, 62, 158
Apennine Mountains, 34, 41, 90-1, 157
Arakan, 66, 73
Ardennes, 106, 136, 167-8
Argentan, 101-102, 191
Armies – Allied & Axis: See Seperate Index
Arnhem, 130, 133-5.
Arnim, General J. Von, 54, 56
Artillery – Allied, 56, 149,176, 177, 183
Artillery – Axis, 47, 109-11, 120, 151, 175, 194
Auchinleck, General Sir C., 18-24, 26, 47-9, 77-80, 109-11, 114, 141-2, 157, 172-5
Augusta, 57, 91
Avranches, 96, 100-101, 123, 159, 166, 184, 191

Badoglio, Marshal P., 33, 88-9
Bare Ridge, 24
Barker, Lieutenant General E., 199
Barrackpore, 66-7
Bayeux, 97-9
Beeringen, 129
Belchem, Lieutenant Colonel R.F.K., 78, 83 , 93, 142, 166
Belgium, Campaigns in, 9, 11-2, 45, 126, 129, 166, 197
Belsen, 139, 199
Ben Gardane, 148
Benghazi, 53, 85, 116, 149, 179
Bennett, Air Vice-Marshal D., 166
Biferno River, 91
Bir es Suera, 52
Bir Hacheim, 172, 174
Bismarck, Major General G., 113
Bizerta, 123, 209
Blumentritt, General G., 125, 139
Bock, General F. Von, 45
Bologna, 42-3, 63-5
Bonesteel, Colonel T., 93
Bourguebus Ridge, 191-5
Bradley, Major General, later Lieutenant General O., 57-8, 92, 94-7, 99, 101-103, 123-4, 126-7, 159, 163, 167-8, 188-91, 196-7
Bras, 195
Bremen, 138-9
Breskens 'Pocket', 131-2
Brest, 96
Briggs, Major General R., 27-30, 51, 117, 120
Brittany, 96, 100-101, 166
Broadhurst, Air Vice-Marshal H., 5-6, 139, 148, 151-2, 164, 198
Brooke, Lieutenant General, later Field Marshal Sir A., 6, 23, 30, 33, 41, 48, 51, 68, 73, 80, 86, 94, 106-108, 136, 140, 162, 180,

192-3, 195, 201-202, 208
Brooke, Major R., 180
Browning, Lieutenant General Sir F., 68-70, 128-9, 134-5, 167
Brussels, 124, 127, 136
Buerat, 31, 53-5
Burma, Campaign in, 65-75, 151

Caen, 94-5, 97-9, 123, 160-6, 184, 189-92, 195-6
Cagny, 194
Cairo, 15, 19, 22-4, 32, 46, 77-8, 80, 83, 86-7, 110, 140, 144, 152
Calabrian Peninsula, 90
Calcar, 198
Cameron, Major A., 177-8
Canal de Caen, 193
Carentan, 99
Carpiquet, 94, 166
Carver, Captain, later Lieutenant Colonel M., 32, 77
Carver, Major R., 85, 106, 147
Casablanca Conference, 88, 152
Casey, Sir R., 67
Cassino, 34-8, 40, 44, 60-2, 70
Cassino, Battles of, 35-8, 60, 158
Castel Benito, 180
Catania, 57-8
Catanzaro, 90
Caumont, 99, 196
Centuripe, 59
Chambois, 103
'Charing Cross', 27, 29
Cherbourg, 94-6, 99, 189
Cherbourg Peninsula: *See* Cotentin Peninsula
Chieti, 91-2.
Chill, Lieutenant General K.: 129.
Chindwin River: 66, 68, 71.
Chott el Fedjadj (Salt Marsh): 55, 118.
Christison, Lieutenant General K., 66-70, 73
Churchill, W.S., 17-8, 23, 34-5, 41, 45, 46, 48, 78, 80, 84, 94, 98, 112, 160, 167, 208
Clark, Lieutenant General, later General M.W., 33, 35-8, 40-2, 63, 89, 90, 155-8
Clarke, Major Sir R., 42
Cleve, 137-8
Cologne, 124
Conigham, Air Marshal A., 151, 160, 163-5, 170, 193
Conolly, Rear Admiral R., 156
Convoys:
  PEDESTAL, 25
  STONEAGE, 30
Corbett-Winder, Lieutenant Colonel J., 115
Coriano Ridge, 64
Cosgrave, Captain H., 27.

Cotentin Peninsula, 94, 99, 184, 190
Crerar, Lieutenant General H., 95, 131
Crocker, Lieutenant General J., 97, 121, 181-2, 209
Crotone, 90
Cunningham, Admiral of the Fleet Sir A., 153-4
Cuverville, 194-5
Cyrenaica, 16-7, 85, 171-2, 179, 186
Cyrene, 52

Daba El, 28-9
Dawnay, Lieutenant Colonel C., 193, 204
De Guingand, Major General Sir F.W.,
  Character, 7-9, 12, 77, 83, 85, 87, 100, 202-203
  Early Career, 7-9
  In Desert Campaign, 17-8, 50, 77-87, 117, 147
  In Tunisian Campaign, 87, 151
  In Sicily Campaign, 88
  In Italian Campaign, 89-92
  In Normandy Campaign, 92-5, 97, 99-104, 163-4, 166, 193
  In Low Countries Campaign, 104-105, 136
  In Germany Campaign, 106
  Post-War Career, 201-204, 207-208
  Relationship with Montgomery, 7-9, 76, 80-7, 92, 104, 201-204, 211-2
  Mentioned, 13-4, 52, 107, 111, 140-1, 148, 152-3, 159, 161-2, 169, 180
Demouville, 194-5
Dempsey, Lieutenant General M., 57-60, 89, 92, 94, 99, 123, 127-9, 134-5, 138, 159, 161-2, 165-6, 170, 186-8, 191-3, 196-7, 199
Derna, 19, 29, 51
Desert Air Force, 5, 20, 78, 81, 90, 112-3, 118, 139, 141, 143, 148-52, 164
De Stephanis, Major General G., 110
Dimapur, 71
Djebel Fatnassa, 118-9
Djebel Garci, 121
Djebel Roumana, 118-20
Dollmann, General F., 189
Dönetz, Grand Admiral K., 199
Dorman-Smith, Major General E., 21-2, 79-80, 110-12, 142-3, 175
Driel, 134
Dunkirk, 45-6, 107-108, 140, 158

Eberbach, General H.:,127, 190, 197
Eden A., 46
Egypt, 13-24, 81, 91, 180, 203
Eindhoven, 133
Eisenhower, Lieutenant General, later General D., 57, 92, 94, 96, 100, 102, 104-

106, 124-7, 129, 136, 138-9, 154, 160, 162, 167, 190-3, 202-203, 206
Elbe River, 199
Elfeldt, Lieutenant General O., 103
Enfidaville, 56, 120, 150, 181
Enna, 57-8
Erskine, Bridgadier, later Major General G., 14, 86, 180
Essame, Bridgadier, later Major General G.: 137-8, 169, 188-9
Essen, 128
Etna, Mount, 58-9.
Ewart, Colonel J., 201

Faid, 44
Falaise, 101-102, 164, 191-3, 195
Falaise 'Pocket', 101-103, 124, 189-90, 197
Fiennes, Lieutenant Colonel Sir R., 177
Finale, 43
Florence, 41, 70
Flushing, 131
Foggia, 91
Fondouk, 44, 181-2.
Foum Tatahouine, 148
Fox, Flight Lieutenant C., 190
Freyberg, Major General, later Lieutenant General Sir B., 24, 27, 36-7, 49-52, 84, 91-2, 111, 114-5, 117-8, 147, 151
Frosinone, 62
Frost, Lieutenant Colonel J., 130, 133
Fuka, 28-30

Gabes Gap, 55-7, 87, 93, 106, 118-20, 181
Gardiner, Major General C., 152-3
Galal, 28
Garian, 31
Gari River, 44
Garigliano River, 33-4, 44
Gascoigne, Brigadier J., 55
Gatehouse, Major General A., 27-9, 47, 50-1
Gazala: 78-9, 172-4.
Gela, Gulf of, 57, 153-4
George VI, King, 3, 41-2, 63, 160
Geyr Von Schweppenburg, General F.L., 163, 190
Ghent, 126
Giffard, General Sir G., 70, 73-4
Goch, 137
Godwin-Austen, Lieutenant General A., 18
Gold Beach, 94
Gort, Lieutenant General Lord, 45-6
Gothic Line, 41-2, 63-4
Gott, Bridgadier, later Lieutenant General W., 158, 206-207
Graham, Lieutenant Colonel M., 78, 80, 93, 204
Grave, 130, 133, 135

Greece, 17, 42, 77, 87
Gruenther, Major General, later General A., 158, 206-207
Gustav Line, 33-5, 39-40, 60-2, 64, 91, 157
Guzzoni, General A., 57

Haifa, 76, 140, 171
Haislip, Major General W., 102
Halfaya, 30
Hamburg, 138
Hamma El, 118
Hammam El, 110
Harding, Field Marshal Baron A.F. ('John'), Character, 3,4, 16-8, 26, 31-2, 38-9, 42-3, 206-207
Early Career, 3-5
In Desert Campaign, 15-9, 21-31, 178-9
Wounded, 31-2, 180
In Italian Campaign 37-43, 45
Post-War Career, 205-207
Relationship with Montgomery, 4, 15, 23-6, 31-3, 38-9, 205-207, 211-2
Mentioned: 6-7, 9, 13, 63, 80, 115, 123, 182, 201, 204
Harris, Air Marshal Sir A., 166
Harwood, Admiral Sir H., 83
Hauser, SS General P.:,103, 189
Heath, Lieutenant P., 199
Hewitt, Vice Admiral K., 156
Hill 112, 187-9
Himeimat,Qarat el (Peak), 110, 113, 143-4
Hitler, Adolf, 16-20, 28, 33 4, 39-41, 55-6, 95, 97, 101, 105, 135-6, 145, 149, 163, 184, 190, 199, 200.
Hitler Line, 61-3, 75
Hochwald, 198
Hodges, Lieutenant General C., 96, 101, 127-8, 166-8
Holland, Campaign in, 128-31, 136, 167, 198
Homs, 31, 53-4
Hore-Belisha L., 9, 76
Horrocks, Lieutenant General Sir B.G., Character, 9-10, 12, 108, 116-8, 122, 127, 136, 138, 209
Early Career, 9-11
In Dunkirk Campaign, 107-108, 140
In Desert Campaign, 47, 75, 108, 111-5, 178
In Tunisian Campaign, 57, 116-22, 182
Wounded, 123, 155, 209
In Normandy Campaign, 123-4
In Low Countries Campaign, 126-36, 167, 198
In Germany Campaign, 136-9
Post-War Career, 208, 209.
Relationship with Montgomery, 11, 112, 115, 121-4, 136, 210, 211

Mentioned, 13-4, 21, 26, 56, 77, 143-4, 151, 165, 169, 204
Horseshoe Hill, 55
Hughes, Major General I., 24

Imphal, 65, 71
Irrawaddy River, 66, 68-9

Jacob, Colonel Sir I., 48
Johnson, Major General D., 140
Juin, General A., 36-9, 41, 60, 62-3
Juno Beach, 94, 97

Kandy, 66, 70
Kasuya, Major General S., 69
Kaulback, Lieutenant Colonel R., 180
Kesselring, Field Marshal A., 19, 25, 33-5, 40-1, 43, 52, 54, 56-61, 64, 75, 91, 109, 114, 149, 156-7, 208
Keyes, Major General G., 34
Khartoum, 80, 141, 143
Kimura, Lieutenant General H., 68-9
Kippenberger, Bridgadier H., 30
Kirkman, Lieutenant General S., 61-.
Kisch, Brigadier F., 78, 93
Kluge, Field Marshal G. von, 190, 200
Kohima, 65, 72
Ksar Rhilane, 150-1

Leclerc, General P., 150
Leese, Lieutenant General Sir O.H.,
 Character, 5-6 ,49-52, 57-8, 60-1, 74-5, 208
 Early Career, 5-7
 In Dunkirk Campaign, 45-6
 In Desert Campaign, 45-54, 84, 117, 180
 In Tunisian Campaign, 55-7, 87, 119
 In Sicily Campaign, 57-9
 In Italian Campaign, 42, 45, 60-5
 In Burma Campaign, 65-70, 72-5
 Post-War Career: 203, 204, 207-209.
 Relationship with Montgomery, 5-7, 47, 50-1, 54, 59-60, 211
 Mentioned, 9-10, 34, 76, 116, 140, 153, 201
Leigh-Mallory, Air Chief Marshal Sir T., 160-1, 163, 165, 193
Le Mans, 101
Leonforte, 57-8
Libya, 15-6, 19, 31, 52
Li Colli Ridge, 92
Liri River & Valley, 34-6, 39, 44, 60-2, 75
Liss, Colonel U., 145
Loire River, 96, 101
Louvain, 9, 11
Lübeck, 199
Lucas, Major General J., 35

Lumsden, Lieutenant General H., 27, 47, 50, 75, 116
Lüneburg Heath, 43, 169, 171, 201
Maas River, 128, 130, 132, 136-7, 186, 198
Mace, The (Ridge), 103
Mackensen, General E. von, 33
Macmillan H., 59, 65
Maginot Line, 12
Mainwarning, Lieutenant Colonel, later Bridgadier H., 78, 85, 91, 93, 106
Malya, 73, 205
Malta, 18-20, 25, 30, 84, 109, 139, 155
Mandalay, 67-70, 75
Mann, Bridgadier C., 165-6
Mantueffel, General H. von, 125, 168
Mareth Line, 55, 56, 70, 106, 118, 148-50, 181
Mareth Line, Battle of, 56-7, 87, 116-9, 150
Martuba, 19, 25, 30, 52, 84, 86, 172, 179
Matmata Hills, 55, 116, 150
McCreery, Major General, later Lieutenant General R., 65, 155
McNeill, Lieutenant Colonel J., 148, 151
Medenine, 55, 87, 148-9
Medjerda River & Valley, 122, 182
Meida El, 118
Meiktila, 69
Melfa River, 62
Mersa Matruh, 20, 27-8, 30, 35
Messe, General, later Field Marshal G., 55-6, 117-8, 120, 122, 181
Messervy, Lieutenant General Sir F., 69
Messina, 18, 57-9, 154
Messnia, Straits of: 59, 89, 154.
Metz, 125
Meuse River, 45, 128, See also: Maas River
Meuse-Escaut Canal, 129
Miteirya Ridge, 50
Monte Artemisio, 62
Monte Cairo, 62
Monte Cassino, 35-8, 60-1
Mont Pincon, 123-4
Montgomery, Field Marshal Viscount B.L.,
 Character: 1-10, 13-4, 26, 32-3, 38-9, 48, 51, 55, 58, 75-6, 100, 104-107, 116, 147, 149, 153, 167-8, 181, 190-3, 210-12
 In Dunkirk Campaign, 107-108
 In Desert Campaign, 23-31, 46-54, 80-7, 108-9, 111-6, 143-8, 171, 179-80
 In Tunisian Campaign, 55-7, 116-7, 119-21, 148-51, 181-2
 In Sicily Campaign, 57-9, 88, 153-5
 In Italian Campaign, 34, 89-92, 155-8
 In Normandy Campaign: 92-103, 123-4, 159-66, 183-93, 195-6
 Strategy after Normandy, 104, 124-8
 In Low Countries Campaign, 104-5, 128-

33, 135-6, 167
   In Germany Campaign, 137-8, 168-9, 199
   Post-War Career, 201-209
   Mentioned: 44-5, 60, 73-4, 78-9, 106, 122, 139, 141, 152, 170, 200
Moro River, 91-2
Morshead, Major General L., 17, 49, 51
Mortain, 101, 197
Mountbatten, Admiral Lord L., 65-7, 70, 73-5, 207
Mussolini, Benito, 15, 33, 88
Mutaguchi, Lieutenant General R., 72
Myebon, 68
Myinmu, 68-9

Naples, 156-7
Neame, Lieutenant General P., 17
Neder Rijn (Lower Rhine) River, 128, 130, 133-5
Neerpelt, 129
Nehring, General W., 110, 113
Nibeiwa, 15, 16
Nichols, Major General J., 56
Nijmegen, 130, 133, 135-7, 167
Nile Delta, 20, 22-4, 81, 175
Nile River, 24, 80, 106, 110, 145
Normandy, Battle of, 2, 33, 60, 92-104, 115, 123-4, 127, 130, 158-66, 168, 183-97, 212
North Atlantic Treaty Organization (NATO), 202-203, 206-7
Nyaungu, 69

O'Connor, Lieutenant General Sir R., 16-7, 186-7, 191-6, 200
Odon River, 184, 187-8
Omaha Beach, 94, 99
Oosterbeek, 134
Operational Code Names:
   ANVIL, 39, 41, 63
   AVALANCHE, 89-90, 155-6
   BAYTOWN, 89, 155
   BERTRAM, 144
   BLUECOAT, 123, 196-7
   CAPITAL, 66
   COBRA, 100, 191-2, 196-7
   COMET, 128-9, 135
   COMPASS, 15-6, 171, 186
   CRUSADER, 18-9, 23, 30, 172-3
   DIADEM, 38-41, 60-2
   EPSOM, 184-5, 187-9
   EXALTATION, 21
   EXTENDED CAPITAL, 68
   FIRE-EATER, 31, 53
   FORTITUDE, 93
   GOODWOOD, 191-3, 195-6
   GRAPESHOT (Alamein), 147
   GRAPESHOT (Italy), 43

GRENADE, 137-8
HUSKY, 57, 87-8, 152, 154
LIGHTFOOT, 48
MARKET GARDEN, 130, 132-6, 167, 198
OLIVE, 63-4
OVERLOAD, 33-4, 38-9, 41, 92, 159-60
PLUNDER, 168-9
PUGLIST, 55
ROMULUS, 67
SHINGLE, 35
SINBAD, 174
SLAPSTICK, 89
SPLENDOUR, 21
STRIKE, 122
SUPERCHARGE (Alamein), 51, 84-5, 147
SUPERCHARGE (Mareth Line), 117-8, 151
TORCH, 54, 84, 120
VARSITY, 169
VERITABLE, 136-8
ZIPPER, 73-4
Orne River, 94, 161, 166, 184, 187-8, 191-4
Oudane el Hachana (Hills), 120

Pachino Peninsula, 57-8, 153
Paget, Lieutenant General B., 1
Palermo, 58, 88, 153-4
Palestine, 23, 76, 88, 207
Paris, 94, 96, 101, 103, 191, 206
Pas de Calais, 93
Patton, Lieutenant General G., 57-9, 96, 100-103, 125, 153-4, 181
Peel Marshes, 128
Perrier Ridge, 197
Pescara, 91-2
Pienaar, Major General D., 49
Pile, Bridgadier F., 8
Pisa, 41
Po River & Valley, 41, 43, 63
Point 29, 51
Point 102, 24, 111, 113-4, 176-8
Ponte Olivo, 153-4
Pownall, Lieutenant General Sir H., 46

Qattara Depression, 20, 110
Queree, Lieutenant Colonel R., 147

Ramree, 68
Rangoon, 67-71, 73, 75
Rapido River, 35, 44, 61
Reggio, 89-90
Reichswald, 137
Rennes, 159
Reno River, 43
Renton, Major General J.M.L., 26, 112

Rhine River, 105, 124, 127-8, 130, 132, 136-8, 168-9, 198
Rhineland, Battle of, 136-8, 168, 198
Richardson, General Sir C.L.,
  Character, 11-2, 143-4, 150, 152, 155, 157-8, 163, 166, 169, 205
  Early Career, 11-3
  In Dunkirk Campaign, 140
  In Desert Campaign, 80, 117, 141-8
  In Tunisian Campaign, 149-52
  In Sicily Campaign, 154-5
  In Italian Campaign, 155-8
  In Normandy Campaign, 159-61, 163-6
  In Low Countries Campaign, 166-7
  In Germany Campaign, 168-9
  Post-War Career, 205, 207
  Relationship with Montgomery, 12-3, 143-4, 149, 154-5, 165, 167, 210-11
  Mentioned, 77-8, 83, 93, 104, 106, 170, 204
Ridgeway, General M., 206
Rimini, 41-2, 64, 70
Roberts, Major General G.P.B.,
  Character, 13, 174-6, 181, 183, 187, 195, 197, 199, 207
  Early Career, 11-3
  In Desert Campaign, 27, 112, 171-80
  Wounded, 175
  In Tunisian Campaign, 180-2
  In Normandy Campaign 183-9, 191-7
  In Low Countries Campaign, 127, 197-8
  In Germany Campaign, 198-9
  Post-War Career, 207
  Relationship with Montgomery, 13, 14, 179-81, 183, 192, 210, 212
  Mentioned, 26-8, 33, 111, 143, 204
Robertson, Brigadier, later Major General B., 78, 93, 204
Roddick, Brigadier M., 27, 30
Roer River, 137
Romagna Plain, 64
Rome, 33-5, 40-1, 60, 70, 91, 156
Rome, Battle for, 38-40, 60-3
Rommel, General, later Field Marshal E., 17-25, 27-31, 44, 47, 49, 51-6, 79-80, 82-5, 95, 109-12, 114, 139, 142-3, 145, 148-50, 162-4, 172, 174-6, 179-80, 184, 186, 190, 200, 211
Roosevelt, President F.D., 88
Route 5, 91
Route 6, 34-5, 40, 61-2
Route 7, 34, 40, 62
Route 81, 92
Route 124, 58
Ruhr, The, 104, 124-5, 127-8, 130, 134, 167
Rundstedt, General, later Field Marshal G. von, 45, 95, 125, 135, 138-9, 163, 190
Ruweisat Ridge, 78, 80-1, 110, 113

St Lambert, 103
St Lô, 96, 100, 184, 192, 196
Sainte Foy de Montgomery, 190
Saar, The, 125, 127
Sacco River, 34
Salerno, 89-90, 123, 155-8
Sangro River, 34, 91-2
Scaletta, 59
Scheldt River, 131-2
Scoones, Lieutenant General Sir G., 71
Sedan, 45
Seine River, 95, 101-103, 124, 164, 166, 196-7, 212
Sfax, 55, 106, 120
Sicily, 5-6, 18-9, 33, 57-9, 70, 74, 87-8, 91, 102, 121-2, 152-5, 161, 164
Sidi Barrani, 15, 30, 171
Sidi el Guelaa, See Horseshoe Hill
Siegfried Line, 125, 128, 137
Simmonds, Lieutenant General G., 198
Simpson, Lieutenant General W., 137-8, 167-8
Slim, Lieutenant General, later Field Marshal Sir W., 65-75, 206-207, 211
Smith, Major General W. Bedell, 106
Smuts, Field Marshal J.C., 160
Somme River, 127, 197
Son, 130, 133, 135
Sousse, 56, 120
South Beveland Peninsula, 131-2
Speidel, Lieutenant General H., 139
Stopford, Lieutenant General Sir M., 68
Stratemeyer, Major General G., 66-7, 70
Student, General K., 129, 134-6, 139
Stumme, General G., 145-6
Suez, 15, 20, 23, 25, 110
Sultan, Lieutenant General D., 66
Sword Beach, 94, 97
Syracuse, 57, 153

Tadjera Khir (Hill), 87
Takrouna, 121
Tanks - Allied:
  Churchill 'Crocodile', 184
  Comet, 198
  Cromwell, 183, 185, 198
  Crusader, 173, 176-7
  Duplex Drive (Ampibious), 93, 98, 168
  Grant, 172-8, 200
  Matilda, 173, 184-5
  Matilda 'Scorpion', 115
  Sherman, 27, 29, 179, 181-3, 185, 194, 198, 200
  Sherman 'Firefly', 185, 198
  Stuart, 173, 176-8
  Valentine, 56, 173, 181, 184
Tanks - Axis:

224 Six of Monty's Men

Mark III, 173
Mark III Special, 20, 109, 173-4, 177
Mark IV, 173
Mark IV Special, 109, 156, 173-4, 177, 185
Mark V 'Panther', 61, 185
Mark V 'Tiger', 185
Taormina, 59
Taranto, 89
Tarhuna, 31, 53-4, 180
Tebaga Gap, 116-7, 122, 150-2
Tedder, Air Chief Marshal Sir A., 85-6, 153-4, 160, 163-5, 191, 193, 195
Termoli, 91
Thoma, Lieutenant General W.R. von, 84
Thomas, Major General I., 124
Tobruk, 17-20, 30, 42, 78, 85, 109, 116, 171-2
Trieste, 43
Trigno River, 91
Tripoli, 16, 18, 31, 53-5, 70, 86-7, 93, 116-7, 122, 148-9, 179-80
Tripolitania, 16, 54
Tuker, Major General F., 36-7, 48-9, 117, 119-20, 146-7
Tunis, 52, 56, 121-2, 150, 182
Tunisia, 44, 54-6, 87, 119-20, 148-53, 181-2
Turner, Colonel C., 32

Udem, 198
'Ultra' Intelligence, 19, 24, 28, 36-7, 39, 44, 56, 71, 78, 85, 145, 149, 162-4, 172, 184, 201
'Unconditional Surrender' Policy, 88-9
Utah Beach, 94, 99
Vaerst, Major General G. von, 109, 113
Valmontone, 40, 62
Vasto, 92
Veghel, 130, 133-5

Velletri, 62
Venice, 64
Venlo, 128
Via Appia, See Route 7
Via Balbia, 52-4
Via Casilina, See Route 6
Vienna, 63-5
Vietinghoff, General H.G. von, 33, 43
Villers-Bocage, 97-8, 161
Vire, 196
Volturno River, 156
Vught, 134

Waal River, 128, 130, 133
Wadi Akarit, 118
Wadi Natrun, 22
Wadi Zigzaou, 56, 118
Walcheren, 131-2
Walsh, Brigadier G., 5
Wavell, General Sir A., 15-8, 20, 77, 172
Wesel, 128, 138, 198
Western Union, 205-206
Westphal, General S., 139
Whistler, Brigadier L., 27, 31.
Wilder, Lieutenant N., 116
Wilder's Gap, 116-7, 150
Wilhelmina Canal, 130
Williams, Captain, later Major E., 78, 83-4, 93, 142, 166, 204
Wimberley, Major General D., 49, 51, 53-4, 119, 180
Wingate, Brigadier, later Major General O., 72

Zuckerman, Professor S., 160
Zuider Zee, 128-9, 134
Zuid Willemsvaat Canal, 130

Index of Military Formations & Units

ALLIED
Eleventh Army Group, 65
Fifteenth Army Group, 33-4, 38-41, 45, 57, 60, 157
Eighteenth Army Group, 54, 120, 148-9
Twenty-First Army Group, 1, 60, 92, 100-106, 124, 126, 137, 159, 165, 167, 169, 192, 201

BRITISH AND COMMONWEALTH
First Army, 108, 120-1, 148
Second Army, 92, 94-5, 99-101, 123, 126-31, 136, 138, 159-63, 165-6, 169-70, 189-92
Eighth Army, 1, 5, 12-4, 18, 20-31, 33, 36, 39-43, 45, 47-8, 52-65, 73-4, 77-87, 89-92, 108, 110-22, 141-58, 172-4, 179-82, 186, 201, 204, 210-11
Twelfth Army, 73
Fourteenth Army, 65-71, 73-5
British Expeditionary Force (BEF), 9, 12, 45, 107
Burma Army, 72
First Canadian Army, 94, 101-102, 131-2, 136, 185
Western Desert Force, 15-7
I Corps, 94, 97, 121, 131, 191
II Corps, 107-8, 140
IV Corps, 66, 69
V Corps, 60, 90

Index

VIII Corps, 33, 126, 130, 138, 183-4, 186-9, 191-6, 198-9
IX Corps, 121-2, 181-2
X Corps, 23, 27, 47-8, 50-1, 60, 89, 116-23, 144, 155-7
XII Corps, 126, 130, 132, 138, 184
XIII Corps, 14, 18, 23, 26, 42-3, 47, 56-9, 61-3, 86, 89, 90, 108, 110-1, 115, 146, 176, 204
XV Corps, 66-8, 70
XXI Corps, 4
XXX Corps, 23, 46-59, 84, 87, 94, 110-1, 116, 123-4, 126-7, 129-31, 133-8, 167, 172, 184, 196-7, 203
XXXIII Corps, 66, 68
I Airborne Corps, 128, 134
Burma Corps, 67, 71
I Canadian Corps, 61-2
II Canadian Corps, 137, 191, 198
New Zealand Corps, 36, 38

1st Airborne Division, 89, 128-30, 134-5, 161
6th Airborne Division, 94, 161, 169
1st Armoured Division, 27-9, 51, 64, 111, 117-20, 175
6th Armoured Division, 43, 61, 121-2, 181-2
7th Armoured Division, 14, 26-33, 52-3, 111-2, 115-6, 119, 121-3, 149, 161, 171, 175, 178-80, 191-4
8th Armoured Division, 144
10th Armoured Division, 27-9, 47, 50, 111, 144
11th Armoured Division, 33, 126, 129, 132, 183-4, 186-7, 191-9
9th Australian Division: 17, 21, 49-51, 110, 146
4th Canadian Armoured Division, 103, 198
1st Canadian Infantry Division, 90
3rd Canadian Infantry Division, 94, 97, 99, 165
Guards Armoured Division, 46, 127, 129, 133, 136, 191-4, 198
51st Highland Division, 31, 49-54, 56, 119-20, 149, 161, 180, 194-5
4th Indian Division, 36, 48-9, 51, 56, 119-21
5th Indian Division, 110
8th Indian Division, 61
10th Indian Division, 43
20th Indian Division, 68
3rd Infantry Division, 9, 94, 97-9, 107-8
4th Infantry Division, 61, 121
5th Infantry Division, 90
43rd Infantry Division, 124, 134, 138, 184, 187
44th Infantry Division, 24-5, 27, 47, 108, 111, 114-5
49th Infantry Division, 8
50th Infantry Division, 56, 94, 98, 115, 119, 123
54th Infantry Division, 4
56th Infantry Division, 121, 182
78th Infantry Division, 34, 59, 61, 91

2nd New Zealand Division, 24, 27, 36, 43, 47, 49-53, 60, 91, 110, 117-9, 121, 149
15th Scottish Division, 184, 187-8
1st South African Division, 49-51, 110
6th South African Armoured Division, 43, 61

2nd Armoured Brigade, 117-8
4th Armoured Brigade, 171-2, 174-5, 187, 198
8th Armoured Brigade, 31, 111-2, 117-8
9th Armoured Brigade, 47, 51, 108
22nd Armoured Brigade, 14, 26-7, 31, 53-4, 111-3, 175-9
23rd Armoured Brigade, 53, 111
26th Armoured Brigade, 181-2
29th Armoured Brigade, 183, 187, 193-8
30th Armoured Brigade, 183
22nd Guards Brigade, 18
32nd Guards Brigade, 133
201st Guards Brigade, 55-6, 121
8th Infantry Brigade, 98
9th Infantry Brigade, 98, 108
11th Infantry Brigade, 108
17th Infantry Brigade, 7
29th Infantry Brigade, 46
69th Infantry Brigade, 119
131st Infantry Brigade, 25, 27, 31, 180
132nd Infantry Brigade, 24, 47, 114-5
133rd Infantry Brigade, 25, 47
151st Infantry Brigade, 119
153rd Infantry Brigade, 31
159th Infantry Brigade, 183, 194-9
162nd Infantry Brigade, 3
185th Infantry Brigade, 98
214th Infantry Brigade, 138
4th Light Armoured Brigade, 27, 30, 52, 112, 178-9
7th Motor Brigade, 112
4th New Zealand Brigade, 24
5th New Zealand, 24, 30, 114, 117
6th New Zealand Brigade, 24, 114, 117

2nd Coldstream Guards, 6
3rd Coldstream Guards, 5
3rd County of London Yeomanry, 176
4th County of London Yeomanry, 176-8
13th/18th Hussars, 98
1/11th London, 3.
12th Machine-Gun Battalion, 3-4
54th Machine-Gun Battalion, 4
1st Middlesex, 10
2nd Middlesex, 9, 107
2nd Northants Yeomanry, 187
2nd Parachute Battalion 130
1/6th Queens, 180
1/7th Queens, 180
1st Rifle Brigade, 176-7

2nd Royal Gloucestershire Hussars, 176
1st Royal Horse Artillery, 176, 178.
Royal Scots Greys, 177-8
1st Royal Tanks, 176, 178
3rd Royal Tanks, 172, 174
5th Royal Tanks, 176, 178
6th Royal Tanks, 13, 176, 178,
44th Royal Tanks, 187
50th Royal Tanks, 56
1st Royal Warwickshire, 8
1st Somerset, 4
Staffordshire Yeomanry, 98
2nd West Yorkshire, 7

3rd Armoured Car Company, 13
Force 141 152, 155
Long Range Desert Group, 116

UNITED STATES.
Twelfth US Army Group, 96, 102, 105, 124-6, 167

First US Army, 92, 94-6, 100, 125, 159, 162, 166-8, 184, 189-90
Third US Army, 96, 100-102, 125, 166
Fifth US Army, 33, 36, 39-43, 63, 65, 89-90, 123, 155-8
Seventh US Army, 33, 57-8, 153-4
Ninth US Army, 137-8, 167-9

II US Corps, 34-5, 40, 43-4, 57 8, 60, 181
V US Corps, 94
VI US Corps, 35, 38-40, 62, 156-7
VII US Corps, 94, 167, 189
VIII US Corps, 100
XV US Corps, 101-102
XX US Corps, 101

17th US Airborne Division, 169
82nd US Airborne Division, 94, 129-30, 133, 136
101st US Airborne Division, 94, 129-30, 133
1st US Armoured Division, 181
1st US Infantry Division, 94.
4th US Infantry Division, 94
5th US Infantry Division, 196
90th US Infantry Division, 103
OTHERS
Belgian Army, 107
French Expeditionary Corps, 36, 39, 41-2, 60, 63
II Polish Corps, 60-1
2nd French Armoured Division, 103
1st Polish Armoured Division, 103
1st Polish Parachute Brigade, 128, 134-5
12th Podolski Lancers, 61

French Force L., 150
AXIS

GERMAN
Army Group A, 45
Army Group B, 45, 95, 139, 190
Army Group C, 33
Army Group H, 139
Panzer Group West, 163, 190

Seventh Army, 95, 103, 127, 189
Tenth Army, 33, 35
Fourteenth Army, 33
Fifteenth Army, 95
Fifth Panzer Army, 54, 122, 168
Panzerarmee Afrika, 19, 145-6, 175
1st Parachute Army, 129, 139

Afrika Korps, 17, 110, 113
LXXXIV German Corps, 103

90th Light Division, 29, 52, 54-5, 109-10, 113, 120, 145-6, 149, 179
164th Light Division, 109-10, 117-8, 146, 149
2nd Panzer Division, 99, 103, 184, 196
10th Panzer Division, 149
15th Panzer Division, 109-10, 118, 120, 149, 177-8
16th Panzer Division, 156
21st Panzer Division, 97, 99, 109-10, 113, 117-8, 145-6, 149, 177-9, 184
116th Panzer Division, 196
15th Panzer Grenadier Division, 154
Panzer Lehr Division, 99, 164, 184
1st SS Panzer Division, 184, 187-8
2nd SS Panzer Division, 184, 187-8
9th SS Panzer Division, 13, 130, 184, 188, 197
10th SS Panzer Division, 103, 130, 184, 188, 197
12th SS Panzer Division, 99, 184
288th Parachute Brigade, 109-10

ITALIAN
First Italian Army, 55, 118, 122
XX Italian Corps, 110, 113
Ariete Division, 110, 145-6, 198
Bologna Division, 109
Brescia Division, 110
Folgore Division, 109-10, 113
Littorio Division, 110
Trento Division, 110, 146
Trieste Division, 110, 145-6

JAPANESE
15th Japanese Division, 72
53rd Japanese Division, 72